The View From Here

Sociology of Health and Illness Monograph Series

Edited by Hannah Bradby
Department of Sociology
University of Warwick
Coventry
CV4 7AL
UK

Current titles:

- **The View From Here: Bioethics and the Social Sciences (2007)**,
  edited by *Raymond de Vries, Leigh Turner, Kristina Orfali and Charles Bosk*
- **The Social Organisation of Healthcare Work (2006)**,
  edited by *Davina Allen and Alison Pilnick*
- **Social Movements in Health (2005)**,
  edited by *Phil Brown and Stephen Zavestoski*
- **Health and the Media (2004)**,
  edited by *Clive Seale*
- **Partners in Health, Partners in Crime: Exploring the boundaries of criminology and sociology of health and illness (2003)**,
  edited by *Stefan Timmermans and Jonathan Gabe*
- **Rationing: Constructed Realities and Professional Practices (2002)**,
  edited by *David Hughes and Donald Light*
- **Rethinking the Sociology of Mental Health (2000)**,
  edited by *Joan Busfield*
- **Sociological Perspectives on the New Genetics (1999)**,
  edited by *Peter Conrad and Jonathan Gabe*
- **The Sociology of Health Inequalities (1998)**,
  edited by *Mel Bartley, David Blane and George Davey Smith*
- **The Sociology of Medical Science (1997)**,
  edited by *Mary Ann Elston*
- **Health and the Sociology of Emotion (1996)**,
  edited by *Veronica James and Jonathan Gabe*
- **Medicine, Health and Risk (1995)**,
  edited by *Jonathan Gabe*

Forthcoming title:

- **Ethnicity, Health and Healthcare: Understanding Diversity, Tackling Disadvantage (2007)**, edited by *Waqar Ahmad and Hannah Bradby*

The View From Here
Bioethics and the Social Sciences

Edited by

Raymond G. De Vries, Leigh Turner,
Kristina Orfali and Charles Bosk

Blackwell
Publishing

First published as Volume 28, No. 6 of *Sociology of Health and Illness*.

BLACKWELL PUBLISHING
350 Main Street, Malden, MA 02148-5020, USA
9600 Garsington Road, Oxford OX4 2DQ, UK
550 Swanston Street, Carlton, Victoria 3053, Australia

First published 2007 by Blackwell Publishing Ltd

Library of Congress Cataloging-in-Publication Data has been applied for

ISBN-13: 978-1-4051-5269-3

A catalogue record for this title is available from the British Library.

Set in 10pt Times
by Graphicraft Ltd, Hong Kong
Printed and bound in the United Kingdon
by TJ International, Padstow, Cornwall

The publisher's policy is to use permanent paper from mills that operate a sustainable forestry policy, and which has been manufactured from pulp processed using acid-free and elementary chlorine-free practices. Furthermore, the publisher ensures that the text paper and cover board used have met acceptable environmental accreditation standards.

For further information on
Blackwell Publishing, visit our website:
www.blackwellpublishing.com

Contents

List of Contributors

Jill Allison
Department of Anthropology
Memorial University of
Newfoundland
Newfoundland, NL, Canada

Renée R. Anspach
Department of Sociology
University of Michigan
Ann Arbor, MI, USA

David Armstrong
Department of General Practice
King's College London
London, UK

Sarah Banks
School of Applied Social
Sciences
Durham University
Durham, UK

Charles Bosk
Department of Sociology
University of Pennsylvania
Philadelphia, PA, USA

Helen Busby
Institute for the Study of
Genetics, Biorisks and Society
University of Nottingham
Nottingham, UK

Larry R. Churchill
Center for Biomedical Ethics
and Society
Vanderbilt University Medical
Center
Nashville, TN, USA

Alan Cribb
School of Social Science and
Public Policy
King's College London
London, UK

Arlene M. Davis
Department of Social Medicine
University of North Carolina at
Chapel Hill
Chapel Hill, NC, USA

Michele M. Easter
Department of Social Medicine
University of North Carolina at
Chapel Hill
Chapel Hill, NC, USA

Bobbie Farsides
Brighton and Sussex Medical
School
University of Sussex
Brighton, UK

Jill A. Fisher
Women and Gender Studies Program
Arizona State University
Tempe, AZ, USA

Adam M. Hedgecoe
Department of Sociology
University of Sussex
Brighton, UK

Gail E. Henderson
Department of Social Medicine
University of North Carolina at
Chapel Hill
Chapel Hill, NC, USA

Klaus Hoeyer
Department of Health Services
Research
Institute of Public Health
University of Copenhagen
Copenhagen, Denmark

Nancy M. P. King
Department of Social Medicine
University of North Carolina at
Chapel Hill
Chapel Hill, NC, USA

Orla McDonnell
Department of Sociology
University of Limerick
Limerick, Ireland

Mike Michael
Department of Sociology
Goldsmith's College London
London, UK

Nissim Mizrachi
Department of Sociology and
Anthropology
Tel Aviv University
Tel Aviv, Israel

Kristina Orfali
Department of Pediatrics
Division of Neonatology, ISERP
and Center for Bioethics
Columbia University
New York, NY, USA

Jackie Leach Scully
Arbeitsstelle für Ethik in den
Biowissenschaften
University of Basel
Basel, Switzerland

Michael J. Selgelid
Centre for Applied Philosophy
and Public Ethics
and Menzies Centre for
Health Policy
The Australian National
University
Canberra, Australia

Tom Shakespeare
Policy, Ethics and Life Sciences
Research Institute
Newcastle University
Newcastle-upon-Tyne, UK

Janardan Subedi
Department of Sociology and
Gerontology
Miami University
Oxford, OH, USA

Sree Subedi
Department of Sociology and
Gerontology
Miami University
Oxford, OH, USA

Mark Tausig
Department of Sociology
University of Akron
Akron, OH, USA

Leigh Turner
Biomedical Ethics Unit
McGill University
Montreal, QC, Canada

Raymond de Vries
Bioethics Program
School of Medicine
University of Michigan
Ann Arbor, MI, USA

Steven P. Wainwright
Division of Health and Social
Care Research
King's College London
London, UK

Heleen Weyers
University of Groningen
Department of Legal Theory
Groningen, The Netherlands

Clare Williams
Division of Health and Social
Care Research
King's College London
London, UK

1

Social science and bioethics: the way forward
Raymond de Vries, Leigh Turner, Kristina Orfali and Charles Bosk

Every moral has a story . . .
Amos Lee, *Dreamin'*

As editors of this volume, we were somewhat surprised that the initial call
for submissions yielded over 60 responses. Constrained by chapter and page
limitations, we faced the difficult task of selecting just 12 chapters from the many
fine proposals we received. Our first task required developing criteria to guide
our decision-making. We sought to produce a volume displaying the variety
of topics undergoing scrutiny at the intersection of bioethics and the social
sciences while ensuring the chapters were united by an organising principle.

As Simmel so long ago recognised, *negative solidarity* is easy to achieve.
Individuals and groups have little difficulty agreeing on the features of the world
that vex them. To convert *negative solidarity* into *positive agendas* for change
is, however, a different matter. As an editorial team, we were an exemplar of
Simmelian *negative solidarity* – we were quickly able to agree on what shape
we did not want this volume to take. Nonetheless, just as Simmel predicted, we
had difficulty determining how to organise this volume so that it remedied
past failures to reconcile the bioethical and sociological imaginations.

As an editorial team, we were aware of the often troubled relationship
between bioethics and the social sciences. Three of us are social scientists
affiliated with centers or departments of bioethics. The fourth is a bioethicist
appointed to a bioethics unit and department of social studies of medicine.
We had all become weary of the repetitive, often simplistic ways that lines had
been drawn to demarcate bioethics from the social sciences. The lines so drawn
had the appearance of reasonableness, the overgeneralisations involved in
creating clear distinctions were grounded firmly enough in the empirical
world, and the resulting debates just entertaining enough that it took a great
deal of unproductive goring each other's ox before the destructive nature
of critique and countercritique became apparent. The starting points of
the debate, when stated baldly, appear innocent. Social science is, by nature,
empirical and limited in its usefulness because it is 'merely descriptive'.
Ethics is, by nature, normative and limitless in its potential for moral reform
because it provides a 'logical method for knowing the good'.

Then, when disciplinary pretensions and vanities on both sides of the divide are added to the simmering debate, the sweet reasonableness of an interdisciplinary stew turns bitter. Since Comte, all sociologists have recognised that, because our discipline integrates knowledge across a range of inquiry, it represents 'the queen of the disciplines'. In contrast, philosophers, insisting that an 'ought' cannot be derived from an 'is', assign to social scientists an inferior task: 'Just describe for us the way things are, we will then – without your help, thank you – determine how things ought to be'. What is justice, equity, autonomy, the nature of good society – all these are issues for philosophy. Anthropologists and sociologists just muddy the water by showing how different societies in different places in different times give empirical form to these unchanging essences.

Veblen spoke of disciplinary knowledge in dismissive terms. Instead of privileging disciplinary knowledge as a perspective for seeing the world, Veblen disparages such expertise as a 'trained incapacity' that renders its holders unable to view the world from a variety of equally valid points of view. The nature of the back and forth between sociologists and bioethicists becomes truly frustrating once we realise how long we have been hurling the same invectives at each other, how much we are each the victim of our carefully cultivated incapacities.

As an editorial team, we had grown weary of a debate that had produced much heat and little light. We were more than weary, in truth, since each of us had contributed to the back and forth in ways that deepened the ruts in which the currently contentious discourse had become stuck.

From the social science side, some of the problems with our standard critique are painfully obvious. We tend to speak of bioethics as if it were a monolithic entity, with a single perspective and mode of inquiry, reinforced by a cadre of leaders whose position and expertise are unchallenged – an orthodox professional group capable of enforcing such tight discipline that the 'field' speaks with one voice on all issues. But, of course, bioethics is a plural noun and its plurality is multiple. There is a set of socially visible activities that we call bioethics. The items in that set are unusually diverse. They range from serving on national commissions, to providing advice to the pharmaceutical industry, to consulting at the bedside when conflict between and among caregivers, family members and patients has stalled decision-making, to debating in journals the wisdom that one's colleagues have shown in their articles, to acting as public intellectuals when the instant op-ed piece is needed or when CNN calls.

Equally plural are those that claim the title of bioethicists. Collected under the unifying label 'bioethicists' are – to create a partial list – physicians, nurses, attorneys, social workers, psychologists, patient activists, theologians, philosophers, narrative theorists, historians, economists, anthropologists and sociologists. In fact, there is no way of preventing anyone from making the claim, 'I am a bioethicist', or invalidating such a claim once made. Given the disparate array of activities that are considered to be bioethics and the diverse collection of people engaged in these activities, the orthodoxy social scientists attribute to bioethics, as a component of the larger monolith biomedicine, is a proposition too preposterous to take seriously, especially since no hierarchical, centralised social organisation exists to enforce the orthodoxy implicit in our characterisations of the 'professionalising project' of bioethics.

We, who would never accept from our undergraduates arguments with such essentialising formulations as 'society feels, thinks, believes, does' need to be reminded that phrases such as 'bioethicists believe, argue, do' are unacceptable and inadequate as empirical descriptions in our own work. Bioethicists are more than justified in taking umbrage at the simple-mindedness of such characterisations. To state this problem is not quite the same as resolving it.

Much of the sociological confusion about what bioethics is and who bioethicists are reflects confusions of three sorts. First, there is the challenge of trying to fix in words a dynamic, changing, multi-sited field. Second, as bioethics has entered the public arena, bioethicists have become exercised about who is, and who is not, a 'real' bioethicist. Our confusion about what is, and what is not, bioethics is reflected in the arguments that have been inspired within the field over the legitimacy of the current incarnation of the President's Council on Bioethics in the United States. Third, while an identifiable body of work known as the 'sociology of bioethics' exists, and while this work seeks to show the socially-structured interests that account for the contours of the issues that bioethicists engage or evade and the positions that are accepted as the conventional solutions to these issues, those of us who contribute to this body of knowledge are not nearly so forthcoming about the values and interests that shape our critiques. We critique with more than a little vehemence bioethicists who write as if they possessed 'a view from nowhere'; yet we are not so forthcoming about explicating where 'the here' of our critique of bioethics is located.

In putting together this volume, we have sought contributions that move beyond arguments none of us is able to advance with much conviction. We have attempted to set aside the classic false dichotomies of 'fact and value', 'empirical and normative', or 'universal and relative'. We have put aside the desire to transform ethicists into empirical social scientists or to make social scientists better philosophers. These are the terms of a debate that has taken neither bioethicists nor social scientists anywhere other than to the place at which each started.

We have operated under the premise that we have not yet entered that utopian space where, to paraphrase Marx, we can be workers in the morning, social scientists in the afternoon, and bioethicists in the evening. Bioethicists need not be social scientists. Social scientists need not be philosophers. We are not obliged to agree with each other or use the same methods of study. We do need to take heed of each other's objections. Instead of trying to erase differences, we need to understand them and find ways to learn from them. Gregory Bateson once wrote that all knowledge began with a conscious awareness of difference. To paraphrase a song title of Guy Clark's, we need to find ways to 'Shut Up and Talk to Each Other'.

Our goal in organising this volume has been to make the awareness of difference productive. Three criteria guided our selection of these chapters. First, we decided to select chapters drawing upon original data. Second, we found empirical evidence that illustrated how the work of bioethics was shaped by the operation of social institutions such as law, religion, politics, and emerging global markets held the greatest promise for contributing to new lines of inquiry. A focus on bioethics and social institutions was a concrete strategy for anchoring the view from 'here'. Finally, we selected the work of authors making an effort to engage, rather than simply criticise, the enterprise of bioethics. These criteria emerged in our first editorial meeting. Surveying the field, we agreed that the time for 'thought pieces' on the nature and status of bioethics – its sins of omission and commission – had passed. After years of reflection on bioethics, the time has come to go into the field and actually watch how this thing works. For the most part, the chapters in this issue accomplish that objective. The chapters grouped themselves into four categories: the ethics of research, bioethics and the work of biomedicine, bioethics and social policy, and the bioethical imagination.

Ethics of research

Highly visible abuses of research subjects' trust brought to light by whistle-blowing investigators or investigative journalists served as one of the pivots for organising in its formative years the interdisciplinary domain of bioethics. Clinician-researchers and scholars from a variety of fields contributed to articulating principles, promulgating local and national regulations based upon these principles, and then designing organisational structures and policies for transforming principles and regulations into bureaucratic practices. Those principles, policies, and structures – fully informed voluntary consent, acceptable risk-benefit ratios, adequate protections of subject anonymity and confidentiality, research ethics committees, university offices of research administration, and, at the national level, various commissions, offices, committees, councils and boards intended to protect the subjects of research and the integrity of researchers – are the concrete, and still contentious progeny of various documents that are foundational for bioethics such as, in the United States, the *Belmont Report.*

The three chapters in the first section do not revisit those controversies that still surround these policies and principles more than a quarter century after their implementation: Is fully informed consent possible? How should human subjects' regulation be applied to ethnographic inquiries undertaken by sociologists and anthropologists? Do our regulations protect human subjects or the institutions in which research takes place? Does all this regulatory activity do any measurable good? Is the cost of the bureaucratic apparatus to put principles into practice worth the benefit?

A literature on these questions grew alongside the administrative structures from the moment that these policies were implemented. These questions remain alive and well. Outlets aplenty exist for debating them and a host of others concerning how best to assure the conduct of ethical research. The chapters in this section open different avenues of inquiry.

Fisher's chapter takes changes in the organisation and financing of clinical research to discuss how principles of research ethics are understood in new settings in which research is conducted. The share of clinical research that was once financed by industry and outsourced to academic institutions has decreased dramatically. Research is increasingly conducted by commercial research organisations. Protocols are reviewed by commercial review boards. With this change – the transformation of clinical research into a business conducted within a market economy-we are likely to anticipate a weakening of human subjects' protection. Fisher illustrates that this anticipation is not fully supported by available evidence. The potential baleful impact of production pressures and market forces on robust ethical regulation are leavened by the emergence of the research coordinator's role. Typically former nurses, research coordinators recruit subjects and oversee the implementation of research protocols. These former nurses do not leave their 'ethic of care' behind when they switch roles. They depend upon personal relations with subjects to succeed in meeting production goals. As a result, their sense of individual obligation to subjects and their reputation for integrity are critical to their continued success. In this case, personal relations and human connections act as a buffer against the degradation of ethical standards.

The chapter by Easter and her colleagues revisits an old question – the conflicting rules and roles, the potential confusions occasioned by the fact that subjects are also patients, researchers are also clinicians. There is no shortage of research on the 'therapeutic misconception'. The contribution of this chapter is to show that, to invoke a phrase from ethnomethodology, neither patient-subjects nor clinician-researchers are 'judgmental dopes'. Both are aware of the research-therapy divide and neither expects a clean separation of research from therapy. The meanings of care are multiple for all participants in the research endeavour. The chapter contributes to our understanding of how all the actors in clinical research understand the meaning of care as well as how these meanings are not fixed but fluid and changing with context.

Finally in this section, the chapter by Anspach and Mizrachi shows the limitations of thinking of questions of research ethics as something finished once a research ethics committee approves protocol. Ethical questions are omnipresent in the conduct of research. Ethnographic research is a particularly fertile field for illustrating this omnipresence if only because the primary data-gathering tool in this research is the manipulation of interaction to produce data. The fact that human interaction is fraught with ethical dilemmas perforce means that research conducted through such relations is especially ethically complex. Anspach and Mizrachi frame their discussion as one of a conflict of interest between obligations researchers owe to their academic fields and those that they owe to their human subjects. In doing so, they engage an important theme that helps the social scientist connect with the bioethicist – all roles embed conflicting obligations, we all possess multiple roles – conflict within and between roles is endemic to the human conditions. Sustained discussion of how role conflicts unfold in one domain provide an oblique lesson to those in other domains with other conflicts.

Setting moral boundaries: bioethics and the work of biomedicine

Three chapters in our collection explore how moral boundaries are negotiated, established, challenged and reconstituted by social actors such as laboratory-based stem cell researchers, citizens, oncologists and regulatory agencies. They prompt reflection concerning what falls inside or outside the scope of bioethics, what tools clinicians, researchers and citizens use to make moral judgements, and how contested social practices are negotiated in particular social arenas.

'Ethical boundary-work in the embryonic stem cell laboratory', by Wainwright, Williams, Michael, Farsides and Cribb, examines how research scientists working with embryonic stem cells grapple not just with legislation and frameworks imposed by regulatory bodies but also with their own understandings of the moral significance of their work as well as the ethical status of embryos. They challenge efforts to draw sharp boundaries demarcating 'science' from 'non-science'. Wainwright and colleagues argue that scientists are not just passive, morally disengaged agents responding to the decrees of bioethicists, jurists and legislators. Rather, scientists play active roles in shaping regulatory arenas and making moral judgements that are sometimes at odds with moral claims embedded in established legislative frameworks. Moral deliberation is not cast outside the sphere of scientific practice; scientific research, the scientists interviewed for this chapter argue, involves moral praxis. Aside from contributing to policy arenas – now part of the practical 'work' of science – researchers must personally and collectively confront what moral norms ought to govern their work. In particular, researchers and research teams working in particular laboratories must decide whether they will use 'spare embryos', only embryos donated following pre-implantation diagnosis programmes, or embryos created solely for research. Wainwright and colleagues do not make the typical move of the philosopher. They make no effort to 'solve' the moral status of embryos or determine which sources of embryos are morally acceptable. Rather, drawing upon interviews with stem cell researchers, they characterise how scientists work within regulatory arenas, shape the content and borders of these arenas, and struggle with moral dimensions of their work, even where 'expert' ethics commentary and established policy guidelines suggest that moral issues are resolved.

'Gift not commodity? Lay people deliberating social sex selection', questions a key demarcation line in bioethics. According to one school of thought in bioethics, the role of the bioethicist is to promote democratic deliberation, contribute to civic public discourse and engage fellow citizens in conversation about the good society. Within this model of moral reflection, the bioethicist engages in careful reasoning and sustained dialogue, but makes no special claims to moral expertise. However, not all bioethicists see themselves in quite such modest terms. The concept of the moral expert is part of the story of bioethics. According to this account of moral reasoning, the ethicist is not just another citizen capable of debating what constitutes morally defensible ethical practice or policy. Rather, possessed of formidable powers of reasoning – whether these tools take the form of conceptual analysis, linguistic analysis or cost-benefit calculations – the bioethicist is supposed to contribute not just 'a' voice but 'the' definitive voice to moral debate. The bioethicist as expert has gained authority in an era when hospitals employ clinical ethicists, ethics experts provide court testimony, bioethics popularisers are widely quoted in news media, and bioethics advisory bodies in many different nations offer 'expert' commentary to governments. Bioethicists gain considerable institutional power by laying claim to the notion of expertise. Scully, Shakespeare and Banks, though they do not provide a detailed taxonomy of various attempts in bioethics to claim expert moral knowledge, make a strong case for the reasonableness of 'lay people' engaged in deliberating social sex selection. They reveal that citizens do not rely upon crude moral intuitions or arbitrary, 'thin' forms of moral reasoning. Rather, at least within the context of discussing particular scenarios within group discussions, citizens could articulate basic moral norms, question them, acknowledge competing moral considerations, and provide cogent arguments in support of their initial presumptions. Scully, Shakespeare and Banks describe how citizens think through the complex moral question of the extent to which 'social sex selection' differs from sex selection performed for 'medical purposes'. Advocates of moral expertise will most likely remain dissatisfied with the intuitionist claims of lay people attempting to make moral judgements about when sex selection is justified. However, their chapter conveys a sense of the thoughtfulness of 'average', 'lay' citizens as they try to address the moral dimensions of a controversial procedure. Whether or not bioethicists can make some distinctive contributions to moral debate, Scully, Shakespeare and Banks challenge efforts to assert that 'expert bioethics' is rigorous and articulate whereas 'lay' conversation is unsophisticated and inarticulate. This effort at claiming expertise and demarcating boundaries is ineffective; citizens are far more capable of engaging in thoughtful moral reflection than ethics experts suggest. Scully, Shakespeare and Banks make a cogent case for more democratic, populist forms of collective moral deliberation.

Adam Hedgecoe, in 'It's money that matters: the financial context of ethical decision-making in modern biomedicine', explores how moral boundaries are drawn, the manner in which bioethicists contribute to moral debate, and the role of economics in setting boundaries for clinical practice. Hedgecoe notes that when bioethicists address topics related to priority setting and resource allocation they commonly address basic questions concerning which interventions ought to receive funding. In contrast, they pay much less attention to scenarios where a medication or medical device is granted regulatory approval but not financial backing from public or private insurers. By focusing upon just one set of questions, Hedgecoe argues, bioethicists neglect important moral issues that emerge both in the practice of medicine and in larger public arenas. They fail to respond to questions concerning how clinicians and healthcare institutions ought to act when medical interventions are permitted but not given space in budget allocations. In such circumstances, Hedgecoe notes, clinicians must engage in constant boundary work. They must decide who will have access to tests and who will obtain access to expensive treatments. Delays in addressing such questions, such as when the United Kingdom's National Institute for Health and Clinical Excellence delayed approving the drug Herceptin, compel individual clinicians and health care systems to make moral judgements about how to allocate scarce resources. Clinical discretion, Hedgecoe observes, is bounded by economic constraints. Caregivers must decide whether to circumnavigate existing limits on practice or devise rationales for refusing to provide access to tests and therapies. Hedgecoe's work attends to numerous demarcation lines. Governments and government advisory bodies set limits on clinical practice by setting economic boundaries on the provision of medical care. Clinicians must set boundaries on clinical practice either by deciding how to interpret rules and policies or by determining how to practice in the absence of regulatory standards. And finally, bioethicists set boundaries on their work by prioritising some ethical issues and neglecting equally significant moral concerns. In particular, Hedgecoe argues, bioethicists privilege debates about whether or not particular treatments ought to be funded while neglecting to address practical questions concerning the moral dimensions of how particular rationing decisions are implemented in everyday clinical practice.

These contributions range in subject matter from the moral deliberations of laboratory-based stem cell researchers to the practical reasoning of 'lay citizens' as they reflect upon the morality of social sex selection and finally to the financial context of moral decision-making in modern biomedicine. All three chapters identify, engage and challenge existing boundaries and exercises in demarcation. The chapters explore how particular social actors set boundaries and make distinctions in biomedical research, public conversation and biomedical practice. In addition, the chapters challenge the emphases and assumptions of contemporary bioethics. Bioethicists, these authors suggest, address particular moral issues while overlooking equally significant ethical concerns. Furthermore, at their worst, bioethicists denigrate the moral insights of concerned, thoughtful social actors and attempt to install themselves as uniquely qualified 'expert' arbiters of moral conduct. Articulating the complex moral worlds of particular social actors, these chapters all prompt reflection upon how moral distinctions are made, who is granted social authority to make them, and why particular topics are seen as morally significant whereas other topics are characterised by bioethicists as falling outside the scope of their work. They both critique bioethics and provide insight into the shape a richer, more sociologically informed bioethics might take.

Bioethics and social policy

Bioethics often has been criticised for being an insular field of general principles and decontextualised norms, and for promoting an overly individualistic approach to medicine and health care. Three essays address the crucial question of how ethical norms and regulations can be produced and implemented, both at a local level and in a broader social and national context. All three chapters deal with the social, cultural and institutional conditions that promote or inhibit the emergence of ethical regulations and the expression of ethical norms and practices. While the three contexts share a common western European background of socialised healthcare systems, the authors show how the content of what counts as ethical is shaped differently in each situation.

The chapter by Hoeyer analyzes how ethics policies are shaped by different agents (policy makers, nurses and donors) around a population-based bio-bank in Northern Sweden. The author studied the varied rhetorics of ethics around informed consent as a way of generating trust. He shows how participants – and particularly the donors – are less concerned with issues of personal choice, confidentiality or protection than with the 'mutual obligations embedded in the State-citizen relationship', reflecting a high level of trust in the Swedish welfare system. The fact that this welfare is largely constructed by popular social movements and is characterised by solidarity and egalitarianism translates into a common sense of public oversight and benefit-sharing, contrasting with the diversity of meanings ascribed to ethical values by the different agents.

Weyers' analysis of the emergence of regulations governing the practice of euthanasia in the Netherlands draws on the sociology of law and the distinction between formal and informal social control to explain the Dutch legal changes. The author shows how an increase in informal social control brings, in turn, formal control. Though several chapters have described the euthanasia debates and legal changes in the Netherlands, the key component in Weyers' explanation of the uniqueness of such emergence is the informal social control which pervades Dutch society through its strong participation and trust at several levels. In the Netherlands, networks of trust are constructed by the unique organisation of healthcare into 'homecare'. People are born and die at home, accompanied by their family doctor. Medicine, therefore, is a high-trust, family-based institution allowing, as Weyers shows, the implementation of a major legal change such as the euthanasia law without much resistance and even with strong support from the Dutch Medical Association. The euthanasia law is seen as allowing extensive informal and formal social control on ethical practices.

Religion has played a well-known role in the emergence of bioethics in the United States. Interestingly, the Catholic Church has never been an *institutional* player in this movement. But in many European countries (Ireland, Italy, Spain), despite increasing secularisation, the Church remains a key institutional partner in framing and constraining bioethical issues and politically and socially acceptable norms. The example of Ireland is analysed by McDonnell and Allison in their chapter 'From biopolitics to bioethics'. They show how the church, the state and medicine engage in 'politics of subterfuge' to maintain a status quo and institutional arrangements that constrain any reference to public debate. Still, the authors show how the Church has to position itself within a bioethical discourse in pragmatic medical rational terms and in the national identity frame to be able to maintain a powerful social role.

These chapters study how values are shaped and negotiated within specific cultures and diverse national contexts. They show that moral problems are generated and framed by the structures, institutions and practices within which they arise. Cultural ideologies- and the power relationships they entrench-can perpetuate moral inertia, as in Ireland, or trigger moral change as in the Netherlands and Sweden. The dynamics of institutions and the interlocking interests of the state, medicine, and in some cases the church, play a central role in bioethical regulation in western Europe, and a sociology of bioethics should therefore encompass a stronger analysis of institutions, structures and healthcare systems.

The bioethical imagination

Different disciplines have different ways of imagining the world. These different imaginations create the 'tower of Babel' problem in the academy. When sociologists and philosophers look at the development, introduction and influence of new biotechnologies, for example, it is no surprise that the concepts and language they use sound foreign to each other. This conflict of imaginations is all the more vexing in bioethics, where the 'stuff' of the field is analysed by members of several disciplines and where a variety of non-academic actors bring their agendas to the conversation. Three chapters in this collection reveal the range and limitation of the bioethical imagination. Each of these chapters shows how social contexts shape the way bioethical problems and solutions are imagined – the reflexive first step in an informed dialogue between members of the different tribes of bioethics.

Tausig and his colleagues offer a chronicle of the awakening of the bioethical imagination to the ethical problems of infectious disease. Their contribution highlights the difficulty of sorting out what is and is not bioethics – for while it is true that 'mainstream' bioethics has, until recently, paid scant attention to complex ethical issues of infectious disease, there have been several scholars writing about the moral questions raised by pandemics, epidemics and infectious disease. Is it fair to define this work as bioethics, even if the authors do not see themselves as bioethicists? Showing more than a hint of the contentiousness that has characterised the sociology-bioethics relationship, Tausig *et al.* go on to explain how the sociological imagination offers a framework for understanding and responding to the ethical quandaries posed by infectious disease and its treatment.

Busby's contribution explores the widely varied understandings of the donation, collection, storage and use of biological materials. Like Hoeyer, she presents an empirically grounded account of the way stakeholders in bioethics debates talk past each other, using the same words and phrases to mean very different things. The public – those doing the donating – see their contribution as a gift to be used to alleviate disease and suffering. But, as Busby shows, the notion of gift, an apt description in the days when blood was donated for direct use by the sick, loses its meaning in a world where commercial enterprises mine biological materials for profit. Industry and government, however, have an economic interest in perpetuating the altruism of would-be donors in order to advance bioscience. Busby offers no solution or policy recommendations but clarifies the issues at stake in bioethical debates.

Armstrong's reflection on the two bodies of medicine – that of the doctor (as professional) and that of the individualised patient – offers a fitting conclusion to this collection. In his historical analysis he uncovers interesting parallels in the way disease and medical ethics were imagined. By refusing to accept the stories medicine tells about its history, Armstrong is able to show how threats to individual health and to the integrity of the profession of medicine shifted over time. In the mid-19th century the concern was with dirt invading the body and 'irregulars' challenging the profession; by the beginning of the 21st century the tables were turned – public health is now concerned with how the human collectivity is harming the environment, and medical ethics is focused on protecting patients and subjects from medical mistakes, unethical practices and unscrupulous researchers. Like Busby, Armstrong is not in the business of providing answers to bioethical questions. He offers, instead, an opportunity for ethicists to see how their concerns are the product of history, social organisation and culture.

Conclusion

Social scientists have some skill in describing general patterns. We are adept at describing central tendencies and recognising variation around a mean. We are not prepared to declare – and have no special tools for identifying in a particular situations – just what to do. After decisions have been reached we are quite good at unpacking rationales of those involved as well as explicating the implications of those rationales. Characterising those rationales often involves us in debunking actors' stated motives by showing grains of self-interest that actors choose not to make public and, in truth, are possibly not aware of themselves. Those at the tail end of our debunking impulses are seldom grateful for the experience.

The outrage of bioethicists at the social scientists' critique, in part, has its roots in having their motives and actions subject to this sort of scrutiny. However, something else contributes to the often strained relationship between social sciences and bioethics. Bioethics – at least in its formative years – was a 'big-tent' discipline. Lawyers, philosophers, theologians, clinicians and other scholars and professionals all contributed to the emergence of bioethics. In contrast, we social scientists entered the tent and behaved as we typically do. We sat on the sidelines, we participated as little as possible in the flow of events, and then we criticised whatever policies were adopted, whatever actions were taken. Social scientists were not simply pushed to the margins of ethical debate. Rather, we chose this off-centre perch to better understand and interpret changes in law, institutions, health professions and social norms.

Bioethicists were, we think, surprised at what seemed like the worst form of rudeness – the team member who does nothing to help but only criticises team performance. Social scientists were startled that bioethicists took such umbrage at our behaviour and our critique. After all, we were behaving as we typically do – so the bioethicists' discontent was itself surprising.

This volume is intended to turn a page in the tiresome back and forth critique by presenting work that displays what social scientists have to offer to bioethics. The contributions reveal how ethics gets done on the ground, how fluid terms pick up specific meaning within institutional contexts, how the same action can be interpreted differently depending upon social location. In so doing, the chapters in this volume specify 'the here' from which social scientists take in their view. These chapters also do another thing characteristic of social science. They often describe dilemmas, they even sketch likely consequences from acting this way or that, but in general they do not offer direct responses to questions concerning how to live and what ought to be done.

Acknowledgements

We would like to thank Hannah Bradby, Allison Pearson and Robert Dingwall for their encouragement, support and work on behalf of this volume and the authors of the chapters collected here for their patience with unusually heavy-handed editors. De Vries' work on this volume was supported in part by a grant (K01AT000054-01) from the National Center for Complementary and Alternative Medicine (part of the National Institutes of Health, US).

2

Co-ordinating 'ethical' clinical trials: the role of research coordinators in the contract research industry
Jill A. Fisher

Introduction

The past two decades have witnessed a radical shift in pharmaceutical drug development. To a large extent, this process has been marked by a change in the location of clinical trials. Before 1990, pharmaceutical companies contracted primarily with academic medical centres for the clinical phase of their research and development (Sox 2001). Shifting from more than 80 per cent in 1990 to less than 35 per cent of pharmaceutical contracts today, universities have been increasingly replaced by private-sector, for-profit research organisations, often being run out of private practices (CenterWatch 2005). Moreover, clinical trials are increasingly conducted outside of the United States (Parexel 2005). This process of privatising clinical trials is driven by pharmaceutical companies' desire to cut costs and to speed up the development of new products (Evans, Smith and Willen 2005). More broadly conceived, these changes are part of larger corporate trends emphasising outsourcing, cutting production costs and maximising profits that have been described as characteristics of globalisation, neoliberalism and post-Fordism (Castells 1996, Harvey 1990, Smith 1990).

As part of the reorganisation of pharmaceutical research, a veritable clinical trials industry has formed. This industry includes companies to support the outsourcing of contracts to independent research sites (*i.e.* 'investigative sites'), companies to provide a corporate infrastructure for small investigative sites (*i.e.* SMOs, 'site management organizations') and companies to provide niche services like recruitment of human subjects and preparation of US Food and Drug Administration (FDA) applications for experimental products (*i.e.* CROs, 'contract research organizations') (CenterWatch 2005). Even the review of study protocols is now outsourced to for-profit institutional review boards (IRBs) that provide centralised review of clinical trials (Lemmens and Freedman 2000). Further, many of these companies have a global presence that allows the co-ordination of clinical trials on human subject populations throughout the world (Petryna 2005).

The new mode of drug development has involved changes in more than the locus and logistics of clinical trials. Pharmaceutical companies are increasingly adding genetic components to studies as a way of banking information they hope will be useful and important in the future (Hedgecoe 2004). In addition, industry insiders report that clinical phases of development are routinely begun before pre-clinical results on animals have been fully analysed, that clinical protocols are more complicated with more information about subjects being collected over longer periods of time, and that more stringent inclusion-exclusion criteria define which human subjects can be enrolled in studies (Personal communication, interview with physician-investigator, 31 March 2004). These modifications to the studies themselves are propelled by the pharmaceutical industry's desire to streamline development, to gather more information about their investigational products for the same or less investment and to ensure the best conditions for proving the efficacy of their products (CenterWatch 2005). The randomised controlled trial may be considered the gold standard in clinical development (Timmermans and Berg 2003), but this does not mean that the design of this type of study is static or exempt from economic and political pressures (Hess 2000).

Changes in the organisation of pharmaceutical research and the subsequent proliferation of a clinical trials industry have produced new professions and roles within the healthcare sector. Although many of these roles are based on more traditional doctor-nurse and doctor-patient relationships, the context of contract research alters older configurations of power and engenders new ethical conflicts within the clinic (Fisher 2005)[1]. Some scholars have done empirical studies of the organisation of medical research (*e.g.* Epstein 1996, 2004, Fishman 2004, Gray 1975). Others have shown that ethical conflicts are inherent in clinical research (*e.g.* Fox 1996, Mueller 1997, Taylor 1992). Yet, to date, only a few researchers have explored the implications of this new mode of drug development (Fisher 2005, Petryna 2005).

In this chapter I examine one aspect of these changes: the role of research coordinators as part of the clinical trials industry in the United States. My focus on coordinators highlights the role and ethical conflicts embedded in clinical trials. In order to show these dynamics, I describe the ways in which coordinators experience, and contend with, the conflict between research and care as part of their position within the clinical trials industry. Specifically, I explain: 1) what co-ordinating drug studies entails, 2) how research coordinators manage the conflict between research and care, and 3) how coordinators frame their jobs explicitly in terms of an ethic that is distinct from formal institutional conceptions associated with human subjects research. My argument is that coordinators use ethics as a vehicle through which they can reinsert individualised care into the context of research.

Method

This chapter is based on findings from 12 months of qualitative research in the southwestern United States[2]. The purpose of the study was to investigate the relations, structures and logics produced through the privatisation of clinical trials. Using a mode of institutional ethnography (Smith 2005), I examined the everyday work lives of those in the clinical trials industry, paying particular attention to the power dynamics that organise the social relations within that industry. In my work I was particularly attuned to the role and ethical conflicts – of various degrees of intensity – that were described by my informants (*i.e.* physician investigators, coordinators, monitors and even human subject volunteers) and observed in their practices (*e.g.* recruitment of subjects, informed consent processes and study retention and compliance).

My research consisted of interviews and observation at more than 20 for-profit research organisations in two major cities. Semi-structured interviews with 57 informants were clustered to get the perspective of multiple employees at individual investigative sites (*i.e.* conducting contract research), including physicians, coordinators, administrators and patient-subjects. The sites I chose represented a diverse sample of organisational forms, including private practices, dedicated research sites and large (non-academic) hospitals. My sample also included interviews at two not-for-profit investigative sites. In general, the types of drugs being tested were targeted at a wide range of medical conditions, including illnesses such as allergies, depression, irritable bowel syndrome and weight loss. A few centres were conducting research on more treatment-intensive illnesses like HIV and cancer. My research also included attendance at industry conferences and the monitoring of publications produced by industry professional organisations.

Apropos this chapter, I interviewed 18 coordinators (15 women and three men, 16 white and two Hispanic) and three recruiters (all women, two white and one African American), who had previously been coordinators. Ten of these 21 individuals were nurses, and one was a physician assistant. Their ages ranged from the late-twenties to the sixties, with the majority being in their forties. My interviewees also ranged widely in their amount of experience in the industry: from as little as three months to over 15 years. Specific demographic information about the individuals I quote in this chapter can be found in the Appendix.

Results: Coordinators' role and ethics

The vast majority of coordinators are women (90%), many of whom have come from nursing (60%) or other health-related positions (CenterWatch 2005). Not unlike the work of nursing, coordinators have the task of educating patients about clinical trials, getting patients to consent and enroll in studies and alleviating patients' fears about medical research (Sandelowski 2000). It is primarily through coordinators that patient-subjects interact with the industry and come to believe that they are being cared for (Mueller 2001). This role is not taken lightly by coordinators because they understand that the quality of their interactions with patient-subjects will determine how well they are able to recruit, enroll and retain those individuals. At the same time, many coordinators explicitly underscore the profound ethical implications of their work and their relationships with patient-subjects.

In spite of the centrality of their position, coordinators are often over-looked in discussions about the ethics of clinical trials (Davis *et al.* 2002). In many respects, this lack of attention to the work of coordinators is related to the more general invisibility and undervaluation of nursing within healthcare (Reverby 1987, Statham, Miller and Mauksch 1988). As is often the case with nursing (Duffy 2005), co-ordinating studies has been devalued because it is seen as unskilled women's work, not because the work is seen as unimportant in the quotidian operation of clinical trials. In fact, coordinators are often described as the most important members of clinical research teams (Fedor and Cola 2003).

Co-ordinating drug studies
The job descriptions for coordinators vary widely, yet the basic tasks that are delegated to them include recruiting, screening and enrolling patient-subjects into particular studies, managing the regulatory documents like IRB submissions and FDA forms, and sometimes even overseeing the financial end of contract negotiation and fee collection (Woodin 2004). The labour associated with co-ordinating a study includes two stages: screening/ enrolling and maintenance. During the screening and enrolling process, coordinators meet patient-subjects who have been referred by physicians or who have responded to advertisements. At these visits, coordinators go through informed consent forms and answer any questions potential volunteers have about a study. Only after patient-subjects have signed their explicit consent do coordinators complete the screening process by taking patients' medical histories and completing all laboratory work (*e.g.* blood tests, urine analysis)[3]. This information about patient-subjects is then used to determine whether or not they are eligible to enroll in studies based on the specific inclusion-exclusion criteria set by the pharmaceutical companies.

Those patient-subjects who do qualify are then enrolled in the clinical trials. This means that coordinators must follow the explicit instructions for randomising patient-subjects into the different arms of the studies. During the phase of study 'maintenance', coordinators ensure that patient-subjects are compliant, meaning that patient-subjects not only take study medications but also attend all study visits and complete associated diaries or other instruments designed to collect data on their symptoms. Coordinators are seen as critical in making sure that the specific details of all the studies being conducted at investigative sites are done according to protocol and on schedule[4].

One of the main functions of coordinators during study maintenance is retention; it is crucial for the pharmaceutical companies' data that patient-subjects who are enrolled in studies complete them[5]. As a result, there is a strong emphasis placed on the interpersonal skills of coordinators for getting patient-subjects to enroll in studies, and motivating them to follow the protocols:

> Compliance and retention can depend on the coordinator . . . If you respect the patient, you understand that they are taking an investigational medication, if you're flexible enough to work with their schedule, in a good mood, stuff like that, it really makes a difference to people . . . A lot of people just like to come in and talk (Coordinator A).

A strong theme in coordinators' descriptions of their interactions with patient-subjects revolves around talking. They see this type of interaction as what is necessary for individuals to feel comfortable about participating in research studies, and they highlight the importance of establishing strong ties of trust with patient-subjects. This tone is often established from the first interaction coordinators have with prospective patient-subjects. According to informants, a personal tone is critical to recruiting and enrolling patient-subjects:

> I try very hard to be very compassionate and understanding. I listen to them . . . The way I recruit probably takes a whole lot longer than some, *but I'm a friend of that woman* before she ever walks in the door. And when she does, I'm delighted to say, 'Oh Mary, I remember speaking with you. It's so good to get to meet you now' (Recruitment Specialist A).

Moreover, the relationships that coordinators build with patient-subjects must be maintained and built upon during the course of the entire study.

Emphasis on the interpersonal skills of coordinators and their work of recruiting, enrolling and retaining patient-subjects results in the job being highly gendered. This gendered component is explicit in what coordinators say about their professional roles. For example, many of my interviewees feel that women are uniquely qualified for co-ordinating, even without a background in medicine or patient care. They emphasise that women's specific interpersonal skills are critical to clinical trials because the job requires a sensitivity to others' needs that is rooted in women's personal identities. Empathy and compassion are coded here as the domain of women and as the human element in clinical trials.

In short, the value placed on coordinators is often determined as much by their gendered interpersonal skills as by their ability to multitask and to keep studies well organised[6]. Less value is placed on the medical expertise that coordinators have as nurses, technicians and physician assistants. Their medical knowledge is often seen as incidental to the work they do managing drug studies. In part, their medical expertise is ignored because these prior positions are not seen as *required* for co-ordinating. Of course, in practice, coordinators frequently make medical decisions and judgements in their interaction with patient-subjects. In the next section I pick up this thread by discussing how coordinators experience the conflict between *clinical research* and *patient care* and how they mobilise a discourse of 'ethics' to combat this role conflict.

Resolving role conflict through ethics

One of the hardest lessons for new coordinators, especially those who are nurses, is that research is not care. Even with training on how to conduct the various aspects of clinical trials, from determining if patient-subjects are eligible for studies, to randomising the patient-subjects into groups, to documenting all of the details of the study, many coordinators experience a conflict between their job description and their role vis-à-vis the patient-subjects. While I am not the first to notice this conflict (Davis *et al.* 2002, Mueller 1997), my research extends this earlier work by analysing how the coordinators' construction of specific ethical practices is generated by their interactions with patient-subjects and *not* from their job descriptions, IRB requirements or formal ethical principles that have been linked to human subjects research.

Most discussions of medical ethics focus on the protection of autonomy through the use of formal measures such as informed consent forms (Beauchamp and Childress 1993), but as with medical interactions more generally, everyday experiences of research ethics are constantly negotiated by the actors in the research setting. It is this informal and constructed sense of ethics that I am engaging here. In order to explain the way ethics comes into play in research settings, I must begin with a description of the way coordinators experience the conflict between the roles of researcher and caregiver.

In one case, a coordinator had been a practising nurse in the same private practice for decades when the physician she worked with began seeking contracts from pharmaceutical companies to conduct clinical trials. After a few months as a coordinator, she described to me how keenly she felt the struggle to understand her role in research as separate from care, and to make this distinction clear to patient-subjects:

> It's just getting that thing in your head that it's *not* a patient-doctor or nurse relationship. It's a *participant-research* [relationship] and making that clear . . . That, 'Yes, you're important as an individual, but it isn't a doctor-patient relationship' . . . [There was a] participant we had that was doing this [study] for psoriasis. It was unfortunate that out of the four people that have [been enrolled in the study], he was the one [whose condition] was the worst and had been getting worse – which was why he came in. Well, we were almost sure he got the placebo. He got no effect . . . Even though he'd read the informed consent and we'd explained it to him, he didn't understand it well: 'How would they pick me to not get the drug when I'm so bad?' . . . He still seemed a little dumbfounded by it because you're in a medical setting, *sort of* . . . We're doing medical tests and they're still expecting medical treatment *appropriate* for their [conditions], even though you've told them otherwise (Coordinator B).

Coordinators understand that randomisation means that patient-subjects who very much need medical treatment might instead receive a placebo as part of a clinical trial[7]. They also understand that a research orientation toward clinical trials (*i.e.* separating the goals of research from care) is key to the retention of human subjects. As part of the training many receive, coordinators are asked to accept the studies' most important goal for the pharmaceutical companies: drug development. It is, therefore, coordinators' duty to deliver patient-subjects and their data to completion in these studies.

Role conflicts intensify for coordinators as they develop relationships with patient-subjects. As I noted above, building these relationships is often crucial for recruiting and retaining patient-subjects in clinical trials. Conflicts intensify because, unlike standard medical care, coordinators are not only allowed but *encouraged* to spend a significant amount of time with patient-subjects. Most coordinators I interviewed emphasised that participation in a clinical trial enabled better care for many patient-subjects because the medical interactions were much richer due to the time spent with coordinators[8]:

It's really neat too because the length of our studies – we have trials that can go on for years: three, four, five years – you get to know those people over time . . . It's more personable, and we don't have that any more with healthcare, [but] *we're* able to give that to people [in research] (Recruitment Specialist B).

By creating these direct ties with patient-subjects, however, coordinators become invested in them as individuals. Subsequently, it is difficult for many coordinators to justify putting the interests of pharmaceutical companies before the interests of the sick people coming to their investigative sites for help. Coordinators describe being torn between their obligation to pharmaceutical companies and to patient-subjects: 'Unfortunately, we have some studies right now that are not a good option [for subjects]. For me, it's difficult when I have a conflict between whether this is really the best thing for the subject or not' (Coordinator C).

Because they interact with patient-subjects as individuals rather than as data, many coordinators I interviewed could not fully accept the separation of research and care. In other words, the relationships they develop with patient-subjects add to their experience of role conflicts within the context of clinical research. Through their interactions with patient-subjects, coordinators cannot help but see their role – at least partially – in terms of helping the patient-subjects. In one remarkable case, a coordinator who had 14 years of experience convinced the physician for whom she was working to stop accepting particular studies. In her telling of this story, she had done multiple studies for several different pharmaceutical companies on cox-2 inhibitors[9] (*e.g.* Vioxx®, Celebrex®, Bextra®) and saw the negative effects that this type of drug was having on patient-subjects:

I finally got to the point where I said, 'No, I don't want to do these studies'. And so I had to talk to Dr. X and say, 'You know these meds? We're supposed to be here helping mankind and these medicines aren't. They're making them worse and [causing] a lot of pain. That's not what we're here for, so I don't want to do these studies. If you want to do these studies, that's fine, but you'll need to find somebody else to do it for you. Because I can't legitimately give people these medications' (Coordinator D).

Although this type of situation is not the norm in contract research, it does illustrate the extent to which some coordinators will go to minimise their own conflict between research and care. It also reveals the sincerity of coordinators' concern for patient-subjects. Given that the relationship-building in which they engage acts as an extremely effective recruitment and retention strategy, coordinators' interest in patients could serve an instrumental purpose for the industry as a whole. Yet, in the context of their interactions with patient-subjects, coordinators clearly value patient-subjects for more than their enrollment quotas. As a coordinator emphasised, 'It's more than just good PR to have somebody care about you as a person, you know? I mean, that's what we're about. The studies don't matter to me; it's this person' (Coordinator E).

In a sense, the role conflict that coordinators experience surrounding the differences between research and care get played out as a professional conflict between the needs of patient-subjects and the coordinators' obligation to pharmaceutical companies. As such, the coordinators I interviewed have come to describe these conflicts not as intrinsic to their roles but as exogenous ethical conflicts. This interpretation of the conflict between research and care shapes their understanding of what is 'ethical' in the management of clinical trials. Through an appropriation of a formalised concept of ethics, coordinators confer their own meaning of ethics through their everyday practices. Importantly, as the remainder of this section argues, coordinators create their own code of ethics by applying a traditionally feminised sense of right and wrong to the work that they do (Bowden 1997).

Pharmaceutical companies, it should be noted, place little formal emphasis on ethics in coordinator training. The only clear link between the explicit preparation for the job and ethics is embedded in the informed consent process that coordinators learn. Within that context, they are trained to establish what is defined as a non-coercive and informative environment by providing as much time as the patient-subjects need to review the form and by answering any and all questions regarding the studies. Additionally, training often emphasises that informed consent is an ongoing process rather than a discrete event, and coordinators are asked to review consent forms with patient-subjects frequently, if not at each study visit.

Although these procedures clearly fit into the ethical principle of autonomy that has shaped the federal regulation of human subjects research (Faden and Beauchamp 1986, Wolpe 1998), the pharmaceutical industry has also emphasised that viewing informed consent as a process can facilitate patient-subject enrollment and retention (Getz 2002). In other words, ongoing informed consent can encourage patient-subject compliance. For the pharmaceutical industry, this alternative focus on informed consent as a process effectively removes it from the ethical realm and into a marketing modality[10]. What pharmaceutical companies emphasise as ethical practice at the research site is less related to the treatment of human subjects and more focused on the data that are produced through the studies[11].

In spite of the limited degree of emphasis placed on ethics in coordinators' training and interactions with pharmaceutical companies, coordinators told me that ethics is much more important to their jobs now than it was five years ago. By way of an explanation, a coordinator who had been in her position for more than 10 years told me that early on in her career there had been such a high learning curve for conducting studies according to the protocols that nobody had had time to consider ethics. She explained that experience had led to a different consideration of her work: 'So it's [still] all about, "Yes, we want the patients in the trials", but your ethics are more involved now. [You ask yourself,] "*Should* this patient be in the trial?" ' (Coordinator F).

What this coordinator and many others are referring to when they discuss this new attention to ethics is a concern with the appropriateness of clinical studies for individual patient-subjects. Their interpretation of this normative dimension to their work has very little to do with inclusion-exclusion criteria that literally determine whether or not patient-subjects *can* be enrolled in clinical trials. For many coordinators, they make an ethical assessment on two levels: the study itself and the individual patient-subject.

In the former category, coordinators with whom I spoke were quite adamant that they evaluated studies to determine if they were acceptable for *any* patient-subjects. What guides their sense of what is appropriate is often explained both explicitly and implicitly in popular articulations of the Kantian categorical imperative. For example, coordinators often mention the 'Golden Rule' and view their responsibility towards patient-subjects in personalised tones, thinking about how they themselves would like to be treated in the same situations:

Recruiting a patient for a clinical trial . . . , it's just like with everything; it's the same value I use with my everyday life; it's what I raised my boys on. It's to treat other people the same way you want them to treat you, and that is something that I strongly hold dear to my heart even in clinical research. I am not going to say or do anything to another woman that I wouldn't want them to say or do to me (Recruitment Specialist A).

Similarly, coordinators told me that they should recruit strangers into drug studies only if they would enroll someone from their own families. If they would not do so, they indicate, they should question the ethics of their involvement with that study, 'If I wouldn't put my own mother or father or brother or sister or children in a study, then don't do it' (Coordinator G). The example of the coordinator who notified her physician that she did not want to co-ordinate any additional studies on cox-2 inhibitors also illustrates a holistic concern about the types of studies offered to patient-subjects.

The second level of coordinators' ethical orientation toward their work involves determining whether or not the clinical trials are appropriate for specific individuals. One of the key ways this manifests is through an evaluation of the severity of the patient-subjects' illnesses. For example, if coordinators feel that potential patient-subjects are very ill, they may decide that a study with a high chance of receiving a placebo is too high a risk for those patient-subjects[12], especially when there are already effective products on the market for the conditions under investigation. One coordinator was particularly emphatic about the appropriateness of studies for individual patient-subjects:

A lot of people think that research might be a way to go, [but] it's not. If they're too sick, I don't want them in the study. They need to seek help. Even if they can't [access healthcare], we'll pick up the phone and call services . . . [to] get them pointed in the right direction (Coordinator H).

When I questioned coordinators about such ethical determinations, many explained to me that assessments of clinical trials were needed to check each study against the broader goal of medical progress and improving the health and welfare of patients. In their view, conducting clinical trials was about the advancement of medicine for the benefit of humanity. Without prompting, few coordinators mentioned the profitability of the pharmaceutical industry. When I questioned them about R&D agendas and the huge profits enjoyed by pharmaceutical companies, all of the coordinators patiently explained to me that the cost of drug development was so high that the pharmaceutical industry was not as profitable as it appeared. In their view, pharmaceutical profits are funnelled straight back into R&D expenses. In fact, many coordinators told me that working in the clinical trials industry helped them understand the high cost of drugs[13].

By understanding the clinical trials industry in humanitarian terms, coordinators construct their professional identities with an altruistic mission and apply it to their understanding of ethics. In some respects, their focus on medical progress replicates the conflict between research and care in a slightly different way. On one hand, coordinators need to minimise their concerns for individual patient-subjects for the potential benefit of society. On the other, they remain focused on the benefits and/or risks to individuals who do participate in the studies. The 'ideal' that is constructed by coordinators is a combination of the two modes: the desire to bring medical progress directly to patient-subjects who enroll in clinical trials.

Thus, for research coordinators, ethical clinical trials are defined quite differently from the way they are by institutional review boards, federal agencies and academic or clinical bioethicists. While these latter groups emphasise the autonomy of human subjects as the means of protecting them from research abuses, coordinators adopt an approach in line with more traditional modes of medical paternalism[14]. Whereas institutionalised bioethics is formalised, and emphasises universalism, coordinators cannot affect such detachment and make no pretence of neutrality. In fact, coordinators' understanding of ethics is so contingent and particularistic that they can and often do disagree with each other about which studies are more ethical and what types of decisions patient-subjects ought to make.

What my research suggests is that coordinators respond to the conflict between research and care by individualising both pharmaceutical studies and potential patient-subjects. They then make determinations about who should participate in which clinical trials. This construction of ethics has little in common with the more abstract goals of protecting the rights and welfare of human subjects, which is the mission of federal regulation. Yet it reinscribes a particular type of care back within the context of clinical trials that is based on a feminised sense of right and wrong and a maternalistic concern with the wellbeing of individual patient-subjects.

This is not to suggest that coordinators' mobilisation of ethics leads to better protection of patient-subjects. Instead, their explicit attention to ethics suggests a disconnection between the ethical principles that currently guide human subjects research and the needs of patient-subjects who are making personal decisions to participate in pharmaceutical research. Limitations in regulatory oversight cannot be overcome by coordinators alone, but their attention to ethics can help to highlight the structural conditions – intractable diseases, lack of health insurance, need for supplementary income, etc. – impacting upon patient-subjects' participation in drug development[15].

While this orientation towards clinical trials is clearly laudable, it is also problematic. Of course, it should be the goal of human subjects research to treat study volunteers with respect and care, yet the sense of ethics adopted by coordinators simultaneously serves the profit motive of pharmaceutical companies by adding a softer, maternalistic face to the rigid demands of drug development. Where this distinction matters is when the focus of drug development becomes the quest for market share, which is then repackaged as narratives of medical progress. Just as nurses have traditionally ensured compliant patients within the system of medicine and healthcare delivery (Sandelowski 2000), through their 'sentimental work', research coordinators are ensuring both current and future consumers of pharmaceutical products.

Discussion and concluding remarks

My focus on the role of research coordinators within the clinical trials industry offers a more complete picture of the way ethics gets constituted on the ground in pharmaceutical research. As this and other scholarship has shown

(Mueller and Mamo 2000, 2002), because co-ordinating is predicated upon the nurse-patient relationship, coordinators experience role conflicts in which their obligation to patient-subjects must be balanced with their obligation to pharmaceutical companies. This conflict catalyses informal ethical practices as part of coordinators' attempt to reinsert care into research.

My findings have particular relevance for sociological and feminist approaches to bioethics. By drawing attention to structural conditions that provide the contexts for ethical action, including analyses of gender, class and race, social scientists are increasingly engaged in complementary empirical research to redirect philosophical and clinical assumptions predominant in the field of bioethics (DeVries and Subedi 1998, Holmes and Purdy 1992). As an emerging field, the sociology and, to some extent, anthropology of bioethics have been framed as a corrective to both the abstraction of bioethics and the lack of normativity within the social sciences (Zussman 1997). Scholars who position themselves within this disciplinary framework have criticised bioethics for its lack of empirical material from which ethical standpoints are constructed and have argued for a new bioethics that is rooted in the social sciences (Hoffmaster 2001). In addition, scholars have called for sociological analyses to be relevant for policymaking (DeVries 2004).

My work does more than simply illustrate the conflict between research and care that is embedded in our current system of clinical trials. I have also shown that the negotiation of ethics is an everyday affair situated in the quotidian work of conducting pharmaceutical studies, not just in exceptional cases that generate the ethical dilemmas that provide the case material for normative bioethicists (Chambliss 1996, Winner 1991). As such, my research signals a place were empirical and normative ethics work hand-in-hand. My focus on the significance of the ethics of everyday practice begins where the work of bioethics has, until recently, left off. The exposé of egregious ethical breaches and the policy-making intended to prevent future violations prepared the ground for my study and others like it. My research broadens the field of ethical concern and opens a new and important area to those who claim expertise in bioethics.

Notes

1   Contract research refers to clinical trials sponsored by the pharmaceutical industry. It is often contrasted with investigator-initiated research, which is generally sponsored by the federal government or private foundations.
2   This research was supported by the National Institutes of Health under Ruth L. Kirschstein National Research Service Award 5F31MH070222 from the National Institute of Mental Health.
3   Elsewhere, I critique the assumptions underlying informed consent and the process used by coordinators (Fisher 2006). See also Corrigan (2003).
4   Coordinators are especially important in light of the problem known in the clinical trials industry as 'phantom investigators'. It is widely acknowledged that

physicians have low levels of involvement, that they delegate most details of study protocols to coordinators, and that they are often quite unfamiliar with the studies they are responsible for conducting (CenterWatch 2005).

5   One of the labour-intensive components of co-ordinating is the task of documenting everything that happens as part of the clinical trial. Information is written in patient-subjects' charts – called the 'source document' – and then the specific information requested by pharmaceutical companies is transferred to 'case report forms' that are then sent to the sponsoring company.

6   My interviewees also saw these latter characteristics as inherent, not as skills that are developed through work experience: coordinators either have them or they do not. Moreover, coordinators argue that these are traits that women are more likely to have than are men because they are similarly needed in the management of domestic activities. Here, these skills, seen as useful in both co-ordinating clinical trials and the care of the home, are naturalised as feminine.

7   The vast majority of pharmaceutical clinical trials are designed to compare investigational drugs against a placebo. Only in the treatment of some illnesses, like HIV/AIDS and various cancers, do pharmaceutical companies use an open-label drug against their investigational products. This is because it is considered easier and cheaper to show efficacy of the new product by comparing it to a placebo.

8   This sentiment about better care being available through clinical research was also echoed by patient-subjects I interviewed. Each of them made a point to tell me that they felt they had received higher-quality care (even when they thought they had been on placebos) because of the attention they received during the studies.

9   It is interesting to note that this interview was conducted on 27 January 2004, before the Vioxx® story broke, so the informant was not merely posturing in response to a scandal.

10   This marketing use of informed consent is often the subject of panels at industry conferences (*e.g.* Getz 2002).

11   In the last decade, pharmaceutical companies and the FDA have grown increasingly concerned about the perpetration of research fraud: fake patient-subjects, fabricated data, and/or tampering with laboratory results. A highly publicised case involved a California doctor who was engaged in severe research misconduct (Eichenwald and Kolata 1999).

12   Studies have different randomisation schedules for the experimental and placebo arms of the clinical trial. For example, studies commonly randomise 25 per cent, 40 per cent or 50 per cent of patient-subjects into the placebo group. In contrast, other studies are designed so that 100 per cent of patient-subjects will receive a placebo at some point during the study.

13   In spite of persuasive refutations about the cost of drug development (Angell 2004), the pharmaceutical industry's claim that profits are re-invested in R&D has remained salient through the industry's strategic marketing (King 2005).

14   Elsewhere (Fisher 2005), I draw the distinction between traditional modes of paternalism and what I call *pharmaceutical paternalism* – an organisational instantiation of medical paternalism occurring within private-sector clinical trials. I see this new form of paternalism as characterised by decision-making for healthcare that is no longer made by physicians or nurses for patients or by patients themselves, but rather by pharmaceutical companies for consumers – both patients and their providers. What is best for patient-subjects is defined

through the development of study protocols designed to prove efficacy of pharmaceutical companies' new products.

15   Scholars who emphasise the importance of structural conditions to patient-subjects' participation in medical research include Corrigan (2003), Eckenwiler (2001), Elliott and Lemmens (2005), King, Henderson and Stein (1999) and Zussman (1997).

References

Angell, M. (2004) *The Truth about the Drug Companies*. New York: Random House.

Beauchamp, T.L. and Childress, J.F. (1993) *Principles of Biomedical Ethics*. Oxford: Oxford University Press.

Bowden, P. (1997) *Caring: Gender-Sensitive Ethics*. New York: Routledge.

Castells, M. (1996) *The Rise of the Network Society*. Oxford: Blackwell Publishers.

CenterWatch (2005) *An Industry in Evolution*. Boston: CenterWatch.

Chambliss, D. (1996) *Beyond Caring: Hospitals, Nurses, and the Social Organization of Ethics*. Chicago: University of Chicago Press.

Corrigan, O.P. (2003) Empty ethics: the problem with informed consent, *Sociology of Health and Illness*, 25, 768–92.

Davis, A.M., Hull, S.C., Grady, C., Wilfond, B.S. and Henderson, G.E. (2002) The invisible hand in clinical research: the study coordinator's critical role in human subjects protection, *Journal of Law, Medicine, and Ethics*, 30, 411–19.

DeVries, R. (2004) How can we help? From 'sociology in' to 'sociology of' bioethics, *Journal of Law, Medicine, and Ethics*, 32, 279–92.

DeVries, R.G. and Subedi, J. (eds) (1998) *Bioethics and Society: Constructing the Ethical Enterprise*. Upper Saddle River: Prentice Hall.

Duffy, M. (2005) Reproducing labor inequalities: challenges for feminists conceptualizing care at the intersections of gender, race, and class, *Gender and Society* 19, 66–82.

Eckenwiler, L. (2001) Moral reasoning and the review of research involving human subjects, *Kennedy Institute of Ethics Journal*, 11, 37–69.

Eichenwald, K. and Kolata, G. (1999) A doctor's drug trials turn into fraud, *New York Times*, 17 May 1999, 1.

Elliott, C. and Lemmens, T. (2005) Ethics for sale: for-profit ethical review, coming to a clinical trial near you, *Slate*, 13 December 2005.

Epstein, S. (1996) *Impure Science: AIDS, Activism, and the Politics of Knowledge*. Berkeley: University of California Press.

Epstein, S. (2004) Bodily differences and collective identities: the politics of gender and race in biomedical research in the United States, *Body and Society*, 10, 183–203.

Evans, D., Smith, M. and Willen, L. (2005) Big pharma's shameful secret, *Bloomberg Markets Special Report*, December 2005.

Faden, R.R. and Beauchamp, T.L. (1986) *A History and Theory of Informed Consent*. New York: Oxford University Press.

Fedor, C. and Cola, P. (2003) Preliminary results of the 'Clinical Researcher' Coordinators' Survey, *Clinical Researcher*, 3, 18–22.

Fisher, J.A. (2005) *Pharmaceutical Paternalism and the Privatization of Clinical Trials*. Troy, NY: Rensselaer Polytechnic Institute.

Fisher, J.A. (2006) Procedural misconceptions and informed consent: insights from empirical research on the clinical trials industry, *Kennedy Institute of Ethics Journal*, 16, 251–68.

Fishman, J.R. (2004) Manufacturing desire: the commodification of female sexual dysfunction, *Social Studies of Science*, 34, 187–218.

Fox, R. (1996) Experiment perilous: forty-five years as a participant observer of patient oriented clinical research, *Perspectives in Biology and Medicine*, 39, 202–26.

Getz, K. (2002) Leveraging the informed consent process as strategic recruitment and retention asset, *Patient Recruitment Strategies for Clinical Trials*, Philadelphia, 10.17.02.

Gray, B.H. (1975) *Human Subjects in Medical Experimentation: a Sociological Study of the Conduct and Regulation of Clinical Research.* Huntington: R.E. Krieger.

Harvey, D. (1990) *The Condition of Postmodernity.* Oxford: Blackwell.

Hedgecoe, A. (2004) *The Politics of Personalized Medicine: Pharmacogenetics in the Clinic.* Cambridge: Cambridge University Press.

Hess, D. (2000) *Can Bacteria Cause Cancer?: Alternative Medicine Confronts Big Science.* New York: New York University Press.

Hoffmaster, C.B. (ed.) (2001) *Bioethics in Social Context.* Philadelphia: Temple University Press.

Holmes, H.B. and Purdy, L.M. (eds) (1992) *Feminist Perspectives in Medical Ethics.* Bloomington: Indiana University Press.

King, N.B. (2005) Pharma porn: making the case for medicalization. Paper presented at the Society for Social Studies of Science Conference, Pasadena, 22 October 2005.

King, N.M.P., Henderson, G.E. and Stein, J. (eds) (1999) *Beyond Regulations: Ethics in Human Subjects Research.* Chapel Hill: University of North Carolina Press.

Lemmens, T. and Freedman, B. (2000) Ethics review for sale? Conflict of interest and commercial research ethics review, *Milbank Quarterly*, 78, 547–84.

Mueller, M.R. (1997) Science versus care: physicians, nurses and the dilemma of clinical research. In Elston, M.A. (ed) *The Sociology of Medical Science and Technology.* Oxford: Blackwell.

Mueller, M.R. (2001) From delegation to specialization: nurses and clinical trial co-ordination, *Nursing Inquiry*, 8, 182–90.

Mueller, M.R. and Mamo, L. (2000) Changes in medicine, changes in nursing: career contingencies and nurses in clinical trial coordination, *Sociological Perspectives*, 43, S43–S57.

Mueller, M.R. and Mamo, L. (2002) The nurse clinical trial coordinator: benefits and drawbacks of the role, *Research and Theory for Nursing Practice*, 16, 33–42.

Parexel (2005) *Pharmaceutical R&D Statistical Sourcebook 2005/2006.* Boston: Parexel.

Petryna, A. (2005) Ethical variability: drug development and globalizing clinical trials, *American Ethnologist*, 32, 183–97.

Reverby, S. (1987) *Ordered to Care.* New York: Cambridge University Press.

Sandelowski, M. (2000) *Devices and Desires: Gender, Technology, and American Nursing.* Chapel Hill: The University of North Carolina Press.

Smith, D.E. (2005) *Institutional Ethnography: a Sociology for People.* New York: AltaMira.

Smith, V. (1990) *Managing in the Corporate Interest: Control and Resistance in an American Bank.* Berkeley: University of California Press.

Sox, H. (2001) Sponsorship, authorship, and accountability, *Annals of Internal Medicine*, 135, 463–6.

Statham, A., Miller, E.M. and Mauksch, H.O. (eds) (1988) *The Worth of Women's Work: a Qualitative Synthesis*. Albany: State University of New York Press.

Taylor, K. (1992) Integrating conflicting professional roles: physician participation in randomized clinical trials, *Social Science and Medicine*, 35, 217–24.

Timmermans, S. and Berg, M. (2003) *The Gold Standard: the Challenge of Evidence-Based Medicine and Standardization in Health Care*. Philadelphia: Temple University Press.

Winner, L. (1991) Engineering ethics and political imagination. In Johnson, D.G. (ed), *Ethical Issues in Engineering*. Englewood Cliffs: Prentice Hall.

Wolpe, P.R. (1998) The triumph of autonomy in american bioethics: a sociological view. In Devries, R. and Subedi, B. (eds) *Bioethics and Society: Constructing the Ethical Enterprise*. Upper Saddle River: Prentice Hall.

Woodin, K.E. (2004) *CRC's Guide to Coordinating Clinical Research*. Boston: CenterWatch.

Zussman, R. (1997) Sociological perspectives on medical ethics and decision-making, *Annual Review of Sociology*, 23, 171–89.

Appendix

Demographic Information for Quoted Informants

- Coordinator A: white, female, 25–35, no prior medical training
- Coordinator B: white, female, 40–50, nurse
- Coordinator C: white, female, 25–35, nurse
- Coordinator D: white, female, 40–50, medical assistant
- Coordinator E: white, female, 55–65, nurse
- Coordinator F: white, female, 35–45, no prior medical training
- Coordinator G: white, female, 40–50, no prior medical training
- Coordinator H: white, female, 40–50, counselling background
- Recruitment Specialist A: white, female, 45–55, former coordinator, no prior medical training
- Recruitment Specialist B: African American, female, 30–40, former coordinator, life science background

3

The many meanings of care in clinical research

Michele M. Easter, Gail E. Henderson, Arlene M. Davis, Larry R. Churchill and Nancy M. P. King

Introduction and background

Clinical research is the testing of experimental medical interventions in humans with the goal of advancing knowledge about improving treatments or procedures for diagnosable illnesses. It is usually done by investigators who are physicians and study coordinators who are nurses, and usually enrolls patients as research subjects. The conduct of scientific research in clinical settings thus involves two distinguishable sets of roles and relationships: researcher-subject and clinician-patient. The presence and impact of these multiple and potentially conflicting professional roles has been described in the sociological literature (*e.g.* Fox 1959, Mueller 1997, Taylor 1992); in bioethics, the issue has been more often framed in normative terms: should these roles be combined and, if so, how? (*e.g.* Churchill 1980, Miller *et al.* 1998).

A well-known body of principles and guidelines stipulates moral duties owed to subjects and norms to guide clinical research. The 1947 Nuremberg Code describes a set of investigator responsibilities distinctive to research to assure voluntary informed consent and protection from harm. The Belmont Report (1979) provides the moral basis for the US 'Common Rule', federal regulations governing human subjects research (45 CFR 46). In the 2002 revision of the Council for International Organizations of Medical Sciences (CIOMS) guidelines, one of 25 essential points of information for subjects in obtaining informed consent is 'whether the researcher is serving only as a researcher or both as researcher and the subject's health care professional' (CIOMS 2002: 15). Yet despite calling attention to the issue, this guidance and others are silent on whether and how care-giving should be incorporated into clinical research, and how to avoid confusion between these two roles.

Some philosophers and ethicists argue that being a patient in a clinical care setting and a subject in a research study are so different that anything that would encourage subjects to see themselves as patients is exploitative and deceptive (Katz 1993, Miller 2000). The concern is that 'investigators who appear before patient-subjects in white coats create confusion. . . . Patients will view an invitation to participate in research as a professional recommendation that is intended to serve their individual treatment interests' (Katz 1993: 29). Others assert that although the researcher-subject and clinician-patient relationships require different ethical rules and principles to guide them, the moral tensions inherent in a combined role can be managed if and only if they are kept in mind (Brody and Miller 2003, Miller and Rosenstein 2003). Still others contend that the clinician and researcher roles are fully compatible, such that physicians' ethics are also the foundation for research ethics (Fried 1974, Grunberg and Cefalu 2003).

Over the past three decades, a number of empirical studies have shown that subjects in clinical trials are indeed likely to misunderstand the difference between research participation and treatment for their condition, and to overestimate the potential for research to offer them direct medical benefits (Gray 1975, Daugherty *et al.* 2000, Joffe *et al.* 2001, Henderson *et al.* 2006) originally identified as a 'therapeutic misconception' for subjects (Appelbaum *et al.* 1982). These studies reinforced concerns about the potential for confusion in patients who are considering participation in clinical research. It is unclear whether this confusion is also fuelled by the presence of treatment relationships and a perception of 'care' in the context of a clinical research study, although this is the assumption of the CIOMS guideline. There are almost no empirical data about how researchers and study participants view the presence of care in research, and whether it is related to increased confusion about the purposes of research. If care and caregiving exist in both worlds, a deeper understanding of the dimensions and meanings of care in clinical research is necessary in order to distinguish appropriate from inappropriate care for research subjects.

In the absence of empirical data about perceptions of care in research or their meaning, theories about what care is owed to research subjects continue to be proposed. For example, Richardson and Belsky (2004) have recently articulated a moral framework for thinking about clinical care responsibilities that researchers owe to their subjects. Their beginning assumption is that researchers do not owe their subjects 'the same level of care that physicians owe their patients', and they seek to frame the surplus of care that is owed over and above the protocol requirements in non-Hippocratic terms, modelled on the legal paradigm of 'bailment', or 'partial and limited entrustment', in which the care of patient-subjects is not completely entrusted to study physicians. Whether or not this is an adequate normative framework, it is clear that any normative model for care in research would benefit from a better understanding of what clinician-researchers perceive their role to be, as well as how patient-subjects understand the nature and meaning of the care they receive in clinical trials. Filling that void in our understanding is the aim of this chapter. We do not begin with theoretical models of care, such as those offered by nursing (James 1992, Webb 1996, Lea *et al.* 1998), philosophy (Gilligan 1982) or the sociology of carework (Hochschild 2003, Strauss *et al.* 1982). Rather, to speak directly to normative debate about care in research, we begin with the most basic categories of that debate – care and research – in order to see if the people involved in research also understand the situation in those broad terms. Like Kohn and McKechnie (1999) we attend to the ways caring practices can 'extend the boundaries of care' and examine how the people involved understand that care.

How do the researchers and subjects who participate in clinical trials understand the presence of care, broadly conceived, in research? We explore whether research personnel are likely to be seen, and to see themselves, as clinical caregivers or as researchers, and why. Our analysis is drawn from interviews with researchers (physician-investigators and nurse-study coordinators) and patient-subjects in early phase gene transfer (often called gene therapy) trials. The purpose of such early phase trials is to provide the first testing of safety and efficacy of experimental interventions in human subjects. Direct medical benefit – the purpose of treatment in clinical settings – is unlikely in this category of clinical trial, even though essentially all early-phase gene transfer trials enroll only patients as subjects. This chapter goes beyond our previous work (Henderson *et al.* 2004, 2006) by focusing on the concept of care rather than either the expectation of benefit or the therapeutic misconception, and by taking into account perspectives by principal investigators (PIs), study coordinators (SCs), and patient-subjects.

Our empirical investigation addresses the ethical issues raised in the normative debate about the clinician-investigator dual role in the following ways. First, we hypothesised that if researchers are seen by subjects as 'mostly taking care of [them] as patients', or if research relationships are described as 'the same as relationships with their personal physician [or nurse]', then research will be seen – erroneously – as individualised treatment. Similar hypotheses have been suggested by bioethics literature and social science (Fox 1959, Bamberg and Budwig 1992, Kass *et al.* 1996, Joffe *et al.* 2001, Mueller 1997, Daugherty *et al.* 2000, Dresser 2002). Second, we also expected that researchers and subjects would perceive a conflict between the physician/ nurse role of caring for patients and the investigator/study coordinator role of gathering knowledge, in early-phase experiments using interventions that are not known to be effective and are potentially harmful to subjects. This hypothesis is supported by social psychological theories of role conflict and cognitive dissonance (Merton 1957, Biddle 1986, Festinger 1962), as well as previous studies of medical roles in research (*e.g.* Taylor 1992, Hicks 1996).

Sample

As part of a larger study of researchers and subjects in early phase gene transfer research (GTR) (Henderson *et al.* 2004, 2006), we contacted principal investigators (PIs) of all trials registered with the Office of Biotechnology Activities (OBA) as early phase GTR studies in adults between December 1998 and December 2000 ($N = 123$). Seventy-eight studies were eligible for inclusion, and 19 had one or more patient-subjects willing and well enough to participate, producing our sample of 37 researcher and 68 patient-subject interviews. To reduce the influence of studies with larger numbers of patient-subjects, we analysed no more than four randomly selected interviews from any given study, yielding a subset of 45 total patient-subjects from the 19 studies. The project was approved by Institutional Review Boards (IRBs) at the University of North Carolina and the National Human Genome Research Institute. Interview and consent form instruments are available at http://socialmedicine.med.unc.edu/scob/.

Of the 19 studies that contributed principal investigators, study coordinators and patient-subjects, about half were studies of cancer, followed by inherited, vascular and infectious disease. Half were phase I studies, and the rest phase I/II and II. We used Fisher's exact test to determine whether there were statistically significant differences in the distributions of disease and study phase for the studies sampled vs. those not sampled, and for subjects interviewed vs. those not interviewed (data not shown). There was no significant difference in the distribution of phase. Our sub-sample under-represents subjects in cancer trials: half are cancer trials, compared to three-quarters of those eligible to be included. This probably reflects the severity of illness experienced by subjects in cancer trials, compared to the other disease categories.

About half of the 19 studies were multi-centre trials, and half had corporate sponsors. With one exception, the trials were conducted at academic or governmental medical centres. Researchers included principal investigators (PIs) and study coordinators (SCs). All PIs in the 19 studies had medical degrees; two had PhD degrees as well. Most PIs were male (13/19), while most SCs were female (15/18). Fourteen SCs had nursing degrees, and two had medical degrees. The average age was 47 for PIs and 45 for SCs. All PIs and most of the SCs had extensive clinical research experience; eight of the PIs and five of the SCs had conducted at least one other GTR trial.

Patient-subjects' ages ranged from 20–83, with a median of 58. Almost all (93%) had graduated from high school, and nearly half had graduated from college (44%). Eight (18%) of the 45 respondents were women. Two-thirds (67%) described their condition as mild, mild-to-moderate or moderate; one-third (28%) said it was moderate-to-severe or severe; two said it varied. Seventeen (38%) subjects had been involved in a research study before.

Methods

Most of the 82 45-minute telephone interviews were conducted by three of the authors (GH, AD and ME) and completed between July 2000 and June 2002. The interviews focused on recruitment and enrollment of subjects in the particular trial; the procedures, activities and roles involved in the conduct of research; and potential benefits expected from participation. The interviews were semi-structured, including closed-ended and open-ended questions, often with follow-up questions asking respondents to explain their answers. Interviews were taped and transcribed verbatim and were electronically coded using QSR N6 software (version 6.0, QSR International Pty. Ltd. 1999). Codes were developed emically based on respondent answers, and applied by three investigators divided into two teams (one investigator coded PI-related questions, another coded SC-related questions, and a third coded both). Differences were reconciled in iterative meetings (Miles and Huberman 1994).

We collected quantitative and qualitative data about research and provider relationships, and perception of the intent of the study. All three kinds of respondents were asked if they saw the PI or SC as 'mostly taking care of patients' or 'mostly doing/conducting research', and asked why they responded as they did. Qualitative coding beyond the response options (mostly care, mostly research, and both) captured the reasons for choosing care, research or a combination. The initial closed-ended question necessarily limited the range of answers to the response options in order to focus attention on the research question, and thus the qualitative data are constrained; these data do not tell us what respondents might have said had we not introduced those categories. All researchers and subjects were also asked to compare investigator-subject relationships with health-care provider-patient relationships. Again, open-ended responses yielded insight into nuances beyond the pre-defined response options (same or different). Subjects who viewed the PI as their personal doctor were identified using a combination of closed-ended questions and text coding, including whether that relationship had started prior to the trial. Subjects also were asked whether they understood the intent of the study as mostly to 'help you as a patient' or mostly to 'gather knowledge', and the reason for the answer given (see Tables 1 and 3 for verbatim questions).

We first present quantitative results of our analysis. In bivariate logistic regression, the intent of the study was treated as the dependent variable, and perceptions of research relationships as independent variables. This analysis was conducted for subjects only because it is their understanding of the relationship that is of greatest concern in bioethics. We then present qualitative analysis of the meaning of clinical care for researchers and subjects, how research comes to be seen as 'taking care' of subjects, and why subjects may prefer research to traditional healthcare relationships. Because our focus is on the thematic variety of responses rather than how representative they may be, we do not present frequencies or percentages for qualitative data.

Findings

Research relationships: mostly care or mostly research?
Subjects had a range of opinions about whether researchers were 'mostly taking care of [them] as patients or mostly conducting research'. As Table 1

Table 1 *Subjects' views of research relationships and study purpose*

Question	Response Options	Frequency (%)
In the [XX study], did you see [PI] as *mostly* taking care of you as a patient or *mostly* doing research?	Mostly taking care	19 (43)
	Both	8 (18)
	Mostly doing research	17 (39)
	Total	*44 (100)**
In the [XX study], did you see [SC] as *mostly* taking care of you as a patient or *mostly* doing research?	Mostly taking care	19 (45)
	Both	7 (17)
	Mostly doing research	16 (38)
	Total	*42 (100)***
Thinking about your relationship with [PI] while you were in the [XX study], do you think it was the same as your relationship with your personal doctor, or was it different?	Same	14 (34)
	Different	27 (66)
	Total	*41 (100)†*
Thinking about your relationship with [SC] while you were in the [XX study], do you think it was the same as your relationship with nurses who have taken care of you, or was it different?	Same	7 (18)
	Different	32 (82)
	Total	*39 (100)**‡*
Subject reports PI is own doctor.	PI is my doctor	18 (40)
	PI is not my doctor	27 (60)
	Total	*45 (100)*
Thinking about the [XX study], would you say it was mostly intended to help you as a patient or mostly intended to gather knowledge?	Mostly to help patients	10 (22)
	Both	13 (29)
	Mostly to gather knowledge	20 (44)
	Don't know	2 (4)
	Total	*45 (100)*

*1 subject could not answer. **1 subject did not know the SC and 2 did not have a SC.
†4 subjects could not answer. ‡3 subjects could not answer.

demonstrates, close to half saw the PI (43%) or SC (45%) as 'mostly taking care', and almost the same proportion said the PI (39%) or SC (38%) was 'mostly conducting research'. A smaller number (18%, 17%) said they did 'both'. Despite these similar percentages averaged across studies, no standard division of labour between care and research is apparent in individual subject views of PI-SC pairs within a study. Table 2 shows that approximately equal numbers of subjects saw the PI-SC team in each possible combination of research and care-giving: for seven subjects, both PI and SC were seen as mostly conducting research; for nine both were seen as mostly taking care of them as patients; for 13 (6 plus 7), the team combined care and research, and two to three subjects perceived each of the other possible combinations.

Table 2 *Subjects' perception of team (PI and SC)*

	Perception of SC			
Perception of PI	SC mostly research	SC both	SC mostly care	Total
PI mostly research	7 (17%)	3 (7%)	6 (15%)	16 (39%)
PI both	2 (5%)	2 (5%)	3 (7%)	7 (17%)
PI mostly care	7 (17%)	2 (5%)	9 (22%)	18 (44%)
Total	16 (39%)	7 (17%)	18 (44%)	41 (100%)*

*4 people could not answer one of these questions (see note at Table 2).

Table 3 *Researchers' views of research relationships*

Question	Response Options	Frequency (%)
In this study, do you see yourself [PI] as *mostly* taking care of patients or *mostly* conducting research?	Mostly taking care	5 (26)
	Both equally	4 (21)
	Mostly conducting research	10 (53)
	Total	19 (100)
In this study, do you see yourself [SC] as *mostly* taking care of patients or *mostly* conducting research?	Mostly taking care	7 (39)
	Both equally	6 (33)
	Mostly conducting research	5 (28)
	Total	18 (100)
Do you think the relationship that subjects in the [XX study] have with you [PI] is the same as the relationship that they have with their personal doctors, or is it different?	Same	2 (12)
	Different	14 (82)
	Both Same and Different	1 (6)
	Total	17 (100)*
Do you think the relationship that subjects in the [XX study] have with you [SC] is the same as the relationship that they have with their personal clinicians, or is it different?	Same	4 (24)
	Different	12 (71)
	Both Same and Different	1 (6)
	Total	17 (100)**

*2 PIs could not answer this question. **1 SC could not answer this question.

Researchers also had a range of opinions about whether they were 'mostly taking care of patients' or 'mostly conducting research'. As Table 3 shows, about half of the PIs tended to see themselves as conducting research, and a third of SCs did so. Like subjects, researchers did not portray one standard division of labour for the research team; that is, despite small numbers, PIs and SCs described their team roles as research-research, care-care, and almost every other combination. This was true both for their self-classifications and when they classified each other (data not shown).

The second measure of researcher relationships was a comparison of relationships in research and treatment settings. Table 1 shows that a clear majority of subjects said their relationships with researchers (PI, SC) were different from their relationships with health-care providers (personal doctor or other). Sixty-six per cent saw their relationship with the PI as different from that with their personal physician, and 82 per cent considered the SC relationship as different from that with their personal nurse (or other healthcare provider if the SC was not a nurse). Five subjects perceived both the PI and SC relationships to be the same as relationships with personal healthcare providers (data not shown). Most PIs and SCs also saw their relationships with subjects as different from those subjects might have with healthcare providers (Table 3). There was more agreement between researchers and subjects about this comparison than about whether a researcher was 'taking care'; most subjects agreed with their researchers that the relationship was different (data not shown).

The third and last examination of research relationships addressed subjects' perception of the PI as their personal doctor. Forty per cent of subjects considered the PI to be their personal doctor (see Table 1), and for half of these the relationship had started before the recruitment phase of the study. The PIs for these subjects also reported that they considered one or more of the subjects in the study to be their patients, though we do not know which subjects. Subjects who saw the PI as their personal doctor were more likely to describe the relationship as 'the same as' relationships with their personal doctor, but were **not** more likely to describe the PI's role in the study as 'mostly taking care of me as a patient' than as 'mostly conducting research' (data not shown).

Study purpose
Patient-subjects' views about the purpose of the study tended to emphasise the research component. When asked whether the study as a whole was 'mostly intended to help you as a patient', or 'mostly intended to gather knowledge', 44 per cent said the purpose of the study was to gather knowledge, 22 per cent saw the intent of the study as mostly to help me as a patient, 29 per cent said both and 4 per cent could not choose (Table 1).

Research relationships and study purpose
The central concern about clinical care in research settings is that research imbued with care will cause subjects to misunderstand the study's purpose, thinking its goal is to help them personally rather than to contribute to scientific knowledge. Yet surprisingly we found no relationship between a care-giving relationship with researchers, as defined by subjects, and the tendency for those subjects to misunderstand the purpose of the study.

Bivariate logistic regression showed that none of the variables measuring relationships was significantly related to subjects' perception of the study purpose (data not shown). If a subject saw the PI or SC as mostly taking care of 'me as a patient', he was not more likely to think the study was 'intended to help me as a patient'. This was true even if the subject thought **both** the PI and SC were taking care of him as a patient. Similarly, if a subject thought her relationship with a researcher was the same as her relationships with other healthcare providers, she was not more likely to misperceive the intent of the study. Even if relationships with **both** the PI and SC were like those with healthcare providers, the subject was not more likely to think the study was intended to help her as a patient. Lastly, subjects who considered the PI to be their personal doctor were no more likely to think the study was intended to help them as patients than those who did not.

Understanding research relationships

How can we explain the finding that patient-subjects perceive 'care' in their relationships with both PIs and SCs, without thinking the purpose of the study is to help them as patients? Qualitative examination of the fuller context of subjects' and researchers' answers to two families of questions – about whether researchers are mostly taking care, and whether the relationship is the same as with healthcare providers – sheds light on why respondents answered as they did.

Defining 'care' and 'research'. When respondents explained why they selected 'mostly taking care' or 'mostly conducting research' to describe the roles of PIs and SCs, it was clear that they understood care to include both physical and emotional components. Subjects who said that care was part of the PI or SC role defined this care as clinical activities, psychosocial support, expressions of concern and close personal relationships with study team members. Many cited monitoring for symptoms and side effects, prescribing medications, discussing medical issues and generally 'performing all of the functions that a doctor would normally do'. Both PIs and SCs primarily supported their care responses with instrumental, clinical activities, though SCs were more likely than PIs to offer descriptions of psychosocial support and relationships.

Secondly, we found that some activities clearly necessary for research or for subject protection, such as monitoring for adverse events and side effects, and discussing the study and its progress, were cited as evidence of care by some respondents. A few described the study intervention itself as therapeutic, and therefore a form of care. Protection of study subjects was occasionally cited as evidence of care by both patient-subjects ('I came before the research') and researchers ('my first responsibility is to them and their wellbeing'). Sometimes the specificity of the description made it difficult to tell whether the activities offered in support of a care answer were part of the research intervention (delivery of the test agent), or a standard of care related to good clinical practice (proper wound management).

Thirdly, some respondents expressed the view that the research part of the clinical trial did not involve interaction with subjects. Many patient-subjects, as well as several researchers, thought research activities were carried out apart from subjects in some other place (the lab), at some other time (after the subject leaves), or with other people (study personnel or sponsors). Interaction with or simply the presence of a researcher was taken as evidence of care by some, even if the researcher was clearly collecting what was understood to be data: 'I wouldn't consider [my SC] a researcher, I think he was more than that . . . I wouldn't think that a researcher in my definition would be in the room when I got the injection'. Other subjects stated that a PI or SC was mostly doing research because he or she did not interact with subjects as much as a caregiver would have, suggesting that time spent was an indicator of care.

Fourthly, some respondents defined research in opposition to individualised standard care. Several PIs made this distinction: 'this would not be part of my standard care of patients'; 'it's about research, not about patient care'. A few PIs revealed discomfort about this, as expressed by this PI: 'From the study perspective, I'm conducting research. Putting them in the study isn't really taking care of them, [but] it's a conflict, there's a tension when you're the investigator and the physician'. It was less common for subjects and SCs to discuss a tension between research and care in this way.

Fifthly, despite the focus of ethics guidelines on the responsibility to protect subjects from harm, some respondents defined research as entailing an inhumane lack of regard. Indeed, several respondents seemed to view research as a pejorative term associated with neglect, depersonalisation and disregard for a subject's comfort, and almost an insult to the caring researcher: 'he never referred to me as a chart or a clinical experiment . . . I mean he's very concerned' and 'you could just say, okay, it's strictly research, [but] she goes beyond that . . . she's got a way to make you feel comfortable, that you know everything's gonna be okay'. Similarly, one PI said he provided 'mostly care' because human subjects were not the same as animal subjects: 'they're not a mouse'. Many SCs appear to be uncomfortable with a purely research role; all described themselves as providing some form of care even when they described their role as 'mostly research'. Respondents who chose mostly research were often quick to add that someone else was providing care to subjects, whether another member of the research team or a healthcare provider outside of the study.

Finally, respondents who said the researcher's role involved research often described research-like attributes, rather than an absence of care-like attributes. For some it was simply obvious; 'the reason we're here is to do research'. Subjects who chose mostly research cited specific activities to support their answers, such as observing researchers checking study results, writing things down, collecting data, spending time in a lab or office (rather than the clinic), and managing study personnel.

Research as a way of taking care of patients. The majority (83%) of subjects said that someone on the study team (PI or SC) was caring for them as patients to an equal or greater degree than conducting research (Table 3). A majority of PIs (68%) and SCs (78%) also said this (data not shown). As described above, it was common to define care in positive terms and research in negative terms, and reconciling the two could be challenging. Several respondents, including researchers, said our questions about care and research were hard to answer, even 'unfair'. This PI's language exemplifies the difficulty of distinguishing and reconciling care and research: 'I tell [subjects] I wear two hats. One hat is the hat I put on when I'm your doctor to take care of you. And the other hat is the hat that I put on when I'm trying to see if something new works, or to find out how to give it . . . And when I'm taking care of you I wear both hats'. On the one hand, there is a difference between the two hats. But on the other hand, the two hats can seem so indistinguishable that the phrase 'taking care of you' encompasses both of them. The struggle to reconcile care and research often depended upon respondents' perception that certain types of care were inseparable from the research, and that research was a way of taking care of patients.

We found three ways in which research was seen as taking care of patients. For some respondents, research was care because of the potential for direct benefit from the gene transfer intervention. One subject felt the investigator was mostly taking care of him as a patient because 'I was in there to get cured . . . of course I felt, surely the study on me was helping the overall study, but I looked at it very much as being hopefully beneficial to my condition'. One PI said, 'I'm a clinician and I spend a lot of time seeing patients but this is a study that I'd really like to know whether it will impact on the patient, especially to cure [his] cancer'.

Others focused on indirect benefits as a source of care. Some researchers felt that research participation itself (without a prospect of direct benefit) could still be considered a form of taking care of patients because it provided extra monitoring, health education and psychosocial benefits such as hope. Such conviction caused one investigator to strongly resist the question: 'Stupid question . . . clinical trials and patient care are one and the same. [I think] that being someone's doctor is more than giving them something which makes a tumour get smaller. I think it's helping them cope with their present problem physically, emotionally, helping them look forward to and prepare for the future. I think clinical trials are an integral part of that'. Typically, when SCs and subjects described psychosocial benefits from the study, they talked about the care and concern shown by study personnel.

Finally, the 'dual nature' of some research activities made it difficult to separate care and research. Even if no benefit is expected from the experimental intervention, care can arise whenever the subject's data are needed for both care and research. As two SCs explained in categorising care and research, 'it's hard to separate out, but that [study] data also represents how well the patient is doing'; 'I think the two go together. Although we are doing research on patients, we have to do care to get the answers that we need. So, I would have to say it's caring for patients in a research capacity'. One investigator may consider the management and monitoring of patient-subjects as care in research, while others may create distinct spheres of care and research based on the specific purpose of the activity required by the research: '. . . while getting a CAT scan could be a patient care issue, it's really a research issue if we have to have that CAT scan for this study'.

Researchers as providing better care than health care providers. Above, we described how research participants defined care and research, and how research could be seen as a form of care for many. Here we describe a striking finding: it was common for research participants to see researchers as *providing better patient care* than healthcare providers. We had expected most researchers and subjects to describe differences between relationships on- and off-study the way PIs in our study tended to: greater specialisation, narrower focus, shorter duration, or that investigators simply were not personal doctors. However, most SCs and patient-subjects who said the relationship was different, said it was better because there were *more* personal care elements and closer personal relationships in research than in clinical care, due at least in part to being able to spend longer amounts of time together. As one subject said about an SC, 'it was more personal . . . you see someone almost every week, you get sort of close to them'. Thus, for many subjects and study coordinators, enrolling in or working for a study was not only compatible with patient care, it was an improvement over patient care delivered in treatment settings.

Discussion and conclusions

The goal of early phase clinical trials is to create generalisable knowledge rather than to provide individualised patient care. We expected that respondents would distinguish between conducting research and taking care of patients according to these separate goals. Similarly, we expected that if subjects and researchers said research relationships were different from healthcare relationships, the difference would involve more emphasis on research and less on patient care.

Instead, we found that researchers and subjects perceived many kinds of care in researcher roles and relationships, and that often these research relationships were both 'different and better' than those in health care. Further, for patient-subjects the perception of care in relationships did not seem to predict how they perceived the overall intent of the study. Seeing researchers as care-givers or as personal doctors did not mean that subjects were more likely to think the study was intended to help them. These factors also did not predict a related construct- the therapeutic misconception- in multivariate analysis (Henderson *et al.* 2006). The many kinds of care in clinical research often offered satisfying care-giving relationships and did not result in the confusion about the purpose of research central to much scholarly debate in research ethics. Normative proposals that aim to clarify the distinction between care and research should take these findings into account. At a minimum, these findings indicate that the notion of 'ancillary responsibilities' as formulated by Richardson and Belsky (2004) may not be a good model for gauging investigator duties to subjects because it fails to recognise the amount and kinds of care-giving already present in research relationships in the eyes of both investigators and patient-subjects.

Our exploratory approach in this study had strengths and limitations. Its strength is the inductive discovery that researchers and patient-subjects alike see care as a fundamental part of research. We found that care is not a synonym for therapeutic intent, but a much broader and potentially more important concept to some researchers and subjects. On the other hand, we acknowledge the limitations of our small sample size and several measurement issues. We must be cautious about any finding of non-significance with a small sample, *e.g.* finding no relationship between subjects' views of researchers as caregivers and the study intent as care. The wording of questions may also affect interpretation of our results. For example, we chose to ask open-ended questions about 'caring for patients' rather than questions that measured the specific emotional and instrumental components of care, or the more specific 'individualised patient care', which might have elicited different answers. Alternatively, we could have framed the question in terms of treating patients rather than caring for them, which with hindsight likely might have excluded many of the emotional aspects of care. Our respondents' negative view of research may have been due in part to the way the question pitted it against care. Although we avoided words known to have negative connotations such as 'experiment' (ACHRE 1995), some respondents might have thought the choice was between caring and un-caring, rather than caring for patients and conducting research, thereby biasing our results toward care answers. Our findings are also limited to subjects who had enrolled and continued to participate in early phase gene transfer trials, and who were healthy enough to participate in our interview. We cannot generalise beyond this population, though we think it is likely that subjects and researchers in other early phase studies have similar views.

Qualitative analysis of responses revealed a variety of combinations of care- and research-related roles, sometimes with evident tension. Some researchers said they combined the roles, others prioritised one over the other. Although some trials appear to divide care and research between the PI and SC, we did not find a standard, widespread pattern in which SCs provided care and PIs research (Mueller 1997), or vice versa. Some respondents explicitly mentioned a tension between the two roles. Others did not, but nevertheless defined research and care in opposition to each other. In some studies, the potential conflict was removed from the study site, because research was thought to be conducted off-site at the lab or company, or care was thought to be given only by non-study physicians. We speculate that some of the phenomena we observed were strategies for resolving a role conflict (Taylor 1992, Biddle 1986, Merton 1957), and we hypothesise that the focus on what care and research have in common was a cognitive strategy to minimise potential tensions: all parties would like the experimental intervention to 'work', to protect subjects from harm, and to provide or receive high quality physical and emotional care.

Although we expected and found evidence for a conflict between research and care, we also found that, according to several definitions of care, clinical researchers were seen as better able to care for patients than healthcare providers. Participants saw clinical activities, psychosocial support, expressions of concern and close personal relationships with study team members as forms of care, which is consonant with definitions of care in nursing and sociological literatures (James 1992, Webb 1996, Lea *et al.* 1998, Hochschild 2003, Strauss *et al.* 1982). Remarkably, these forms of on-study care were often seen as superior to care outside the study, particularly by subjects and study coordinators; the definition of the professional nursing role as providing care in particular was difficult to shed even when nurse-researchers had a mostly research role (Hicks 1996, Reverby 1987). These trials offered the personalised attention, clinical care and psychological support that often get short shrift in the treatment setting (Mechanic and Schlesinger 1996, Anders 1996), which is appealing to researchers and subjects who are also providers and patients.

Subjects perceived care in research relationships regardless of the intent of the study. Their judgements appear to be based on cultural expectations about how researchers and care-givers will behave. It is evident from our study and others that there are common stereotypes about scientists that portray them as distant and uncaring (Rahm and Charbonneau 1997, Haynes 1994, Rowan 1995). The 'different and better' relationships in the study did not conform to those negative expectations, but rather than softening and expanding the definition of researcher to encompass kind and compassionate individuals, researchers were often simply classified as care-givers. Ethical reasoning in practice may thus be guided by cultural expectations for occupational identities, exemplifying its 'social embeddedness' in institutions (Light and McGee 1998).

For many respondents, care seems to stand in for the moral duties researchers owe to subjects. There is a moral framework in research that protects people from harm, which guides IRBs and researchers as they design and carry out studies in accordance with principles such as non-maleficence, and careful risk-benefit analysis. However, subjects and researchers articulated the duties owed to subjects in terms of the more familiar clinical care framework, not the research framework. This suggests that the moral framework for research is less robust than for clinical care; in practice the latter is credited not only with attentive physical and emotional care, but sometimes also for human subject protection, a duty generally accorded to investigators in research activities. Researchers do have an obligation of beneficence, but it is directed toward society and science, not toward individuals. Without a separate moral framework for clinical research, participants in research appear to rely on the 'similarity position' identified (and criticised) by Brody and Miller, in which 'the ethics of clinical research is merely a special case or application of the ethics of clinical medical practice' (Brody and Miller 2003: 330).

Although empirical investigations focus on describing what 'is', we do not wish to abandon a normative commitment to what we think 'ought' to exist, that is, clarity about the difference between research and treatment. We are concerned that if researchers are able to provide 'different and better' care, subjects may be unduly influenced to join and remain in studies. However, we resist the temptation to rewrite clinical research ethical standards based on our findings; we do not believe 'that a moral "ought" can be deduced from a factual "is" ' (Callahan 1999: 286). But neither can ethical norms be separated from the larger social context and the felt experiences of researchers and subjects. So we take seriously the relevance of the complex definitions of caring offered by our respondents; clearly the experience of clinical research provides no easy and unambiguous distinction between care in research and care in routine healthcare encounters.

Our findings are useful for both ethics and social science. This study was designed, carried out and analysed by a team including lawyers, philosophers, physicians and sociologists. This sort of inter-disciplinary scholarship is necessary for the sociological study of bioethical issues (Hedgecoe 2004). We shed light on how research relationships are understood in practice, and propose that these data provide a new and more robust context for understanding whatever normative aspects for caring may be proposed. Ethicists should keep in mind that research participants tend to hold the 'similarity' position referenced above, and that normative models that do not recognise a place for care in research are unlikely to be implemented into research practice.

Our study cannot tell us precisely what norms should govern clinical investigators, but it does clearly indicate that several different and powerful forms of care-giving cannot be excised from research. Even researchers outside a clinical context employ forms of emotional and supportive care that might confuse subjects (Bosk 2001), and at least some personal attention seems necessary if only to recruit and retain subjects in a study (Groves *et al.* 1992). It appears that research in any context, by necessity and inclination, is very unlikely to be 'care-free'.

Acknowledgements

This research was supported by a grant from the Ethical, Legal and Social Implications of the Human Genome Program, NHGRI, 2R01 HG002087. Investigators include authors of this chapter, and Daniel K. Nelson, Barbra Bluestone Rothschild,

Benjamin S. Wilfond and Catherine R. Zimmer. The authors wish to thank the anonymous reviewers for their helpful comments.

References

ACHRE (Advisory Committee on Human Radiation Experiments) (1995) *Final Report*. Washington, D.C.: U.S. Government Publishing Office.

Anders, G. (1996) *Health against Wealth: HMOs and the Breakdown of Medical Trust*. Boston: Houghton Mifflin.

Appelbaum, P.S., Roth, L.H. and Lidz, C. (1982) The therapeutic misconception: informed consent in psychiatric research, *International Journal of Law and Psychiatry*, 5, 3–4, 319–29.

Bamberg, M. and Budwig, N. (1992) Therapeutic misconceptions: when the voices of caring and research are misconstrued as the voice of curing, *Ethics and Behavior*, 2, 3, 165–84.

Biddle, B.J. (1986) Recent developments in role theory, *Annual Review of Sociology*, 12, 67–92.

Bosk, C. (2001). Irony, ethnography and informed consent. In Hoffmaster, B. (ed.) *Bioethics in Social Context*. Philadelphia, PA: Temple University Press.

Brody, H. and Miller, F.G. (2003) The clinician-investigator: unavoidable but manageable tension, *Kennedy Institute of Ethics Journal*, 13, 4, 329–46.

Callahan, D. (1999) The social sciences and the task of bioethics, *Daedalus*, 128, 4, 275–94.

Churchill, L.R. (1980) Physician-investigator/patient-subject: exploring the logic and the tension, *The Journal of Medicine and Philosophy*, 5, 3, 215–24.

CIOMS (Council for International Organizations of Medical Sciences) (2002) *International ethical guidelines for biomedical research involving human subjects, Commentary on Guideline*, 13.

Daugherty, C.K., Banik, D.M., Janish, L. *et al.* (2000) Quantitative analysis of ethical issues in phase I trials: a survey interview of 144 advanced cancer patients, *IRB*, 22, 3, 6–14.

Dresser, R. (2002) The ubiquity and utility of the therapeutic misconception, *Social Philosophy and Policy*, 19, 2, 271–94.

Festinger, L. (1962) *A Theory of Cognitive Dissonance*. Stanford, Calif.: Stanford University Press.

Fox, R.C. (1959) *Experiment Perilous: Physicians and Patients Facing the Unknown*. Glencoe, Ill.: Free Press.

Fried, C. (1974) *Medical Experimentation: Personal Integrity and Social Policy*. Amsterdam, New York: North-Holland Pub. Co., American Elsevier.

Gilligan, C. (1982) *In a Different Voice: Psychological Theory and Women's Development*. Cambridge, MA: Harvard University Press.

Gray, B. (1975) *Human Subjects in Medical Experimentation: a Sociological Study of the Conduct and Regulation of Clinical Research*. New York: Wiley.

Groves, R., Cialdini, R. and Couper, M. (1992) Understanding the decision to participate in a survey. *Public Opinion Quarterly*, 56, 475–95.

Grunberg, S.M. and Cefalu, W.T. (2003) The integral role of clinical research in clinical care, *New England Journal of Medicine*, 348, 14, 1386–8.

Haynes, R.D. (1994) *From Faust to Strangelove: Representations of the Scientist in Western Literature*. Baltimore: Johns Hopkins University Press.

Hedgecoe, A.M. (2004) Critical bioethics: beyond the social science critique of applied ethics, *Bioethics*, 18, 2, 120–43.

Henderson, G.E., Davis, A.M., King, N.M., *et al.* (2004) Uncertain benefit: investigators' views and communications in early phase gene transfer trials, *Molecular Therapy*, 10, 2, 225–31.

Henderson, G.E., Easter, M.M., Zimmer, C.R., *et al.* (2006) Therapeutic misconception in early phase gene transfer trials, *Social Science and Medicine*, 62, 1, 239–53.

Hicks, C. (1996) Nurse researcher: a study of a contradiction in terms? *Journal of Advanced Nursing*, 24, 2, 357–63.

Hochschild, A.R. (2003) *The Managed Heart: Commercialization of Human Feeling*. Berkeley: University of California Press.

James, N. (1992) Care = organisation + physical labour + emotional labour, *Sociology of Health and Illness*, 14, 4, 488–509.

Joffe, S., Cook, E.F., Cleary, P.D., *et al.* (2001) Quality of informed consent in cancer clinical trials: a cross-sectional survey, *Lancet*, 358, 9295, 1772–7.

Kass, N.E., Sugarman, J., Faden, R. *et al.* (1996) Trust, the fragile foundation of contemporary biomedical research, *Hastings Center Report*, 26, 5, 25–9.

Katz, J. (1993) Human Experimentation and Human Rights, *St. Louis University Law Journal*, 38, 1, 7–54.

Kohn, T. and McKechnie, R. (eds) (1999) *Extending the Boundaries of Care: Medical Ethics and Caring Practices*. Oxford: Berg.

Lea, A., Watson, R. and Deary, I.J. (1998) Caring in nursing: a multivariate analysis, *Journal of Advanced Nursing*, 28, 3, 662–71.

Light, D. and McGee, G. (1998) On the social embeddedness of bioethics. In De Vries, R. and Subedi, J. (eds) *Bioethics and Society: Constructing the Ethical Enterprise*. Upper Saddle River, NJ: Prentice Hall.

Mechanic, D. and Schlesinger, M. (1996) The impact of managed care on patients' trust in medical care and their physicians, *Journal of the American Medical Association*, 275, 21, 1693–7.

Merton, R.K. (1957) The role-set: problems in sociological theory, *The British Journal of Sociology*, 8, 2, 106–20.

Miles, M.B. and Huberman, A.M. (1994) *Qualitative Data Analysis: an Expanded Sourcebook* (2nd Edition). Thousand Oaks, Calif., Sage.

Miller, F.G., Rosenstein, D.L. and DeRenzo, E.G. (1998) Professional integrity in clinical research, *Journal of the American Medical Association*, 280, 16, 1449–54.

Miller, F.G. and Rosenstein, D.L. (2003) The therapeutic orientation to clinical trials, *New England Journal of Medicine*, 348, 14, 1383–6.

Miller, M. (2000) Phase I cancer trials. A collusion of misunderstanding, *Hastings Center Report*, 30, 4, 34–43.

Mueller, M.R. (1997). Science versus care: physicians, nurses, and the dilemma of clinical research. In Elston, M.A. (ed.) *The Sociology of Medical Science and Technology*. Oxford: Blackwell Publishers.

Rahm, J. and Charbonneau, P. (1997) Probing stereotypes through students' drawings of scientists, *American Journal of Physics*, 65, 8, 774–8.

Reverby, S. (1987) *Ordered to Care: the Dilemma of American Nursing, 1850–1945*. Cambridge: Cambridge University Press.

Richardson, H. and Belsky, L. (2004) The ancillary-care responsibilities of medical researchers, *Hastings Center Report*, 34, 25–33.

Rowan, A.N. (1995) Scientists and animal research: Dr. Jekyll or Mr. Hyde? *Social Research*, 62, 3, 787–800.

Strauss, A., Fagerhaugh, S., Suczek, B. *et al.* (1982) Sentimental work in the technologized hospital, *Sociology of Health and Illness*, 4, 3, 254–78.

Taylor, K.M. (1992) Integrating conflicting professional roles: physician participation in randomized clinical trials, *Social Science and Medicine*, 35, 2, 217–24.

Webb, C. (1996) Caring, curing, coping: toward an integrated model, *Journal of Advanced Nursing*, 23, 5, 960–8.

4

The field worker's fields: ethics, ethnography and medical sociology

Renée R. Anspach and Nissim Mizrachi

Introduction

In an address to the Royal Society of Anthropologists published shortly after his death, Pierre Bourdieu outlined his approach to reflexivity in ethnographic field work, which he calls 'participant objectivation'. In contrast to the 'narcissistic reflexivity of postmodern anthropology' or 'the ego-logic reflexivity of phenomenology', Bourdieu uses the tools of anthropology and sociology to examine the researcher's field and its assumptions, biases, rewards and constraints that s/he unconsciously projects onto the social world. He notes that:

> [the ethnographer's] most decisive scientific choices (of topic,
> method, theory, etc.) depend very closely on the location she
> (or he) occupies within her professional universe, what I call
> the 'anthropological field', with . . . its habits of thought, its
> mandatory problematics, its shared beliefs and commonplaces,
> its rituals, values, and consecrations, its constraints in matters of
> publication of findings, its specific censorships, and . . . the biases
> embedded in the organizational structure of the discipline, that
> is . . . all the unconscious presuppositions built into . . . categories
> of scholarly understanding (Bourdieu 2003: 283).

Bourdieu's concept of 'field' sheds new light on a dilemma that occurs when researchers' very efforts to do good research cause harm to those they study (see, for example, Cicourel 1964, Anspach 1993). The present paper suggests that this tension between doing good work and doing good, occurs because the researcher is situated in two very different fields. The first is the ethnographer's field or discipline as Bourdieu uses the term – that is, the organisation of the discipline and its assumptions, constraints and rewards attached to various kinds of analysis (Bourdieu 2003, Wacquant 2004). At the same time, the researcher is situated in a second kind of field, as ethnographers commonly use the term: the setting s/he studies, the web of relationships in which s/he comes to be embedded, and the obligations and mutual expectations that develop between researcher and researched. When the canons of their disciplines collide with what researchers view as their normative obligations to research subjects, the two fields become the horns of an intractable dilemma.

In the following pages, we use our own research experience to show how ethical quandaries result from the collision of these two fields. While we do refer to the published work of other ethnographers, our primary strategy, suggested by Bosk (2003), is to 'revisit' the sites of our ethnographic research in neonatology (Anspach), and an institution for severely disabled children (Mizrachi), and to 're-view' this ethnographic work through the prism of the present. The analysis we present is the result of collaborative reflection on our individual projects; when we talk about our work in the field we indicate whose work it is (in end notes) and use the first person singular voice to describe our experience.

The ethnographer's fields

Nowhere are the tensions between the ethnographic and academic fields more apparent than in sociological ethnographies of medicine. Comparing anthropological and sociological work on bioethics (and, by implication, medicine), De Vries (2004) observes that medical sociologists are more likely to antagonise their subjects than are anthropologists. The role of medical sociologists as perennial irritants to those we study – a 'fly in the ointment', to use De Vries's phrase – can be traced to its quest for 'bounded originality', its origins in the Chicago School, and its location in 'post-Parsonian' medical sociology (Rier 2000).

The hallmark of academic fields is, according to Bourdieu, a relentless 'quest for distinction'. For this reason, part of professional socialisation involves learning to recognise sociology's distinctions between brilliant and competent, important and trivial, original and banal, and interesting and boring work. Sociologists also strive to distinguish themselves from their peers by producing work that differs from other work-work viewed as original or interesting – that is, work that challenges either the conventional wisdom or, better yet, the conventional sociological wisdom (Davis 1971).

If sociology values ideas that challenge taken-for-granted assumptions, it also limits how far an idea can stray from the conventional sociological wisdom to be taken seriously – boundaries that are policed by the field's gatekeepers. Some of this 'forbidden knowledge' (Kempner et al. 2005), while contested, has a long history: sociology's taboo against psychological explanations has persisted since Durkheim, who, in his quest to distinguish sociology from other disciplines, placed psychological explanations outside the boundaries of the fledgling discipline. In short, sociologists strive for originality that remains safely within the boundaries of acceptable theorising or what might be called 'bounded originality'.

This quest for distinction or bounded originality helps explain the unique mandate of Chicago ethnographers: to 'elevate the humble and humble the proud', in the words of C. Everett Hughes (quoted in Bosk 1992: xiv). When applied to those the conventional wisdom deems discredited, deviant and disadvantaged, Chicago ethnography revealed morality and dignity. When applied to powerful professions, notably medicine and psychiatry, the goal was to demystify professional authority. This debunking impulse, fuelled by the research on New Social Movements that flourished in the 1960s, was central to what later came to be called 'post-Parsonian' medical sociology (Rier 2000). Medicine, which at the time enjoyed a degree of power and prestige unparallelled in the Western world, came under attack for failing to regulate itself in the public interest and for medicalising deviant behaviour, death and reproduction. The overall tenor of the times is best summarised by Eliot Freidson's (1970) view of the expanding role of the expert as the greatest threat to a free society.

The classic medical ethnographies reflect this debunking ethos. Throughout *Asylums* are metaphors that elevate the humble mental patient, who has a 'moral career', and that humble the proud psychiatrist, who works in a 'tinkering trade' (Goffman 1961). Irony became ethnographers' master trope as they detailed the unanticipated negative consequences of mental hospitals that ironically drove patients crazy, and 'helping professions' that functioned as agents of social control. (For discussions of irony, see Matza 1968, Gusfield 1981, Pollner 1987 and Bosk 2001). These ironic inversions of the conventional wisdom are a *leitmotif* running through medical ethnographies. Other ethnographies attacked professional dominance at the micro-level, finding that doctors dominated the medical interview, withheld information and deflected patients' concerns (see Anspach 1988, Rier 2000). It should come as no surprise that physicians and mental health professionals are offended when they read our work.

Not only does medical ethnography lead us to antagonise those we study, but it also can be the source of significant ethical problems. As Bosk (2001) observes, we do not really obtain informed consent from research subjects, since we fail to disclose the most significant risk: the damage to self-esteem and reputation that ensues when we portray them in an unfavourable light. Thus, 'we betray our subjects twice: first, when we manipulate our relationship with subjects to generate data and then again when we retire to our desks to transform experience to text' (Bosk 2001: 206). In describing these ethical dilemmas, we follow Bosk's lead.

In short, medical sociologists' ethnographies show that the academic and medical fields may be at loggerheads, and, moreover, that this tension can produce ethical problems. What is often unexplored and undertheorised is the fact that, in addition to pursuing knowledge and data, ethnographic medical sociologists also pursue careers. This omission is striking for, as medical sociologists, we have detailed how careerism shapes the medical work but rarely acknowledge its role in shaping our thinking.

It is at this point that Bourdieu's conception of field can play a constructive role. For Bourdieu, fields are arenas in which actors compete over resources and economic, symbolic and, in this case, cultural capital: degrees, book contracts, publication in scholarly journals, citation counts, awards and honours. If we view writing not as the work of a solitary scholar, but as a form of social interaction with an implied audience, then it follows that when writing, sociologists will consider that audience, paying particular attention to the gatekeepers who control access to valuable resources. This is not to say, however, that careerism is the only, or even the most prominent, consideration for field workers, for to do so would be to reduce ideas to socially structured interests (Bosk 2001). Rather, as the next section shows, the 'imagined reader' is an inescapable component in the complex melding of facts, values, ideas and interests that shapes the ethnographic imagination.

Revealing and concealing

From the first moment of contact with host members to review of the last page proof, researchers make decisions about what to reveal, what to conceal, which questions to ask, and which topics to avoid. These decisions are in part an effort to navigate the thicket of conflicting demands of the academic and ethnographic fields. Throughout the research process, field relations are affected by members' dual role as both informants and gatekeepers who control access to potential research sites. The need to obtain and maintain access to the research setting contributes to what Bosk (2001) calls the first betrayal of research subjects: the proverbial 'cover stories' ethnographers spin to package descriptions of their research that host members will find palatable. Were they fully candid about the purpose of their research, field workers would have to admit that host members would find sociological research irrelevant, arcane or potentially harmful:

> I had been invited by the municipality of Jerusalem to investigate why residents of Nila, an institution for severely disabled children, experienced adjustment problems when they attended school. My interest lay elsewhere: I wanted to study how forms of knowledge shaped the social organization of Nila, using my ethnographic data to explore how the mind/body dualism shaped Nila's social life. Realizing that officials and professionals would have little to gain from such a study, I convinced them that only through a detailed ethnography of Nila would I be able to determine the cause of the childrens' difficulties.

This passage, from Mizrachi's work, shows how researchers translate the language of the sociological gaze into the idiom of the clinical gaze in order to convince municipal officials that this research would be helpful. The actual purpose of the study was lost in the translation.

Unasked questions[1]

In contrast to Bosk's (2001) experiences, problems of revealing and concealing, loyalty and betrayal did not appear at the point of entry nor resurface when my writing began, but rather continued relentlessly throughout my time in the field, intensifying as I developed hunches, interpretations and working hypotheses. As my research proceeded, I developed nagging doubts about the ethicality of neonatal intensive care itself. Do the many healthy newborns saved by newborn intensive care justify the survival of infants with serious disabilities? How many infants leave the nursery with cerebral palsy, blindness or severe developmental disabilities? Can nursery follow-up studies answer this question, or are they biased because dissatisfied parents of seriously disabled children are lost to follow-up? Many of these questions flowed predictably from critical medical sociology, a field that clashed with physicians' own world views. Fearful of offending the nursery staff – to say nothing of losing entrée – I kept these questions to myself.

This reluctance to raise sensitive issues reflects what I call (Anspach 1993) the 'dilemma of discretion', in which researchers avoid violating members' boundaries by asking questions and broaching topics that might offend them. Ethnomethodologists have also demonstrated how incessant questioning and probing violate the demands of everyday polite discourse and make normal social relationships impossible (Garfinkel 1967, Cicourel 1964). Tacit prohibitions against excessive or inappropriate questions pose a problem for ethnographers who must ask questions to learn about an organisation's social life.

Not all researchers conceal their criticisms from research subjects in the name of discretion. In fact, occasionally field workers attempt full disclosure. When she was a graduate student studying fetal surgery, Monica Casper (1998) interviewed a mother who had undergone fetal surgery and her husband, both pro-life activists and fervent supporters of fetal surgery. When, at their request, Casper sent them some of her work, the couple was so enraged by Casper's criticisms of fetal surgery that they convinced the surgeons to curtail her access to the centre. Whatever Casper's intent – whether to begin a dialogue with the couple or to raise their consciousness – the likely benefits from her candour were modest compared to the risks that materialised as the reaction to her forthrightness played out.

Only after spending many months in the nursery did I dare to raise critical questions. Once I had completed most of my research and had less to lose from being asked to leave, I became more assertive. Then, much to my surprise, nurses and residents talked openly about sensitive issues. Many residents who rotated through the nursery with no commitment to neonatology were more critical of newborn intensive care than I. Nurses shared their concerns about the future of extremely low birth weight infants and, to my surprise, admitted favouring some patients. The boundaries of discretion seemed more permeable than I had envisioned.

In contrast, my relations with attendings (attending physicians) remained formal and distant to the end. During my first week in the nursery, I had incurred the wrath of Dr. Nelson, the nursery's leading neonatologist, when I asked a question that revealed my medical ignorance. Because of this incident, coupled with differences in our age and status, I spent most of my eight months in Randolph terrified that one of the attendings would throw me out of the nursery. My data reporting on attendings' perceptions, attitudes and beliefs rested in large measure on their public pronouncements during rounds or conferences and a few impromptu interviews. As a result, I learned the least about those most likely to shape the outcome of life-and-death decisions.

For fear of damaging field relations, seeming confrontational, or hurting members' feelings, field workers typically err on the side of discretion, avoiding the hard questions and failing to explore the most sensitive issues. My own unasked questions led to a view of the nursery's professionals 'from the bottom up': my knowledge varied inversely with the status of the nursery's staff. Had I explored the attendings' views more thoroughly, I would have written a richer, more multi-vocal ethnography. I had sacrificed the standards of good ethnography, as I understood them, in the interests of felicitous field relationships. Such trade-offs between the two fields have significant consequences, for in designating certain topics as taboo, in avoiding persons we view as off-limits, in failing to ask critical questions, we censor ourselves from the outset.

Not only is it ethnographically important to ask tough questions to the extent that this is possible, but, by airing our concerns openly, we avoid some of the guilt toward members of our research site that complicate the writing process. We also avoid the sense that we have acted in bad faith by not sharing with our subjects the misgivings about their actions that we are willing to make public later and at safe remove (Bosk 2001). Members may be disappointed, but they are less likely to feel ambushed in the end.

Conflicting audiences[2]

The tension between the academic and ethnographic fields follows field workers when they leave the field to write. At this point, members seem less powerful, for they no longer hold the keys to the setting. Group members do not, however, simply vanish from the researcher's consciousness. As one implied audience among many, they remain a continued presence. To be sure, most medical ethnographers are primarily oriented to their academic field. They have, however, incurred obligations to their hosts and often hope to inform, if not reform, the host community. This ever-present tension between fields affects, for example, how researchers choose to frame arguments, to evaluate data, and to choose whether or when to treat members' stories as reports of 'what happened' or as subjective narratives. This tension also shapes the way ethnographers represent disputes between patients and professionals.

The process of transforming field notes into text presents a myriad of interpretive choices and challenges. When professionals attribute patients' and families' 'difficult' behavior to 'guilt' or 'denial', are the staff psychologising what is reasonable behaviour on the part of the parents, or, alternatively, are professionals interpreting the parents' behaviour correctly? When faced with a choice between the medical and the sociological gaze, I followed the latter, and depicted professionals as 'psychologising'. Consider the following use of metaphor and irony to debunk professional authority:

> A frequently cited 'folk' psychological theory was that parents who are asked to play an active role in life-and-death decisions would later experience guilt . . . This belief . . . is clearly paternalistic, insofar as it justifies reducing the power of the parents on the basis of what is presumed to be their best interest. I refer to this view as a 'folk' psychological belief because it has little support in the social psychology of decision making (Anspach 1993: 102).

In this passage, the irony results from the disjuncture between what medical professionals believe and what social psychologists who study decision making provide as empirical data. Using the term 'folk' psychology to describe professionals' beliefs debunks professional authority by exposing it as common sense. As this example suggests, irony cuts both ways producing the prized counterintuitive finding while also driving a wedge between researchers' and subjects' interpretive worlds.

In the end, we are held accountable for our interpretive choices when the imaginary audience of our hosts becomes the actual reviewers of our work in their professional journals. At this point, the ethnographic field resurfaces in the guise of physicians who review our work. The day of reckoning comes when the critics find themselves criticised:

> Anspach . . . accurately observes the strategies used by physicians to alleviate guilt, take responsibility and authority away from the parents, and obtain compliance with desired decisions. When conflict does occur, she asserts that professionals 'psychologize' and transform parents from rational decisionmakers into second-order patients . . . In addition, she describes nurses as 'emotion managers,' functioning to evaluate and direct parents' attachment to their babies . . . What Anspach overlooks is the overwhelming emotional impact of the birth of an abnormal child on the family. Appropriate concern for the family's emotional and personal needs is a major part of the care rendered by professionals (Fleischman 1993: 41).

This review makes explicit the conflicting interpretions a neonatologist/bioethicist and a sociologist/ethnographer use to make sense of the nursery's culture. At stake is which representation should prevail? Irony is piled upon irony as the reviewer, a neonatologist and bioethicist, describes my ironic interpretations in the ironic mode, using quotation marks to emphasise the subjective nature of my interpretations. In this final interpretive collision of two fields, it is the reviewer, not the author, who has the last word.

Non-beneficence (sins of omission)[3]

A second common problem occurs when field workers are asked by members of a host group to participate more actively in the group's social life than ethnographers feel is appropriate. The literature is replete with examples of such 'inclusive overtures' (Emerson and Pollner 2001), in which researchers are asked to do things they consider unethical or illegal. Although medical sociologists' predicaments seem relatively tame when compared to the tales of researchers who study, for example, the drug culture – we are more likely to be asked to hold retractors than to wield a scalpel – they nonetheless are troublesome. 'Inclusive overtures' in medical settings result from the natural tendency of members of host groups to assimilate researchers to familiar roles. In hospitals, where the 'natives' are physicians, researchers are often asked to assume the role of consultants.

In my study of two newborn intensive care units, I was sometimes cast in this role when attendings asked my advice about a life-and-death decision. I typically resisted these requests not only because they transgressed professional boundaries, but also because they were beyond the limits of my expertise as a medical sociologist. Moreover, field work texts are repositories of cautionary tales warning of the dangers of intervening in the setting's social life. If the medical decision rule favours active intervention, the ethnographic decision rule is 'Stay out!'. In short, it is much easier to observe from the sidelines and to rationalise that decision as both methodologically and ethically scrupulous behaviour than it is to enter the fray.

In the course of doing ethnography, occasions arise when the researcher by withholding information or refusing to give advice creates real, and easily avoidable, harm. If the researcher gives advice, s/he may be changing the events s/he is supposed to be observing. If, however, s/he refuses, s/he is guilty of a 'sin' of omission or 'nonbeneficence'. Perhaps no dilemma so clearly epitomises the conflict between the academic and ethnographic field, for the demands of good research and our sense of moral obligation to research subjects are at odds. On some occasions, our sense of obligation to research subjects trumps the norms of unobtrusive research:

After treating a critically ill baby actively for some time, the attending and residents questioned whether their efforts were futile during rounds. The attending had heard that the mother wanted everything done, whereas a resident reported that he 'heard that the mother really didn't want us to do anything aggressive'. When the attending asked for my advice, I protested that I was a sociologist rather than an ethicist. The attending did not buy my disclaimer, and replied that I had been working with [the bioethicist], which was 'just as good'. When after more discussion, the attending asked again for my advice, I gave in. I asked him what additional information would be needed in order to make a decision, noting that there seemed to be some confusion about what the parents thought. The attending said he would go over and talk to the mother himself on his way home (taken from Anspach 1993).

At first glance these actions look like nothing more than a pragmatic response to an organisational dilemma, an effort to facilitate communication in a bureaucratic environment in which numerous people talk to the parents and misunderstandings proliferate. From my perspective, however, my actions were shot though with moral implications. I was acting on my firm conviction that parents should play a larger role in life-and-death decisions and was attempting to make certain that this happened. In acting in what I saw as the parents' best interest, I was also consciously violating my field's standards of good ethnographic field work. At the same time, I was responding as a human being to a straightforward request for help from another.

Today sociologists differ as to either the moral or methodological wisdom of consciously intervening in an organisation's social life. John van Maanen (1983), for example, argues that once researchers gain access to the back stage of a setting, they enter into an implicit contract with host members to provide help, refraining only when their actions would create harm. New varieties of ethnography, such as action research, have emerged that encourage active intervention. Even today, however, the broad consensus among sociologists who do field work does not favour advice giving. This general rule is honoured both in the observance and in the breach.

Ethnographers have offered two rationales for refraining from advice-giving and active intervention. A first, proposed by Emerson and Pollner (2001), foregrounds the distinctive nature of ethnographic knowledge. Because field research derives its creative sustenance from the tension between participation and observation, both immersion and detachment are essential. By acceding to members' inclusive overtures, then, researchers may lose the distance necessary to reflect upon the social worlds they study.

If Emerson and Pollner's argument focuses on the effect of active participation on the *researcher*, a second, better-known, rationale focuses on 'reactive effects' or the effect of active participation on the *researched*. The dangers of advice-giving are said to be the risk of 'Hawthorne effects' or self-fulfilling prophecies in which the researcher actually produces the findings s/he purports to describe. Even fieldworkers who do not view reactivity as a source of bias caution against intervening actively. Emerson, for example, notes that 'the less the researcher actively intervenes in the setting, the fewer and more easily identified are any reactive effects' (2001: 301).

Recently, however, this position has been challenged. Bosk (2001) has argued that it is pointless to maintain the empiricist fiction that it is possible to minimise 'reactive effects', if only because the researcher's questions or scribbling in notebooks suggests to research subjects what behaviours capture the ethnographer's interest. Moreover, it is virtually impossible for the researcher to determine the impact of everyday interactions on research subjects, since s/he has no way of knowing how members behave in his or her absence – that is, the ethnographer does not know the counterfactual. However, if we take Bosk's argument to its logical conclusion, there is no *a priori methodological* reason to refrain from giving advice. Given that the researcher *always* has an undetermined impact on the setting, there is no reason s/he should not give advice when s/he believes that is the right thing to do. When viewed from this standpoint, decisions about advice-giving are more properly framed as moral choices rather than as methodological ones.

Bosk is correct in noting that the ethnographer's effect on the scene is unknowable, and the goal of 'unobtrusive' research elusive and unattainable. This being said, there is an experiential and methodological, if not a moral, difference between researchers' routine interactions and cases in which they are consciously and intentionally intervening to change outcomes. In such cases, although it is impossible to *determine* whether the researcher's advice affected a particular decision, it is nevertheless possible to have a 'pretty good idea' of its impact. By the time many researchers are comfortable giving advice, in all likelihood they will have observed a sufficiently large number of cases to know what usually happens in similar instances in which they did not participate actively. Drawing inferences about the counterfactual and reflecting on one's impact on the setting is an ineluctable and necessary component of the research process.

What was my impact in the case I have described? In all likelihood, the baby would have died anyway, and I may simply have accelerated the process. At the time, I was astounded at my influence when the attending immediately decided to talk to the mother. Looking at the situation many years later, I am impressed by both my ability to alter the course of events and by the limited impact of that ability. Before rounds, the baby had not responded to highly aggressive treatment, and the attending and residents looked to me for a justification for forgoing treatment in the absence of a medical signpost. Only when uncertainty was greatest did attendings shift decision-making downward and incorporate parents, social workers and various 'strangers at the bedside' into the deliberative process. Despite exhortations from many quarters to democratise decision-making, the Randolph attendings remained firmly in control of the process.

Untold stories: revealing and concealing redux

In the course of their research, most ethnographers witness actions they view as ethically questionable, improper or illegal. These situations raise difficult questions: Should researchers share their disapproval with those they study? Should they report highly questionable actions to supervisors or administrators? Should they report illegal actions to authorities? Should they record these events in their field notes, knowing that these notes enjoy no protection or privilege in legal proceedings? Should they report these incidents when writing dissertations, articles and books?

As in the first kind of dilemma, these decisions are about revealing or concealing. In both cases, researchers decide what they are to say (or not to say), what to record (or not to record) and what to write (or to censor). Whereas in the first dilemma the researcher must decide what to reveal or conceal from research subjects, in this case s/he must decide whether to reveal members' secrets to outsiders.

These dilemmas typify the conflict between the academic and ethnographic fields, for the norms, rewards and values of sociology collide with complicated obligations to host members. If ethnographers intervene or report these incidents to superiors and authorities, they alter the setting dramatically and consciously produce the very reaction that they describe and interpret. Whatever good is accomplished is accompanied by the betrayal of confidences, this betrayal is magnified by researchers' earlier promises to provide confidentiality and anonymity. By the same token, by failing to intervene, researchers become unwitting accomplices in these acts or, at the least, participants in a 'conspiracy of silence'. (for a related discussion, see Johnson 1983). When they break with this conspiracy by reporting problematic incidents in their texts, ethnographers run the risk of exposing their research subjects to harms that that can occur should readers succeed in decoding pseudonyms.

In American hospitals, decisions about what to record and write are complicated as the state impinges on decision-making. Civil law relating to medical malpractice, child abuse and neglect statutes, regulatory law mandating informed consent – all can be tools in the hands of parents and professionals who take their disputes to the courts (Heimer 1999). There have also been several cases in which ethnographers' field notes have been subpoenaed, and two field workers have been jailed for failing to turn over their field notes (van Maanen 1983, Emerson 2001). The possibility of subpoena places ethnographers in a bind. On the one hand, good ethnographers are obliged to provide complete 'thick descriptions' of the social worlds they study. Unethical or illegal actions are part of an organisation's social life, which good ethnographers are obliged to report. On the other, researchers who reveal such issues in publications may find their field notes subpoenaed, their research subjects sued, prosecuted or harmed by negative publicity, and their access to future research settings compromised.

To illustrate these dilemmas, we describe four incidents witnessed in the course of our research. They are arrayed along a continuum, beginning with behaviour many would view as unethical and ending with what many would view as criminal. Each case involved tensions between the two fields, for deciding whether to record or report each incident entailed trade-offs between its sociological importance and its risks to research subjects – a calculus that changed with each slide on the slippery slope.

A case of neglect[4]

The first incident occurred during field work at Nila, an institution for severely disabled children:

> At Nila, counselors were responsible for residents' daily care and developed close relationships with the children. The institution also employed physicians and psychologists whose contact with residents was quite limited. Counselors frequently complained of what they viewed as physicians' callous, indifferent attitude toward the children, and the events surrounding a resident's death epitomized this indifference. One of the counselors found the patient dead in her room. He put the body in the basement and turned on several fans. Meanwhile, the counselors waited for the physicians to pronounce the patient dead and to decide how to dispose of the body. They also hoped that the doctors would talk to the kids, who by now had become quite agitated. Despite repeated phone calls imploring physicians to come to Nila, it was two days before a doctor finally arrived (Mizrachi 2001).

In this case, doctors clearly failed to carry out their professional obligations, leaving the children frightened and agitated after one of their friends died. I was so outraged by this blatant breach of professional ethics that I considered reporting it to the municipal authorities or even to the press. Although the ensuing scandal may have led Nila to reform its practices, it would also have effectively ended my field work. Ultimately, I did not report the incident until I published it many years later.

On the edges of the law[5]

The next three incidents took place during my research on life-and-death decisions in two newborn intensive care units. To understand these cases, it is necessary to understand the tense zeitgeist surrounding neonatal intensive care units during the period shortly before the case of Baby John Doe. An active right-to-life movement had made the case of Phillip Becker into a cause célèbre. Conservative legal scholar John Robertson had proclaimed that attending physicians, residents and nurses who withheld treatment from infants deemed 'defective' risked criminal prosecution for 'homicide by omission' – an article that the nursery's ethicist cited often (Robertson 1975). Everyone in the nursery knew that it was only a matter of time before a disgruntled nurse, an unhappy resident, a dissatisfied parent – or an indiscreet sociologist – would involve the right-to-life movement in a life-and-death decision that would explode into a public issue. Baby Doe was a problem waiting to happen.

During periods when medicine's moral boundaries are publicly contested, some decisions become the source of serious conflict:

> When I first arrived in the nursery, I observed a case that was similar to that of Baby John Doe, in which parents, a pediatric surgeon and

one attending decided to withhold treatment from an infant with Down syndrome and an intestinal obstruction. At the conference that followed the baby's death, an acrimonious argument erupted between Dr. Nelson and another neonatologist, Dr. Williams, who had participated in the decision. When Dr. Nelson castigated Dr. Williams for not consulting his colleagues, Williams protested that he had tried unsuccessfully to reach Nelson by phone. 'Right' Dr. Nelson said sarcastically, 'our phones were off the hook'.

The ethics of this decision were debatable, but not illegal at the time it was made. However, I wrote *Deciding Who Lives* in the post-Doe era, when withholding routine treatment from babies with birth defects was already considered a legal violation of the rights of the disabled. Deciding whether or not to write about this case and several others in which decisions were premised on the infant's probable 'quality of life' raised both ethical and sociological questions. Clearly, the norms of both sociology and ethnography weigh heavily in favour of reporting these important cases. However, by writing about these cases, even 10 years after they occurred, I potentially expose members of the nursery staff to legal risks. After some deliberation, I reached a compromise between the demands of my academic field and my obligations to research subjects. I discussed the cases, with a *caveat* that they would not occur in today's nurseries although the sociological 'message' remained valid.

This case and others raised the question of whether as a good ethnographer I was obligated to write about the instances of 'doctors behaving badly' that I had recorded faithfully in my field notes. During my research, I observed several unbridled displays of temper, particularly from two attendings. In a formal conference concerning a baby with spina bifida, an attending excoriated the social worker publicly for having 'fucked things up' by involving other professionals in the case, claiming this action would only confuse the parents. Several months later, during rounds, a serious argument erupted between another neonatologist and a neurologist over whether the neurologist should make recommendations about life-and-death decisions or should limit his role to diagnosing the patient. In contrast to the life-and-death decision described above, I did not feel these displays of temper, particularly the first two examples, were central to the book's arguments. These episodes resembled an incident which Bosk (2003) decided not to report in *Forgive and Remember*. Though the attending's public rebuke of the social worker may have had a gendered subtext, there were plenty of incidents that I discussed in *Deciding Who Lives* in which gender (or race) issues were more explicit. The central question was one of decorum. Ultimately, I did not report the incidents in *Deciding Who Lives*, convinced that they added little of value to sociological knowledge but had a large probability of embarrassing research subjects.

When deciding whether to include a particular incident in *Deciding Who Lives*, I balanced its importance and relevance to my sociological story against potential harm to research subjects. (Relevance is relative. Now these incidents add to sociological knowledge by providing data to support this story line, a narrative explicating tensions inherent in the production of good ethnography.) This decision rule usually served me well. However, the issue of self-censorship was more complex than I recognised at the time. For instance, the dispute between the neurologist and the neontatologist concerned professional boundaries, the role of consultants, and contrasting conceptions of expertise. Even today, I would only include examples of 'doctors behaving badly' when the sociological payoff was large enough to outweigh potential embarrassment of subjects, charges of sensationalism or gratuitous 'doctor-bashing'.

Excluding the parents[6]
Another case violated the clear norm that mandated consultation with parents in decisions to discontinue treatment:

> The decisions concerned very small, very premature twins, born to
> Latino farm workers. Both had suffered large brain hemorrhages, and
> were viewed as unlikely to survive. The parents were told that their babies
> would probably not survive and, if they did survive, would have serious
> brain damage. When the attending met with the parents, the father did
> not want to discontinue treatment and expressed hope for 'his girls'.
> The babies were treated for a period of two weeks. One twin died. The
> following Monday I was told that the attending had taken the second twin
> off life support without asking the parents, who were simply told that their
> baby died. Several nurses and residents were highly critical of this action.

Should I have reported this incident in the book? Since one chapter concerned communication between parents and professionals, the case was indeed relevant to the book. However, emphasising this incident exposed participants in the decision to legal risks, however remote. Caught between the demands of the academic and ethnographic fields, I finally reached a compromise. The case was an exception to the nursery's usual practice of informing parents of life-and-death decisions. Readers were likely to mistake a deviant case for a routine decision. Thus, emphasising the incident in the text would not have been faithful to the setting and might also have exposed nursery professionals to legal risks. I therefore briefly mentioned in passing that with the exception of two cases, the parents were incorporated into life-and-death decisions.

Illegal acts[7]
Further down the ethical and legal slippery slope was the most difficult dilemma I encountered when I observed an action that, in my view, if reported, was subject to criminal prosecution. Once again, I faced the decision of whether or not to include the case in my dissertation. Before making the

decision, I consulted a member of my dissertation committee. We both realised my notes were subject to subpoena, and even if I recorded no notes I was subject to deposition, if knowledge of my presence as a researcher became known to a member of the pro-life movement. When my mentor asked how central the case was to my dissertation, I found it difficult to answer this question. On the one hand, the incident had little bearing on the book's central arguments. On the other hand, it *was* important in answering the major research question: how life-and-death decisions were actually made. There were other, careerist considerations as well. Including this 'dramatic' incident would most probably increase the likelihood that my dissertation would be published as a book, and, if published, would get considerable attention. Against these possible benefits, I had to weigh the worst-case scenario: the spectre of subpoena, jail, and, above all, the feeling of having betrayed members of the nursery staff in the process of advancing my career.

The case raised other troublesome issues. Was I obliged to report the incident to the Head of the Nursery? By failing to report the incident, was I complicit? So troublesome was this case that two decades later, I found it necessary to request a 'stat' ethics consultation before presenting a version of this chapter at a conference.

More is at stake in these cases than our conflicting mandates to protect research subjects and to advance knowledge. Our field favours revealing the ethically problematic or illegal acts of those we study. Just as non-participant observation has historically been associated with the public sphere, so has ethnography typically been identified with the deviant, the hidden, the covert – in a word with the private sphere, with what Goffman (1959) calls the 'back stage'. Consider such titles as: the *backrooms* of medicine (Millman 1977), or the *underlife* of a public (mental) institution (Goffman 1961). Observations of ethically problematic behaviour are highly prized data, secrets revealed only to a few, attesting to the ethnographer's skill and the degree to which s/he had been trusted. The point is not to reduce ethnographers' motives to self-interest, but rather to note that, in addition to the highly negative consequences of violating subjects' trust and the value of protecting research subjects, there are few incentives to betray them.

Such cases become even more complicated as the state inserts itself into life-and-death decisions and as field notes are subpoenaed in civil and criminal proceedings. The subpoena of field notes threatens the research enterprise itself, since potential research subjects, fearing that the protection of confidentiality is not wholly within the researcher's control, are wary of participating in research. However, the use of field notes as legal documents affects the researcher as well as the researched. Although I took notes shortly afterward on the incident, simply not recording the incident would have still left me vulnerable to legal action. Ethnographers who observe illegal activities but refuse to take notes, fearing that their field notes will, like medical records, become legal documents, need to remember that, once their presence is a matter of record, they are still subject to deposition.

There are even more troubling issues. In his amended appendix to *Forgive and Remember*, Bosk (2003) describes his decision to omit two incidents involving racism and sexism, noting that including one of them would have made for a richer, more thought-provoking account. Including some of the incidents that have been described would undoubtedly have enriched my text. But there is another, even more serious consequence of my self-censorship. Recall what I omitted from *Deciding Who Lives:* I 'buried' in the text two cases in which the parents had not been consulted in life-and-death decisions. I omitted any reference to attendings' displays of temper – to say nothing of gossip and nurses' and residents' complaints about each other and attending physicians. Finally, I censored any mention of what I view as an illegal action. Taken individually, none of these omissions is in itself significant. Taken *together*, however, these deletions of physicians' worst behaviour result in a somewhat idealised view of the decision-making process. If other medical sociologists systematically censor descriptions of medicine's darkest side, the view of medicine that will emerge is distorted. (Of course, focusing on unrepresentative cases of physicians' 'outrageous' behaviour distorts accounts in the other direction.) How such self-censorship, undertaken in the name of protecting confidentiality, affects ethnographies of medicine is the focus of the conclusion.

Concluding remarks

The concept of fields helps us understand some recurrent ethical dilemmas in field work. By directing attention to the effects of the academic field on the ethnographer, Bourdieu's approach reminds us that more is at issue in ethical dilemmas than conflicting principles. The concept of fields helps us understand the value attached to certain kinds of argument. We learn how the quest for distinction and the pursuit of the 'interesting' leads us to demystify and debunk medical authority, sending us on a collision course with those we study. We notice the effects on our work of careerist considerations – often considered a taboo topic in discussions of field work ethics.

Ethical dilemmas arise from the tension between an academic field that promulgates a critical perspective toward medicine and our relationships to research subjects, who represent the very field we debunk. At every point, we are forced into difficult choices between sociology and our obligations to host members, as we decide how much to reveal or conceal about our research agenda, whether to disclose or hide our criticisms, whether to ask tough questions, and whether to give advice that produces the phenomenon we then describe. The tension between fields follows us after we leave the field to write, for we must decide how to frame our arguments, how to interpret what we have seen, whether to frame accounts as objective descriptions or as subjective narratives, and whose voice should be privileged in our texts. In the conflict between sociology and the ethnographic field described here, the former usually won the day – though other choices are possible. These choices are consummately ethical, for they involve integrity and opportunism, truth-telling and deception, trust and betrayal.

The concept of fields directs our attention to the ways in which medical sociology shapes (or stifles) our ethnographic imaginations. But the chain of influence can also run in the opposite direction: equally important are the effects of field relations and the complex choices we make in the field on our *sociological* imaginations. If, in the name of discretion and concerns for our careers, we avoid asking tough questions and designate particular topics and people as taboo, we censor ourselves early in the research process and foreclose subsequent interpretive possibilities. Through this early censorship we have stifled our sociological imaginations and created silences in the stories we can tell. In the particular case described in this chapter, the result was an ethnography centred on the lower levels of the medical hierarchy, focusing on those with the least authority in life-and-death decisions. Conversely, if in the interest of decorum, confidentiality or fear of legal entanglements, we censor what we witness, record and present to the reader about medicine's darkest side, we will have also stifled our sociological imaginations. Ultimately, the silences in our sociological stories limit and distort what comes to be known as medical sociology. In short, our choices about what to ask, record or present to the reader – decisions that have little to do with what is usually seen as 'science' – shape what is known about the social world. It is through these choices that we *create* our academic field even as it shapes us.

Acknowledgements

The authors thank Raymond de Vries, Charles Bosk and Melvin Pollner for their helpful comments.

Notes

1   Anspach
2   Anspach
3   Anspach
4   Mizrachi
5   Anspach
6   Anspach
7   Anspach

References

Anspach, R.R. (1988) Notes on the sociology of medical discourse: the language of case presentation, *Journal of Health and Social Behavior*, 29, 357–75.

Anspach, R.R. (1993) *Deciding Who Lives: Fateful Choices in the Intensive-care Nursery*. Berkeley: University of California Press.

Bosk, C.L. (1992) *All God's Mistakes: Genetic Counseling in a Pediatric Hospital*. Chicago: University of Chicago Press.

Bosk, C.L. (2001) Irony, ethnography, and informed consent. In Hoffmaster, B. (ed.) *Bioethics and Social Context*. Philadelphia, PA: Temple.

Bosk, C.L. (2003) *Forgive and Remember: Managing Medical Failure*. Chicago: University of Chicago Press.

Bourdieu, P. (2003) Participant objectivation, *Journal of the Royal Anthropological Institute*, 9, 281–94.

Casper, M.C. (1998) *The Making of the Unborn Patient: a Social Anatomy of Fetal Surgery*. New Brunswick, NJ: Rutgers.

Cicourel, A.V. (1964) *Method and Measurement in Sociology*. New York: Free Press.

Davis, M. (1971) That's interesting: toward a phenomenology of sociology and a sociology of phenomenology, *Philosophy of the Social Sciences*, 1, 1309–44.

De Vries, R.G. (2004) How can we help? From 'sociology in' to 'sociology of bioethics', *Journal of Law, Medicine, and Ethics*, 32, 2, 279–92.

Emerson, R. (ed.) (2001) *Contemporary Field Research: Perspectives and Formulations*. 2nd Edition. Longrove, IL: Waveland Press.

Emerson, R.M. and Pollner, M. (2001) Constructing participant/observation relations. In Emerson, R. (ed.) *Contemporary Field Research: Perspectives and Formulations*. 2nd Edition. Longrove, IL: Waveland Press.

Fleischman, A.R. (1993) Unraveling the process, *Hastings Center Report*, November–December, 40–1.

Freidson, E. (1970) *Profession of Medicine*. Chicago: Aldine.

Garfinkel, H. (1967) *Studies in Ethnomethodology*. Englewood Cliffs, NJ: Prentice-Hall.

Goffman, E. (1959) *The Presentation of Self in Everyday Life*. Garden City, NY: Doubleday.

Goffman, E. (1961) *Asylums: Essays on the Social Situation of Mental Patients and Other Inmates*. Garden City, NY: Doubleday.

Guillemin, J.H. and Holmstrom, L.L. (1986) *Mixed Blessings: Intensive Care for Newborns*. New York: Oxford University Press.

Gusfield, J. (1981) *The Culture of Public Problems*. Chicago: University of Chicago Press.

Heimer, C.A. (1999) Competing institutions: law, medicine, and family in neonatal intensive care, *Law and Society Review*, 33, 17–66.

Johnson, J.M. (1983) Trust and personal involvements in fieldwork. In Emerson, R.M. (ed.) *Contemporary Field Research: Perspectives and Formulations*. 1st Edition. Longrove, IL: Waveland Press.

Kempner, J., Perlis, C.S. and Merz, J.F. (2005) Forbidden knowledge, *Science*, 307, 854.

Matza, D. (1968) *Becoming Deviant*. New Jersey: Prentice-Hall.

Millman, M. (1997) *The Unkindest Cut: Life in the Backrooms of Medicine*. New York: Morrow.

Mizrachi, N. (2001) When the hospital becomes home: visibility, knowledge and power at Nila, *Journal of Contemporary Ethnography*, 30, 2, 240–68.

Pollner, M. (1987) *Mundane Reason*. Cambridge: Cambridge University Press.

Rier, D. (2000) The missing voice of the critically ill: a medical sociologist's first-person account, *Sociology of Health and Illness*, 22, 1, 68–93.

Robertson, J. (1975) Involuntary euthanasia of defective newborns: a legal analysis, *Stanford Law Review*, 27, 213–69.

Van Maanen, J. (1983) The moral fix: on the ethics of field work. In Emerson, R.M. (ed.) *Contemporary Field Research: Perspectives and Formulations*. 1st Edition. Longrove, IL: Waveland Press.

Wacquant, L. (2004) Following Pierre Bourdieu into the field, *Ethnography*, 5, 4, 387–414.

5

Ethical boundary-work in the embryonic stem cell laboratory

Steven P. Wainwright, Clare Williams, Mike Michael, Bobbie Farsides and Alan Cribb

Introduction

Innovative technologies have the potential to diagnose, treat and possibly even prevent illness and disease but they also raise new risks. In this chapter we highlight a set of important questions linking social studies of medical and scientific technologies with debates around the ethical, legal and policy dimensions of innovative but controversial biomedical practices (Cribb 2002, Williams *et al.* 2002a, 2002b, Callahan 2003). These technologies are redefining the scale, scope and the boundaries of science and medicine, and the relationship between biomedical technologies, science and the social (Brown and Webster 2004). As Thompson (2005) argues:

> The biotech mode of (re)production will have, and is already beginning to have, its own characteristic systems of exchange and value, its own notions of the dimensions we currently think of as time and space, its own epistemic norms, its hegemonic political forms, and its own hierarchies and definitions of commodities and personhood (2003: 5, cited in Franklin and Lock 2003: 7).

More specifically in relation to the escalating procurement of human body materials, Lock (2001) states that:

> the commodification of human cells, tissues and organs incites particular concern because boundaries usually assumed to be natural and inviolable are inevitably transgressed, raising concerns about 'self' and 'other', 'identity', 'genealogies', group continuity and so on (2001: 65).

Our work highlights the ways in which bioethics is grounded in the practices and units of analysis (particularly human embryonic stem (hES) cells and embryos) of laboratory scientists. In so doing, we support David's (2005: 18) assertion that different scientific fields have different social relations and histories which need to be studied, rather than attempting to apply one overarching model (not least of ethics) to 'science'.

Stem cell biology is one of the most rapidly developing areas within the life sciences (Kiessling and Anderson 2003). Stem cells are believed to hold the capacity to produce every type of cell and tissue in the body, suggesting huge potential in the fields of regenerative medicine and bioengineering. Proponents contend that stem cells promise a medical revolution in the treatment and cure of diverse and intractable degenerative illnesses such as Parkinson's disease and diabetes (Williams *et al.* 2003, Wainwright 2005). This optimism creates 'promissory capital', or capital raised for speculative ventures on the strength of promised future returns (Thompson 2005). According to Rabinow (1996a), this results in an important shift for the biosciences:

> More than ever before, the legitimacy of the life sciences now rests on claims to produce health . . . The bioscience community now runs the risk that merely producing truth will be insufficient to move the venture capitalists, patent offices, and science writers on whom the biosciences are increasingly dependent for their newfound wealth (1996a: 137).

Within this emerging context, scientists must nevertheless demonstrate their commitment to 'ethics': after all, over and above venture capitalists, patent offices and science writers, the audiences of science include various public and regulatory constituencies who, in one way or another, lend the whole bioscientific enterprise legitimacy. Importantly for us, the ethical and public policy debates on hES cells represent the concatenation of debates on cloning, genetic engineering, pre-implantation genetic diagnosis (PGD) and the human genome that have taken place in Europe (Nerlich *et al.* 2002) and the USA (Shostak 2002, Snow 2003). As such, stem cell research comprises a fruitful case study within which to explore the broader processes of the evolving bioscientific engagement with ethics.

Much of the literature on the scientific, political and ethical dimensions of stem cells originates in North America, but there are significant differences between the UK and USA that affect research, policy and practice, including regulations regarding hES and fetal stem cell research (Holland *et al.* 2001, Weissman 2002, Maienschein 2003). For example, in the UK the *Human Fertilisation and Embryology (HFE) Act 1990* requires the Human Fertilisation and Embryology Authority (HFEA) to regulate the creation, storage and use of embryos for research. Initially, research was permitted for five reasons, mostly relating to reproductive medicine. In 2001 the HFE Act was amended to allow the use of embryos for therapeutic research, including the use of hES cells (House of Commons Science and Technology Committee 2005).

Since 1998, when hES cell lines were first isolated (Thompson *et al.* 1998), a series of social science papers have begun to map the key discourses, debates and shifts in the area of stem cell research (*e.g.* Franklin 2001, Waldby

2002, Kerr 2003, Parry 2003, Cooper 2004, Franklin 2005). All these papers, however, draw upon analysis of documentary sources. In contrast, our data come from interviews with laboratory scientists who describe their views on the ethics of biomedical science research using embryonic and foetal stem cells. We use the idea of 'ethics' to draw together a range of considerations, particularly the distinction between forms of conventional ethics on the one hand, and normative ethics on the other. That is, we pay special attention to what *is* deemed socially acceptable, good or right, and to what principles and other normative frameworks suggest *ought* to be so considered.

We use Gieryn's concept of boundary-work (Gieryn 1983, 1999) to introduce the notion of 'ethical boundary-work'. According to Gieryn, boundary-work – 'The discursive attribution of selected qualities to scientists, scientific methods and scientific claims for the purpose of drawing a rhetorical boundary between science and some less authoritative residual "non-science"' – highlights the negotiated character of science (Gieryn 1999: 4–5).

Gieryn (1999) argues that important areas for exploration include the ways in which scientists defend their intellectual territory and how the demarcation of science from non-science works to maintain an image of expertise, authority and credibility. In our research we use Gieryn's idea to explore how scientists draw the boundaries of ethical scientific activity. While Gieryn's formulation suggests that non-science must be excised from science, our data show that non-science, in the form of 'ethics', is becoming an integral part of maintaining the image of science. Ethical boundary-work, however, comes in a form not predicted by Gieryn. For example, we find that ethical boundary-work differentiates between scientists, enhances the authority of 'non-science' (*e.g.* regulatory bodies) and de-privileges science.

Methods

Based on an ethnography of two leading embryonic stem cell laboratories in the UK, our data form part of the findings from a larger project mapping the scientific, medical, social and ethical dimensions of innovative stem cell treatment, focusing on the areas of liver cell and pancreatic islet cell transplantation (Wainwright *et al.* in press a, in press b, in press c). In this chapter we draw on interviews with 15 biomedical scientists who work in these laboratories, both of which are situated on one geographical site. Eight of the scientists in one laboratory derive and characterise hES cells, whilst the seven scientists in the second laboratory use hES cells and fetal stem cells to make insulin producing beta and islet cells, with the long-term aim of curing diabetes. We should point out here that, rather unusually, these two laboratories currently obtain the majority of their hES cells from embryos donated by couples attending for pre-implantation diagnosis (PGD), as opposed to in vitro fertilisation (IVF). The technology of pre-implantation genetic diagnosis can be offered to women/couples at risk of having a child with a serious genetic condition, or in some cases, to women who have experienced repeated miscarriage due to chromosomal rearrangements. Women undergo IVF followed by genetic testing of embryos, and only genetically unaffected embryos are transferred. As will be seen, this is important in terms of interpreting our respondents' views on ethical sources of embryos for the derivation of hES cells.

To preserve anonymity we do not include the specific titles of scientists, describing them in our text as either junior scientists or senior scientists. The eight senior scientists have PhDs, are usually in a tenured post and have an average of 20 years in science (five male; three female). Seven are junior scientists, who are PhD students with an average of six years in science (all female). Following ethics committee approval, interviews lasting between 1–2 hours, took place within the laboratory offices, and with permission, were taped and transcribed. Open-ended questions and an informal interview schedule were used, in order to encourage scientists to speak in their own words about their experiences.

Transcripts were analysed by content for emergent themes (Weber 1990) which were then coded (Strauss 1987). All the research team read the 15 interview transcripts and contributed to the generation of the identified themes. Sections of the transcripts relating to these initial categories were grouped together into broader categories and then into the three major themes of this chapter. The chapter then underwent numerous rewritings as the team discussed and enacted analysis of our data. There was a broad consensus amongst the team as categories were expanded, collapsed and refined through an iterative process. This enabled the different perspectives of the team to be incorporated, and adds to the richness and validity of our analysis. The quotes drawn on below are representative, and illustrate saturated themes. The themes and sub-themes were identified as areas which scientists themselves saw as central in relation to stem cell science and ethics.

Themes

Three major themes emerged from our interviews; each theme contains a number of sub-themes, many of which present a line of cleavage around which our scientists agree to differ.

1. Sources of embryos

Scientists discussed the ethical issues surrounding four sources of embryos for laboratory work with hES cells.

Spare embryos
Much was made of the fact that if 'spare embryos' were not used for scientific research they would be discarded:

With rare exceptions, the embryos that are used in stem cell research are embryos that have no future, either because they are not implantable . . . or they've been screened by PGD and been shown to have, or be at high risk of having, a genetic disorder . . . If all we're doing is using something left over and destined to be discarded, then if some good can come out of it, it's worth doing (Senior Scientist 8).

In their analysis of media coverage of the stem cell debate in the UK in 2000, this was one of the rhetorical strategies Williams *et al.* (2003) identified as used by proponents of stem cell research to assert an ethical position, that embryos would otherwise be 'discarded' or 'left to perish'. This meant that not only could stem cell research be presented as 'less wasteful' of spare embryos, but also that stem cell research could be presented as a form of rescue. Similarly, Waldby (2002) states:

Advocates of stem cell research generally portray the spare embryo as a precious substance. If it is not freely donated it will be simply wasted, a recklessly squandered resource . . . Stem cell technologies are, in these terms, particularly productive sources of biovalue precisely because they can rehabilitate what would otherwise be needless waste and transform it into a spectacularly active, flexible and manageable tissue resource (Waldby 2002, 314).

Only PGD embryos
A few scientists stated that they would only work on embryos donated from PGD and were not prepared to work with embryos from IVF programmes:

I've got large ethical problems with using spare embryos from routine IVF cycles for stem cell research. I believe if an embryo is rejected as too poor quality to freeze on day three for potential future implantation, and then it turns into a blastocyst suitable for stem cell derivation, it may have some clinical potential and should probably be frozen. PGD doesn't have the same ethical baggage – those embryos can't be replaced (Senior Scientist 10).

Here Scientist 10 is arguing that some 'spare' IVF embryos may turn out to have the clinical potential to be used in treatment by the couple, and should therefore be frozen. This situation cannot arise if only genetically affected PGD embryos are used as a source of stem cells as, by definition, such embryos would be deemed unsuitable for replacement. Scientist 10 supports the work of Throsby (2004), who draws attention to the way in which PGD embryos are constructed as 'pre-discursively *spare*, and therefore unproblematically available, obscuring the [social] process of their production and acquisition' (2004: 22).

Unsure about IVF embryos

A few scientists agreed that PGD embryos were a good source for stem cell research, but were uncertain whether they would work on IVF embryos:

> We use embryos created by PGD – yes, they are created, but they're created because people want to have kids that are not going to suffer. That's the main thing, these conditions are so severe that you can justify doing it. I'm not so convinced that IVF is a necessity – would I work on IVF embryos? I'm not sure (Junior Scientist 9).

This line of reasoning ascribes various meanings to the notion of 'waste'. For Scientist 10, the ethical issue is that IVF embryos may have treatment potential, leading her to doubt that IVF embryos are really available as waste, whereas Scientist 9 questions whether they should exist at all. However, both are drawing a distinction between unavoidable waste that can be redeemed, and avoidable waste that perhaps should be avoided rather than redeemed. In addition, whilst IVF embryos can be viewed as 'surplus to requirement', PGD embryos are viewed as 'biologically dysfunctional'. These different meanings of waste are thus implicitly deployed as a means of drawing an ethical boundary between IVF and PGD embryos as sources of stem cells.

Further, all the scientists were keen to articulate how, once human embryos were obtained, there was a strong commitment to ensuring that this resource was not itself 'wasted' by inefficient scientific practices:

> You're not going to start your research straight onto human stem cells. You tend to get as much information as you can out of the mouse stem cells and then apply it . . . You can have this technique that you want to make sure works perfectly and you might need to do it five or six times, then the material . . . from stem cells or whatever, it's very limited, it's your precious material, you are not going to waste it looking for ways to perfect your technique for those cells. It's as simple as that I think (Junior Scientist 1).

This comment also illustrates how work on animals could be represented as waste, in comparison to the more valuable hES cell work.

Using embryos created solely for research

All the scientists interviewed were prepared to use 'spare' embryos for research, although their definitions of 'spare' varied. In contrast, many of the scientists we interviewed were opposed to creating embryos solely for research:

> At the moment the way you grow human stem cells is you get embryos that will be thrown away if you don't use them, and the parents have given informed consent for them to be used by researchers. I don't think that's unethical. I think it would be unethical to let those embryos be thrown

away when there's a choice. But I wouldn't agree with working with embryos that have been created solely for the purpose of harvesting stem cells – I would definitely refuse to work on those cells (Junior Scientist 1).

We get embryos from IVF and PGD and those embryos would be thrown away so it's not as if we're making them specifically for cell work. I wouldn't do that, I wouldn't be happy to produce just a continuous supply of fertilised embryos for lab work (Senior Scientist 2).

This stance is interesting in view of the fact that the UK House of Commons Science and Technology Committee (2005) has recently recommended that, 'where necessary, embryos can be created specifically for research purposes' (Volume 1: 24). Scientists are often portrayed as pushing the ethical limits of biomedical work, but here we see examples of scientists resisting a more permissive public policy on stem cell research. This is an example of our respondents distinguishing between two forms of waste: material that has been created unnecessarily; and existing material that risks not being used. The agency and responsibility of these scientists is deeply embedded in this distinction and, in particular, in not straying into the former zone. Their accounts suggest that they view the source of embryos along an ethical continuum. At one end scientists are simply redeeming the situation, whilst at the other end, embryos are being created for their 'own' purposes alone. The ideal for many of our respondents is the redemption and transformation of material created for other purposes – in other words, the agency of the scientists enters after the 'waste' appears, and not before. However, it is important to note that although the scientists agree that there is an obligation, hovering between the ethical and the social, not to waste sources for the supply of stem cells, there is disagreement about what a legitimate supply constitutes, and what non-usages would be considered wasteful. Thus, agreement about broad principles can obscure differences in the application of those same principles.

The scientists' views also echo the global politics of hES cell science, in that whilst the formal government policy of 18 countries allows the procurement of hES cells from supernumerary embryos, only six, including the UK, also allow the creation of human embryos for research purposes, which includes cloning (Salter 2005). Salter argues that in these countries which allow procurement of hES cells from supernumerary embryos, 'the IVF "supernumerary embryo" is the morally superior option (ironically, because it is "spare" to the needs of reproduction it is then seen as having less intrinsic value) over . . . cloned embryos' (2005: 20). So rather than supporting the UK's more liberal regulations, many of our respondents seem to be aligned with the majority global view. Indeed, we believe that in the context of the ethical contrast between PGD and IVF, our scientists present themselves as *predisposed* to taking a more ethically stringent position. By performing such ethical boundary-work around the sources of human embryos used in their work, our respondents are able to articulate and enact an ethical position that aligns them with the more ethically cautious countries amongst those who permit hES cell research. This example of boundary-work is therefore not about differentiating science from non-science, but rather, about drawing boundaries between what is ethically preferable – in this case, between scientists of higher and those of lesser ethical standards.

2. Perceptions of embryos

The status of the embryo is highly contested. At one end of a continuum some claim that the embryo is a human being, sacrosanct and sacred, whilst at the opposite end the embryo is viewed as a collection of cells, scientifically useful and secular (Bortolotti and Harris 2005).

As 'just cells'

Debates about the status of the embryo are usually presented, particularly in the media, as polarised views, and as incompatible choices (Williams *et al.* 2003, Kitzinger and Williams 2005). However, by viewing early embryos as 'just cells', the scientists we interviewed with religious beliefs had been able to reconcile their scientific and religious beliefs:

> That really depends on your personal stance and whether after fertilisation you've got something that is a being. I don't happen to think that, I think that there's a stage where we are just talking about cells . . . I'm a Christian and I go to church and have quite strong beliefs – for example, only in exceptional circumstances do I agree with abortion. However, my intellectual situation, knowing about a human embryo in the early stages . . . I haven't got a problem with it (Senior Scientist 2).

The view that hES cells are 'just cells' was universal amongst the scientists we interviewed, who further argued that although hES cells were derived from embryos, they were no longer embryos:

> Stem cells growing in a dish are not embryos . . . stem cells are derived from embryos but are not embryos. A placenta is derived from an embryo but it's not a person, and I think that's where some of the difficulty in understanding comes about. My personal view is, we have eight cells in a dish, that is not a real person (Senior Scientist 16).

Gradualist approach

The majority of scientists adopted a gradualist approach, similar to that adopted by the Warnock Committee (House of Commons Science and Technology Committee 2005: 16–17), to the developing human embryo:

I don't perceive very small microscopic collections of cells, that are going to be put in the bin, to be equatable with a person . . . We attach huge moral significance to early embryos and cells derived from them, but not [*to cells*] from a six-week-old fetus – we do abortions all the time . . . A six-day-old embryo has a different status to a six-week-old fetus, but I'd argue that six weeks is closer to being something than a six-day-old (Senior Scientist 8).

Implantation

For some scientists, implantation of the embryo into a woman's uterine wall (a process which begins around day nine in humans) was the key factor in delimiting their perceptions of embryos:

An embryo to me is on its way to being a fetus when it's implanted, but while it's still in the dish, personally I don't feel it's got the capabilities of becoming a human – once it's implanted, yes, I really believe that's what it's going to be, and that it's untouchable. At the stage we see them, at five days old, 20 cells, you can't see any features, you don't know if it's going to survive, whether it would take implantation . . . It's hard, sometimes I do think about it, 'Should I really be doing this?', taking the natural course away, but then I think, 'Well, what about the benefits that are going to possibly be realised?' (Junior Scientist 9).

A senior scientist contrasted the distinction between the developmental potential of the embryo within the environment of the woman's body (*in vivo*) with the development of the embryo outside this environment (*in vitro*):

If you plot the likelihood of a fertilised egg becoming a baby, you can put it in on day one, it's quite low, day two, and day three, it's quite good, day five is particularly good. But then it ceases, because it starts to hatch, so by day seven, day eight, although this is more developed, it has no potential of developing. So the curve starts to go to zero again, because it is not an organism that is capable of implantation . . . It loses its potential although it is developmentally more senior (Senior Scientist 16).

As Waldby (2002) argues, stem cell research highlights conflicting ideas about life and death. Opponents of the research perceive the life of the embryo as biographical, in contrast to advocates, such as our respondents, who view the life of the embryo as 'a form of raw biological vitality. From this point of view, the embryo is not killed. Rather, its vitality is technically diverted and reorganised' (Waldby 2002: 314). In this way, the humanist biography of embryos/hES cells is erased, to be replaced by a material biography of embryos and hES cells as a biological entity (*cf.* Appadurai 1986).

Respect for all tissue

Another common view of the scientists we interviewed and observed was that all tissue, including embryos, should be treated with respect:

> I can't look upon an embryo as a baby or a potential person when
> I'm moving it around the lab all day, and there's a chance I could
> drop it on the floor. I'm poking it, taking bits out of it, I can't possibly
> think that and carry on working in this area . . . But I do think you
> have to treat all tissue with respect, and that runs through everything
> I do (Senior Scientist 10).

Here, we find 'respect' to be another strategic route which enables scientists to rise above the issue of whether the material is biographical or abstractly vital. That is to say, it shifts the ethical boundary from human-biographical/ nonhuman-vitality, to respect/'irrespect'.

These accounts of embryos and hES cells as 'just cells', as tissue to be respected, and of the importance of implantation, all seek to ensure that the embryo does not have a biography in the humanist sense. This key distinction allows scientists to draw an ethical boundary which enables them to work on embryos and hES cells.

3. Deferral to regulatory frameworks

The regulatory framework produced by the UK Parliament, the Human Fertilisation and Embryology Authority (HFEA) and various other bodies provides a legal and ethical landscape for the practice of UK stem cell science. A series of reviews have outlined the development of a UK/European legal, regulatory and policy framework on stem cell research and therapy (Romeo-Casabona 2002, Kerr 2003, Parry 2003, Hauskeller 2004). None of this research, however, includes primary interviews with practising stem cell scientists.

All our scientists argued that the UK provided a well regulated environment in which to undertake fetal and hES cell work. This regulatory environment acted as a legitimating framework against which, and through which, scientists were able to present their own personal accounts. For example, clear guidelines and strict rules were seen as enabling scientists to pursue their lab work:

> I work with fetal material which we get through the MRC [Medical
> Research Council] and I am much happier that it's quite strict so that
> if the shit did hit the fan I can say, 'Well, I was following very clear
> guidelines', because I am a bit uncomfortable about using those materials.
> I'm much happier that there are strict rules . . . I'm squeamish about it,
> partly because I'm a father (Senior Scientist 3).

The regulatory framework that governs such research in the UK was seen as pre-empting the potential ethical issues that surround such work. Personal unease at using the more 'biographical' human fetal cells in the laboratory were inevitably put aside so that scientists could get on with practising their craft of laboratory experimentation. Thus regulation enables biomedical scientists to engage in personal/public boundary-work, separating the former, such as their role as father, from their professional/public role in the laboratory.

Traditionally, the doctrine of scientific neutrality separates science and society, thereby allowing scientists to engage in purely 'objective' work, leaving society responsible for ethical decision-making (David 2005). For our scientists, this ethical work is in key respects sequestered from the space of the laboratory and placed with public regulatory bodies, such as the MRC Tissue Bank and the HFEA:

> I don't feel altogether comfortable doing it but the view that I take is that this is [fetal] material that would otherwise be destroyed, and a person has made that decision to terminate their pregnancy and that hopefully some benefit will come out of the material which we can obtain for research purposes . . . All of our material comes from the MRC tissue bank so I would hope that the ethical issues had been addressed (Senior Scientist 5).

The regulatory framework that governs the production of stem cells from human embryos was seen as central, in that it allowed scientists to pursue research that was authoritatively and demonstrably legal and ethical:

> [In the UK] you know that somebody is keeping track of how many embryos people are using and that it's all adhering to whatever local and national ethical guidelines there are, you know, what the commercial concerns are, so it's just done at a completely different level . . . The HFEA . . . have done a really good job, particularly in stem cell biology . . . I think they have been very, very thoughtful, conservative, deliberate and I think they have done exactly the right thing . . . So yes, I think most stem cell biologists in this country are pretty happy with the regulations, happy with the climate, happy with the government support (Senior Scientist 8).

The public (mis) understanding of science was a theme touched upon in all our interviews. In the example below, regulation is seen as a vital means to reassure both scientists and the public that research is being conducted appropriately:

> There are very strict regulations regarding, say, animal experiments, human tissue, and I think a lot of people aren't aware really of just how strict they are . . . A lot of people have fears about what mad scientists are

doing. They don't realise that they are very constrained by these
regulations . . . I wouldn't be happy working in a field where there weren't
any regulations, or where people were just free to do as they wished
(Junior Scientist 6).

These quotes indicate a complex boundary being drawn between responsibility
and 'non-responsibility', where the bulk of responsibility is effectively
allocated elsewhere, through the process of regulation. Here, ethical boundary-
work is primarily between private and public ethics, drawing on the rhetorical
claim that any suspicion about personal ethical standards can be deflected
because constant surveillance by regulatory authorities ensures high ethical
standards. Scientists thereby become responsible for pursuing the ethically
valuable ends of helping people through research, whilst concurrently being
'non-responsible', through allowing regulating authorities to ensure their
ethical accountability (Salter and Jones 2002).

Of course, regulatory frameworks are created with the input of scientists:
it is senior scientists who shape and help implement the regulations (Mulkay
1997, Jasanoff 2005). But notice: the differentiation between science and
regulation is itself an accomplishment, partly enacted through boundary-work.
The ethical boundary-work that gets done requires *deferral* to non-science –
a reversal of Gieryn's formulation where boundary-work serves to *privilege* science.

Discussion and conclusion

In this chapter we have explored the views of 15 scientists in two UK laboratories,
and as such, we make no claims for our participants being 'representative'
of the wider scientific community. Our study is however ongoing and, to date,
we have found no systematic variation in scientists' views on ethical issues
in relation to age, gender, religious convictions or their main scientific interest.
We also recognise that from these interviews it is not possible to determine
to what extent these scientists' views might relate to their actions if they were
asked to undertake procedures they were uncomfortable with, such as creating
embryos solely for research: currently, neither laboratory has an HFEA
licence for this. Despite these limitations, our account of scientists' deliberations about working with human embryos and stem cells contributes to the
development of a more 'socially reflexive healthcare ethics' (Cribb 2005).
Furthermore, our work shows how 'ethical problems' are framed and managed
by individuals and institutions, and by a dialectical relationship between the
two (Alderson *et al.* 2002, Cribb 2002, Farsides *et al.* 2005). Such research
is important. As Waldby (2002) argues:

Contemporary biotechnology demands a bioethics that can understand
the complex reciprocities and technical mediations between human and
non-human entities, and frame ways of living that acknowledge this. The

kinds of social relationships that may develop around stem cell technologies must be understood as part of a broader social negotiation over this network of production, and the kinds of humans and non-humans, entities and hybrids, health and illness it should produce (Waldby 2002: 319).

When we document aspects of the ethical boundary-work done by scientists, what precisely are we witnessing? Most obviously, we are observing the delineation of a positive 'ethical space' which scientists occupy – a space which signals both ethical reflection and rectitude. The rectitude is largely underpinned by reference to the formal legal and ethical framework that defines and allows 'ethical science', but it is also signalled by the reflection itself, by preparedness – at least in many cases – to venture into ethical argumentation. Our respondents thus present themselves as ethical, as well as expert, actors. Indeed, in the contemporary context where the 'traditional' borders of science are being eroded in numerous ways (*e.g.* Nowotny *et al.* 2001, Irwin and Michael 2003), ethics have become another line of demarcation, not so much from 'non-science' as from 'less ethical' positions. Practical ethics here takes the form of a number of choices over how to conduct oneself in a complicated political, moral and epistemic context. As we have seen, such choices include the use of different sources of embryos, and deferral to regulatory frameworks.

The ethical boundary-work of scientists involves working across a dichotomous and even contradictory terrain. It means maintaining the distinction between 'real science' and 'associated ethics', whilst at the same time incorporating ethical acceptability into the heart of the scientific work. It means both owning the ethical issues as a sign of responsible and thoughtful engagement in a highly contested domain, whilst concurrently devolving ethics to authorities outside science, especially those charged with regulation. Our research indicates that the boundary-work of science has become an altogether more complex process than that initially described by Gieryn (1983). One instance of this increased complexity is the way that ethical boundary-work involves a process of social demarcation – where ethical talk is not only about representing a contradictory set of ethical terrains but is also about ordering such terrains, by making social divisions which speakers identify with, or differentiate from.

These scientists' accounts are very different from 'narrow' philosophical accounts of bioethics because they do not situate themselves in a position of detached abstract rationality, but rather, are centrally implicated in the substantive ethics of practice. They are being deliberative and 'right seeking' (*i.e.* ethically serious) in a way that is akin to bioethics as a discipline, but they are also doing this as part of institutional and social practices of self-justification. Talking to scientists allows us to provide a more grounded and detailed analysis of perspectives, processes and practices that are often erased or 'skated over' by purely philosophical analyses. Appraising their coherence, credibility and defensibility means, amongst other things, attending to how institutions and agents (such as those considered here) embody and enact ethical work. Normative positions in philosophical bioethics – if they are to have any purchase at all – have to be socially embodied, institutionally enacted and 'peopled' (Cribb 2005).

In conclusion, our analysis of the ways in which ethics is embodied in, and mediated by, ethical boundary-work extends Gieryn's original concept (see Ehrich *et al.* 2006). Our chapter illustrates how the ethics-talk of stem cell scientists functions at a normative level and simultaneously serves to define and defend the work of scientists involved in ethically sensitive research.

Acknowledgements

We would like to thank all those who participated in this research, and acknowledge the support of the ESRC Stem Cell Programme (grant no: RES-340-25-0003). The authors also thank the referees and the Monograph Editors for their comments, which have helped refine the original manuscript.

References

Alderson, P., Williams, C. and Farsides, B. (2002) Examining ethics in practice: health professionals' evaluations of in-hospital ethics seminars, *Journal of Nursing Ethics*, 9, 518–31.

Appadurai, A. (1986) Introduction: Commodities and the politics of value. In Appadurai, A. (ed.) *The Social Life of Things: Commodities in Cultural Perspective.* Cambridge: Cambridge University Press.

Bortolotti, L. and Harris, J. (2005) Stem cell research, personhood and sentience, *Reproductive Biomedicine Online*, 10 (Supplement), 76–9.

Brown, N. and Webster, A. (2004) *New Medical Technologies and Society: Reordering life.* Cambridge: Polity.

Callahan, D. (2003) *What Price Better Health?* Berkeley: University of California Press.

Cooper, M. (2004) Regenerative medicine: stems cells and the science of monstrosity, *Journal of Medical Ethics: Medical Humanities*, 30, 12–22.

Cribb, A. (2002) Ethics: from health care to public policy. In Jones, L. and Siddel, M. (eds) *The Challenge of Promoting Health: Exploration and Action* (2nd ed.). London: Macmillan.

Cribb, A. (2005) *Health and the Public Good: Setting Healthcare Ethics in Social Context.* Oxford: Oxford University Press.

David, M. (2005) *Science in Society.* London: Palgrave Macmillan.

Ehrich, K. Williams, C. Scott, R. Sandall, J. and Farsides, B. (2006) Social welfare, genetic welfare? Boundary-work in the IVF/PGD clinic, *Social Science and Medicine*, 63, 213–14.

Farsides, B., Williams, C. and Alderson, P. (2005) Aiming towards 'moral equilibrium': health care professionals' views on working within the morally contested field of antenatal screening, *Journal of Medical Ethics*, 30, 505–9.

Franklin, S. (2001) Culturing biology: cell lines for the second millennium, *Health*, 5, 335–54.

Franklin, S. (2005) Stem Cells R Us: emergent life forms and the global biological. In Ong, A. and Collier, S.J. (eds) *Global Assemblages: Technology, Politics and Ethics as Anthropological Problems*. New York: Blackwell.

Franklin, S. and Lock, M. (eds) (2003) *Remaking Life and Death: Toward an Anthropology of the Biosciences*. Oxford: John Murray.

Gieryn, T.F. (1983) Boundary-work and the demarcation of science from non-science: strains and interests in professional ideologies of scientists, *American Sociological Review*, 48, 781–95.

Gieryn, T.F. (1999) *Cultural Boundaries of Science: Credibility on the Line*. Chicago: Chicago University Press.

Hauskeller, C. (2004) How traditions of ethical reasoning and institutional processes shape stem cell research in Britain, *Journal of Medical Philosophy*, 29, 509–32.

Holland, S., Lebacqz, K. and Zoloth, L. (eds) (2001) *The Human Embryonic Stem Cell Debate: Science, Ethics and Public Policy*. Cambridge: MIT Press.

House of Commons Science and Technology Committee (2005) *Human Reproductive Technologies and the Law, Fifth Report, Volume 1*. London: House of Commons.

Irwin, A. and Michael, M. (2003) *Science, Social Theory and Public Knowledge*. Maidenhead, Berks.: Open University Press/McGraw-Hill.

Jasanoff, S. (2005) *Designs on Nature: Science and Democracy in Europe and the United States*. Princeton, Princeton University Press.

Kerr, A. (2003) Governing genetics: reifying choice and progress, *New Genetics and Society*, 22, 111–26.

Kitzinger, J. and Williams, C. (2005) Forecasting science futures: legitimising hope and calming fears in the embryo stem cell debate, *Social Science and Medicine*, 61, 731–40.

Kiessling, A.A. and Anderson, S. (2003) *Human Embryonic Stem Cells: An Introduction to the Science and the Therapeutic Potential*. Boston: Jones and Bartlet.

Lock, M. (2001) The alienation of body tissue and the biopolitics of immortalized cell lines, *Body and Society*, 7, 63–91.

Maienschein, J. (2003) *Whose View of Life? Embryos, Cloning and Stem Cells*. Cambridge: Harvard University Press.

Mulkay, M. (1997) *The Embryo Research Debate: Science and the Politics of Reproduction*. Cambridge: Cambridge University Press.

Nerlich, B., Dingwall, R. and Clarke, D.D. (2002) The book of life: how the human genome project was revealed to the public, *Health*, 6, 445–69.

Nowotny, H., Scott, P. and Gibbons, M. (2001) *Re-thinking Science: Knowledge and the Public in an Age of Uncertainty*. Cambridge: Polity.

Parry, S. (2003) The politics of cloning: mapping the rhetorical convergence of embryos and stem cells in parliamentary debates, *New Genetics and Society*, 22, 145–68.

Rabinow, P. (1996) *Essays on the Anthropology of Reason*. Princeton: Princeton University Press.

Romeo-Casabona, C.M. (2002) Embryonic stem cell research and therapy: the need for a common European legal framework, *Bioethics*, 16, 557–67.

Salter, B. (2005) *Working paper 2, Project: The global politics of human embryonic stem cell science, ESRC stem cell programme*. University of East Anglia.

Salter, B. and Jones, M. (2002) Human genetic technologies, European governance and the politics of bioethics, *Nature Reviews Genetics*, 3, 808–14.

Shostak, S. (2002) *Becoming Immortal: Combining Cloning and Stem-cell Therapy.* Albany: State University of New York.

Snow, N.E. (2003) *Stem Cell Research: New Frontiers in Science and Ethics.* Notre Dame: University of Notre Dame Press.

Strauss, A.L. (1987) *Qualitative Analysis for Social Scientists.* Cambridge: Cambridge University Press.

Thompson, C. (2005) *Making Parents: The Ontological Choreography of Reproductive Technologies.* Cambridge: MIT Press.

Thompson, J., Liskovitz-Eldor, J., Shapiro, S. *et al.* (1998) Embryonic stem cell lines derived from human blastocysts, *Science*, 282, 1145–47.

Throsby, K. (2004) *When IVF fails: Feminism, Infertility and the Negotiation of Normality.* London: Palgrave.

Wainwright, S.P., (2005) Can stem cells cure Parkinson's disease? Embryonic steps toward a regenerative brain medicine, *British Journal of Neuroscience Nursing,* 1, 3, 61–66.

Wainwright, S.P., Williams, C., Michael, M., Farsides, B. and Cribb, A. (in press) From bench to bedside? Biomedical scientists' expectations of stem cell science as a future therapy for diabetes, *Social Science and Medicine.*

Wainwright, S.P., Williams, C., Michael, M., Farsides, B. and Gibb, A. (in press b) Remaking the body? Scientists genetic discourses and practices as examples of changing expectations on embryonic stem cell therapy for diabetes, *New Genetics and Society.*

Wainwright, S.P., Williams, C., Persaud, S. and Jones, P. (in press c) Real science, biological bodies and stem cells: constructing images of beta cells in the biomedical science lab, *Social Theory and Health.*

Waldby, C. (2002) Stem cells, tissue cultures and the production of biovalue, *Health,* 6, 305–23.

Weber, R. (1990) *Basic Content Analysis.* London: Sage.

Weissman, I.L. (2002) Stem cells–scientific, medical, and political issues, *New England Journal of Medicine,* 346, 1576–79.

Williams, C., Alderson, P. and Farsides, B. (2002a) 'Drawing the line' in prenatal screening and testing: health practitioners' discussions, *Health, Risk & Society,* 4, 61–75.

Williams, C., Alderson, P. and Farsides, B. (2002b) Is nondirectiveness possible within the context of antenatal screening and testing? *Social Science and Medicine,* 54, 17–25.

Williams, C., Kitzinger, J. and Henderson, L. (2003) Envisaging the embryo in stem cell research: discursive strategies and media reporting of the ethical debates, *Sociology of Health and Illness,* 25, 793–814.

6

Gift not commodity? Lay people deliberating social sex selection

Jackie Leach Scully, Tom Shakespeare and Sarah Banks

Introduction

Recent developments in genetics and reproductive medicine have had an increasing impact on the choices available to parents and families over reproduction and health. While there seems to be general support for technologies that offer promise in fighting disease, there is also deep anxiety about their implications, especially for personal identity and family relationships. One particularly contentious issue is prenatal sex selection for social reasons (SSS), by methods that include preimplantation genetic diagnosis (PGD). PGD was developed in the late 1980s to enable families at risk of genetic disease to select unaffected embryos without having to undergo prenatal diagnosis and abortion of affected pregnancies (Braude *et al.* 2002). Medical sex selection, to avoid male embryos potentially affected by X-linked conditions, was the first clinical application of PGD (Handyside *et al.* 1990), and PGD for medical sex selection continues to be regarded as acceptable clinical practice in the United Kingdom. The same technique, however, could be used to give couples the option of selecting a male or female embryo if they prefer children of one sex or wish for a 'balanced family' with children of both sexes. Social sex selection is prohibited under Article 14 of the Council of Europe's 1997 Convention on Human Rights and Biomedicine. To many commentators it represents an important boundary between therapeutic uses of technology to promote health, and the adoption of technologies for non-medical reasons (*e.g.* to increase choice, or satisfy individual desires). For critics concerned about the extension of genetic and reproductive technology, SSS seems another step on a path leading to 'designer babies' (Human Genetics Alert 2002, Center for Genetics and Society 2004).

In the UK, policy decisions on these and related areas of reproductive medicine have been delegated by act of legislation to regulatory bodies such as the Human Fertilisation and Embryology Authority (HFEA). Such bodies aim to make policy that is based on expert judgement and that also retains broad public confidence. Their membership covers a range of expertise in science, philosophy, law and business, and usually includes members drawn from lay interest groups. Regulatory authorities are also expected to consult formally with the wider public as part of their process of deliberation. Several problematic issues remain unresolved here. In practice, such consultations draw on rather limited constituencies, and there is uncertainty about the forms of consultation best suited to enabling the lay public to effectively contribute their views (Levitt 2003). There is also the question of what to do with the material obtained from public input. What kind of authority do lay contributions have? How can they best be interpreted and contribute to policy deliberations?

Using lay concerns to inform policy can be problematic. In particular, dilemmas arise where there is disparity between the views of expert scientists and ethicists and the consensus of lay views. Should regulation be crafted on the basis of broad social consensus, or should it prioritise the arguments of the experts? The divide between 'expert' and 'lay' knowledge and identities is being subjected to increasing critique (Callon and Rabeharisoa 2003, Nowotny, Scott and Gibbons 2001), with attention being paid to the ways members of the public perform as 'scientific citizens' (Irwin 2001, Irwin and Michael 2003, Michael and Brown 2005). A recent example of these questions arose in 2002, when the HFEA ran a public consultation on the acceptability of SSS (HFEA 2002). The use the HFEA made of public opinion in its final report (HFEA 2003) was controversial, prompting discussion by leading medical ethicists in the United Kingdom (Harris 2005a and b, Baldwin 2005, Holm 2004, Tizzard 2004), and was implicitly rejected by the response of the House of Commons Committee on Science and Technology to its recommendations (2005).

A key issue raised in the HFEA discussion was that many expert scientists and bioethicists find lay people's ethical judgements less trustworthy than professional ethicists', arguing they are based solely on intuitions and prejudice rather than on knowledge and rational argument (Levitt 2003). These experts suggest that, instead of weighing the evidence and the arguments, non-philosophers usually have an immediate response to an issue, and then search for reasons to legitimate their intuitions. There is some evidence from moral psychology to support this claim about decision-making processes in general (Haidt 2001, and references therein). A further reason for caution is the culture-bound nature of popular intuitions. There are numerous historical examples to show that the public often find new developments initially threatening and distasteful. Responses such as 'it's unnatural' or 'we should not play God' are common when faced with novel technologies, and are sometimes encapsulated in the phrase 'the yuck factor' (Kass 1997). When it has previously not been possible to exercise choice in an area of social or family life, people initially seem to believe that it would be morally wrong to do so in the future. And so advocates of SSS argue that it is simple *unfamiliarity* with the idea of choosing the sex of children that makes people think it is wrong. Although moral philosophy does make use of appeals to intuition, and conservative bioethicists such as Leon Kass have approvingly cited 'the wisdom of repugnance' (Kass 1997, 2002), yuck factor arguments have not gained widespread philosophical backing.

The Ordinary Ethics study

Our research project, entitled 'Ordinary Ethics: the moral evaluation of the new genetics by non-professionals', and funded by the Wellcome Trust, studied lay people's ethical evaluations about biomedical technologies. One of our fundamental aims was to see whether the ethical evaluations made by these lay participants were indeed based solely on prejudice or whether they had any reasoned basis. We investigated the kinds of opinions lay people expressed; the sorts of arguments they used; and how both their evaluative approaches and their conclusions compared to dominant forms of contemporary bioethical discourse. We chose SSS as our focus topic because the technology involved is relatively simple, there is an existing academic literature, and because the phenomenon of wanting a child of a certain sex would be familiar to most participants. In this chapter we use some findings from the study to demonstrate how lay people's ethical arguments can be revealed, focusing on one motif in particular: that children are 'a gift'. A broader discussion of the methods and findings in relation to the overall processes of ethical evaluation can be found in Banks *et al.* (2006).

Building on previous work (Scully 2002, Kerr *et al.* 1998), we used the method of group discussions based on a scenario about prenatal sex selection by PGD. Ten group discussions were held with different groups of people during 2002–4 in the north east of England. The groups covered a range of age, gender, class and disability perspectives, although no groups were convened from specifically religious, cultural or minority ethnic organisations or groupings. Participants included a women's community education group; postgraduate community and youth work students; a rural youth group; a group of Soroptimists (an organisation for women in management and the professions); a group from a regional user-led disability organisation; one group each of men and women aged over 65; a group of male social workers; a group of less professionalised men active in community and youth work; and a group from the Woodcraft Folk group (an educational movement for young people aiming to develop self-confidence and social participation).

All groups received a brief introduction to PGD and sex selection. We then used a fictional scenario about a couple wishing to use PGD to select the sex of their next child. The discussions lasted between 50 and 90 minutes, and were facilitated by a researcher who, after introducing the scenario and asking people to reflect individually, invited initial reactions. In the majority of groups, the following starting scenario was used:

> Imagine a couple who have three daughters. They plan to have another child, and want to use PGD to make sure they have a son.

Offering a sketchy scenario like this opens a space for a less abstract discussion, inviting participants to imagine a plausible situation, consider what other information they would need to know about this particular case to make a judgement about it, take account of other people's reasons and motives, and so on. The facilitator introduced modifications of the scenario to explore the effect on the evaluation, for example if there were existing children of the 'wrong' sex in the family-balancing scenario; if the parents came from another culture; if they wanted to select to avoid an inherited disability instead of a particular sex; or if they wanted to select *for* a disability. Additionally, we conducted one-to-one, follow-up interviews with selected group members when we wanted to explore their comments in more depth than was possible in a group discussion.

At the end of each discussion participants were asked for their final opinion on the general question of whether SSS by PGD was acceptable. The majority opinion in all groups was that it was not morally justifiable. Forty out of 48 participants (83%) reported holding this view.

The taped discussions were transcribed, organised using the qualitative data analysis package NVivo (Bazeley and Richards 2000, Gibbs 2002), and analysed in detail for ethical themes and argumentation.

Metaphors of 'gift' and 'commodity'

While each discussion group differed in the interactions taking place and the configurations of views and arguments expressed, some common themes were observed throughout[1]. Among the most prominent were the psychological consequences for the individual child and the family, potential social consequences (such as gender imbalance), the individual right to choice, the nature of society and the individual, and the characteristics of the good parent. In the rest of this chapter, we focus on one of the most common and extensively discussed themes, the idea that children should be a 'gift' (and not a 'commodity' or, less frequently, a 'right'). As one of the group discussants commented:

> I think that having a child is not some kind of human right to which you can attach conditions, whatever those conditions are . . . I feel that quite strongly. I think that's actually wrong, to me that is a wrong way of looking at having children. I would prefer to look at it as a gift, something like that (Social workers' group).

Clearly the description of the child as a gift was not being used literally. A literal gift would imply a giver. This could be a person in cases of egg or sperm donation, or adoption, but these were not the topics being considered. In other instances the notion of a giver might be a reference to God. But in fact only one participant made explicit reference to God as a giver, and she was referring to pregnancy termination rather than SSS. In all other instances, the context in which participants referred to children as a gift did not suggest they were framing their concern in overtly religious terms. That is, they were not drawing *explicitly* on the idea of a child as a gift from God.

The claim that 'children are a gift' is therefore a metaphorical one. Lakoff and Johnson (1980) define metaphor as conceiving of one thing in terms of another, in order to further understanding of the first concept. A metaphor is not a definition, but a way of getting a handle on a concept, and has the advantage that it can convey complex ideas succinctly. Metaphors are particularly important in understanding conceptual abstractions in concrete or physical terms. As a metaphor, 'children are a gift' is being used to convey something important about how the speaker believes parents should relate to their children, and the responsibilities this relationship involves.

Metaphors have entailments. Complex metaphors can carry multiple sets of entailments, and which set is mobilised depends on exactly what the user intends the metaphor to express. By using gift as a metaphor, then, what were our participants trying to say? This question has to be investigated by looking at the context in which the metaphor was being used, statements in which it was elaborated, and other metaphors with which it was compared. The large sociological and anthropological literature about gifts (for example, Mauss 1960, Cheal 1988, Osteen 2003) is predominantly framed in terms of economic models of exchange or of gift-giving's social function. Based in real-life gift-giving involving giver and recipient, these models focus on the function that the gift performs in the community. But in our setting, and in the absence of a giver, participants' attention was instead directed to the relationship between recipient and gift and in particular to the appropriate response to receiving a gift. Here, it appeared that the key gift entailment being mobilised was acceptance. In the traditional pattern of gift-giving in western European culture, when someone gives you a gift you do not quibble about its specifications: you accept it unconditionally, with gratitude. The notion of gift implies a lack of control over what is received. To speak about children as a gift is therefore to say that they should be accepted as they are, and that it is not appropriate to refuse them or to want to change their characteristics. This interpretation of the entailment being drawn on is supported by numerous accompanying statements. For example, one focus group participant commented:

> I just don't think it's right that people can actually just sit down and choose what colour hair they want [for the child], what colour eyes they want, what job they want the father to do, because you're not loving a baby if you've got to sit and create it like that (Women's educational group).

The metaphor of the gift was often used in counterpoint with the metaphor of the commodity. In this case, however, the parallel was *rejected*: people said that a child is *not* a commodity. Again, the metaphor of commodity has numerous entailments. Although in some contexts it implies the role of the market and market forces, for our participants it seemed to be more about choice than about money. 'Treating children as a commodity' was less about the wrongness of buying and selling children than it was shorthand for 'exceeding an appropriate level of choice'. Other comments indicated that by commodity people were describing an inanimate object rather than a subject, something that is uniform and not unique, and whose characteristics it is legitimate to select according to one's desires. Choosing the features of what one gets is seen as morally acceptable when buying a car or washing powder, but not when the object is actually a person:

> It's about treating people as commodities which come off a shelf, rather than thinking of them as people (Soroptimists' group).

> It smacks of shopping for the child (Disability group).

Commodification is about treating a child not as a person, but as a thing: an 'it' rather than a 'thou', in Buber's (1937) terms.

We noted previously that complex metaphors like these are overdetermined – they carry diverse, sometimes incompatible associations and entailments, and careful exploration of what is actually being said and not said is needed to tease out the salient meanings. For example, in principle 'gift' might also be associated with marking a special event, repayment for past favours, and so on. However, in practice we saw no examples where participants' speech indicated that they were drawing on these entailments when using the gift metaphor.

In considering how the metaphor of gift is being used in ethical evaluation, the question is whether the notion that children should be accepted (almost) unconditionally, as gifts, is an isolated free-floating intuition, or whether it is grounded in further reasons. As we followed the different discussions in close detail we noted that participants linked the virtue of acceptance with two things in particular: (i) an ontological claim about the nature of children and the person, and (ii) an aretaic claim about the characteristics of the good parent.

Nature of the person
As the following quotes illustrate, participants said that this level of choice (choosing the sex of a child for non-medical reasons) represents the placing of expectations on a child that fails to respect its individual personhood:

> It's not accepting every person as an individual. It's not respecting the individual (Disability group).

> The child isn't the parent's property, they are their own person, and putting expectations on them doesn't seem to respect them or treat them as autonomous . . . There is something there that you don't have

control over you know, there is something I think intrinsic there.
I don't know what it is but there is something. They are people . . .
(Social workers' group).

This participant was asked to expand on this in a follow-up interview.
He said:

> So it is something around that I think, around the detraction from, you
> know, who the individual really is. Actually seeing the person for what
> they are worth in their entirety rather than trying to put things onto them
> and sort of saying, well, actually you are this and this and everything.
> [Parents who select for sex] see them as different types of people [not
> individuals] if you start with ideas that are so definite about how a girl or
> boy should be (Social worker, follow-up interview).

Part of what people felt was wrong was indicated by another entailment of
the gift metaphor. In the traditional pattern of gift-giving, the lack of
control means the gift is a surprise. The following exchange comes from the
older men's group:

A:	Interesting question that, explain the surprise thing. Now providing the surprise is pleasant, everybody is happy about it, but it is difficult to explain the feeling. It's rather like Christmas in the days when you're old-fashioned enough not to know what you were going to get for Christmas.
B:	Anticipation.
A:	Yes.
Facilitator:	And that's a pleasant thing?
All:	Yes.
A:	And how you explain that I don't know, but that's the feeling.

For a small minority of participants the value of surprise seemed to cover
knowing the sex ahead of the birth at all. But the majority were less inclined to
take the 'gift as surprise' entailment that far: their reservations were directed
at attempts to *control* the sex, and they were less or not at all concerned
about simply knowing the sex beforehand (which is after all still a surprise,
albeit brought forward in time).

By drawing on this entailment of gift, participants were saying that in the
reproductive context, unpredictable outcomes are appropriate and indeed
can have special value:

> In a way [SSS] could be setting limits to what that child is going to be
> instead of letting the random element come into it. I don't know enough
> about the science. Perhaps a random element comes into it anyway. In
> which case, good! (Participant in disability group, follow-up interview).

To restate this concern in more conventional ethical terms, choosing the characteristic of sex is seen as a failure to respect the intrinsic value of the individual child. Moreover, this does not appear to be a *consequentialist* claim. It does not rest on the belief that choosing the sex will have bad results for society, the relationship between parent and child, or the child itself (although claims like these were made as part of separate arguments). Rather than any direct harmful consequences, the metaphor seems to be chosen to express a judgement about the ontological implications of the act:

> If it [SSS] happened and . . . the dire consequences didn't materialise . . . I think I would still be sad at the lack of, I'd still feel we'd lost something (Participant in disability group, follow-up interview).

By drawing on the entailments of the gift metaphor, therefore, our respondents are expressing something similar to a deontological idea of 'respect for persons'.

The good parent
The metaphors of 'gift' and 'commodity' could also be viewed in terms of virtue ethics – sometimes known as an aretaic model – thereby calling attention to the behaviours that identify a good parent. Participants expressed their concern that people choosing the sex of their child are placing their own desires or ambitions above the needs and interests of the child, and that this is not behaviour characteristic of good parents. In the group of male social workers one said:

> I think as a parent I'm at my best when I'm not imposing my expectations on my children but rather providing them with the wherewithal to do what it is they want to do. I don't mean that quite literally in that they can go and wreck the place if that is what they want to do, but I mean you know within social confines and all the rest of it, to achieve what they want to achieve. . . . That doesn't mean pushing them down a particular route that actually meets *my* needs.

Similarly, a postgraduate student respondent argued that:

> There is something really selfish about it: I want my child to be like *this*. When being a parent you have to be so unselfish, and it can be such an enriching experience to have this level of unselfishness.

And a member of the older men's group linked the lack of choice with ideas about love in families that were not definable but were, he claimed, shared:

> I also think you're in grave danger of disturbing something here, that is hard to define. I love my family, each and every one of them, not because

of what they are but in spite of what they are. I love them because they are there . . . It doesn't matter to me whether they are tall, short, fat, thin or what. No, I didn't put in an order to have them the way they are, that just happens to be the way they are and as I see it, who can define love. That is something that none of us can really define. You can't put an equation down. We're all family men here and I'm quite sure these two think as I do.

To these participants, then, the good parent is one who allows and enables the unfolding of their child's potential. Doing so means that good parents limit the interventions they make. Permissible interventions are those that protect the child or really do enable it to develop:

As a mother I would want to make my child's life as good as possible. And I think most parents try and do that. . . . I think the parenting bit would want to protect . . . at the end of the day if I knew before that I had a hereditary problem with a boy or a girl, and somebody told me we could do something about that, I think as a protective mother I would ask for something to be done (Soroptimists' group).

This meant that although most of the participants took the virtue of acceptance as a marker for the good parent, the degree of acceptance expected of a good parent is not unlimited and in fact varied from participant to participant. Elsewhere (Scully *et al.* 2006) we discuss in greater detail the participants' reasoning about the limits to chance and choice in reproductive decision making. To give one example, most participants drew a distinction between using PGD to *choose sex* and to *avoid disability*, the latter including sex selection to avoid sex-linked conditions:

The other thing is that I have no objections or no fears about using this system where there is a medical reason for it, where, you know, something in the genes can be carried on to a certain sex, that doesn't upset me at all. It's just in this case, just choosing, well we've got three of one so it's high time we had one of another. I don't like that at all (Older women's group).

Like it could be valid though, you know, you have diseases that can only be passed on to one sex? I don't know . . . there is one that only happens to men, but like if their family had a history of that, they might want to have a girl just for the sake of that, (Facilitator: So that would be okay?) That would be fine (Woodcraft Folk youth group).

The consensus in eight groups was that there was a morally valid distinction to be made between using PGD to select for sex and using it to select against disease and impairment. But all discussions also recognised the difficulty of deciding where the cut-off point might fall between impairments, and two groups contained participants who were adamant that parental acceptance should always be unlimited, even to accepting disease and impairment where termination or PGD might have been options.

Normative status

Our participants were also sensitive to the normative status of their own opinions. That is, most of their discussion was about what they thought would be the morally correct thing to do for themselves. But they acknowledged the difficulty of making normative statements about other people in situations of which they themselves had no experience:

> People who would argue against the technology may be people who have no understanding of what it's like to be in that situation (Postgraduate students' group).

Nevertheless, acknowledgement of this did not affect participants' normative ethical evaluation. Referring to a hypothetical Asian family introduced as a modification of the scenario, one participant in the disability group's discussion said:

> As far as I'm concerned it doesn't affect my decision. I can understand more why they would want a boy than a European family who had three girls and fancied a boy, it does make a difference . . . I don't think that makes it right, though I can understand the pressures they would be under.

On the other hand, although this awareness did not alter their ethical evaluation, it did make them reluctant to advocate drawing a hard and fast line in legislation:

> . . . I would find it very difficult to impose that principle on somebody else, because I wouldn't know what their situation was . . . I wouldn't be able to say no, you shouldn't do that (Social worker).

However, knowing that this line was already drawn (since UK law currently forbids SSS) meant they saw no reason to change it.

Status of the metaphor

Close scrutiny of the metaphors of gift and commodity helps identify which entailments our participants felt were the relevant ones, so clarifying the complex set of beliefs that they were trying to express through them. In drawing on associations of acceptance and surprise, participants were underlining the unpredictable nature of having children. In their emphasis on the individuality of persons against the reproducibility of commodities, participants were saying that a child's individual personhood was worthy of special respect. Taken together, these two metaphors suggest that the important thing about treating children as gifts and not as commodities is that the former shows appropriate respect for unique personhood. It is ethically unacceptable to encroach too much on the characteristics of children because this demonstrates precisely a lack of this respect, and in practice can infringe their autonomy by preventing them from doing 'what they want to do'. In this way the gift metaphor succinctly imports a cluster of deontological beliefs about the child's personhood, individuality and autonomy into the ethical discussion.

Our participants' thinking drew on the resources of interlocking ethical concepts: of respect for the personhood of the child; the obligation to show this respect by minimising the constraints placed on the child's future choices; the characterisation of a good parent as one who does this by accepting children 'as they are'; and a model that sees the parent-child relationship as vulnerable to encroachments in this respect, by such acts as choosing the sex. These are background concepts that are, at least initially, expressed through metaphor and analogy rather than directly articulated, and they seem to provide a set of constraints that enable participants to make moral sense of an unfamiliar situation. (See Holland 2003 for a similar discussion of cases where appeals to 'nature' express something about the need for a particular set of background constraints.)

Citing a metaphor is not an argument in itself. Nor would it be correct to think of either the gift or the commodity metaphor as a premise from which the participants argue to a conclusion about the permissibility or not of SSS. People did not *ground* their moral claims in the child's status as a gift. Rather, selected entailments of the gift metaphor express what these participants felt was the appropriate way to treat a child, and (we argue) in turn express an interlocking set of beliefs about the child's moral status and the moral responsibilities of parents in terms of protection and control. The metaphor is a condensed articulation of this set of beliefs rather than a philosophical premise.

Relevance of 'ordinary ethics' to bioethics

What relationship do these processes bear to the bioethics of academia and policy? How much can what people actually think and do, morally, contribute to ethical theorising?

Bioethics is an interdisciplinary field that encompasses a variety of analytical approaches and theoretical traditions (Jonsen 1998: 118). In recent years, however, it has come under attack for what critics view as its narrowness of approach. One side of this critique relates to the *sources of material* drawn on for ethical analyses – the 'social and cultural myopia' of bioethics (Light and McGee 1998: 1). Some critics argue that this should be remedied by greater use of empirical data from a range of cultural settings (Solomon 2005, Borry *et al.* 2005, Hedgecoe 2004, Zussman 2000, De Vries 2004, De Vries and Subedi 1998, Walker 1998).

But there is a separate issue to do with the *ethical analyses* themselves – how moral positions and arguments, wherever they come from, are handled. As commentators have noted, most of the philosophical work in bioethics comes from within the Anglo-American tradition of analytic philosophy (Light and McGee 1998). It is true that alternative traditions and approaches are present in bioethics, such as virtue ethics (*e.g.* Weed and McKeown 1998), care ethics (*e.g.* Tong 1998), feminist ethics (*e.g.* Wolf 1996, Rawlinson 2001, Mahowald 2001, Moazam 2004), and narrative ethics (*e.g.* Nelson 1997), not to mention the Continental bioethical traditions. Some of these alternatives more closely resemble the approaches of our lay participants with respect to their ontology of the person, the normative weight given to relationships between parent and child, and the styles of reasoning they prioritise. Nevertheless, we share the opinion of the critics that the most influential strands in contemporary Anglo-American bioethics are liberal (and in the United Kingdom at least predominantly secular), prioritising logic and abstract rationality, and drawing extensively on the formalism of consequentialist, utilitarian and rights-based approaches to ethics (Jonsen 1998: 378–380).

This form of bioethics, which for the sake of conciseness we call here 'secular-liberal bioethics', also appears to provide the bulk of bioethical input into policy, at least in the United Kingdom and much of Europe. Our own impression of media discussion, political debates and the make-up of advisory and regulatory bodies is that the most substantial ethical contributions are currently made by bioethicists from within these traditions, and, although the literature here is sparse, this impression is supported by other commentators (*e.g.* Capps 2005: footnote 31, Salter and Jones 2005). This may be because the conclusions of secular-liberal analyses, and the analytical processes through which they are reached, are easier to integrate into the procedures of policy making than the more relational, socially embedded approaches of alternative traditions. Thus Salter and Jones note both that the disciplinary breakdown of national and international bioethics committees shows a predominance of medical genetics and law, and that 'The rationality of science [and, we would add, of philosophy and law] resonates easily with the rationality of the policy process' (2005: 728).

Secular-liberal bioethics overall takes a broadly permissive view of SSS. Its moral position is generally grounded in support for a citizen's reproductive liberty or procreative autonomy, defined by Ronald Dworkin (1993) as the 'right to control their own role in procreation unless the state has a compelling reason for denying them that control'. Reproduction is seen as central to personal identity and freedom and values, and a range of authors have argued for the right of individuals to choose their own lifestyle and pursue family life in their own way, and in accordance with their own notions of their children's wellbeing, unless exercising this right infringes other adults' liberty (Harris 2005 a and b, Robertson 2003, Savulescu 1999, Savulescu and Dahl 2000, Buchanan *et al.* 2000). According to this line of argument SSS might undermine the public good if the sex ratio were affected, or if sexism were reinforced through preference for one sex over the other. In the absence of these effects, however, the freedom of parents to choose should be defended. Examining the possible consequences of SSS, most secular-liberal bioethicists find that there is no empirical evidence of such psychological or social harms, and they conclude from this that there is no good or sufficient cause for restricting the freedom of others to create children via different forms of sex selection (see also McCarthy 2001, Dickens 2002, Robertson 2003, Pembrey 2002).

Both the conclusion and the style of reasoning contrast markedly with the ethical concerns articulated by participants in our study. Although they did not exclude issues of principles and rights, or the narrower issues of reproductive autonomy and harm, they were primarily concerned with questions of the relationship between children and their parents, and what it means to be a good parent. These questions are certainly not absent in the wider academic bioethical literature, but are given limited coverage in the secular-liberal approaches of the UK and US.

We conclude from this study that the ethical views of our participants were not, as has been suggested, either uninformed or 'simply incoherent' (Harris 2005b: 287). Their views were grounded in intuitions that were usually presented through metaphor rather than through the logical argument that is more familiar to moral philosophy. These intuitions were of genuine moral salience to the lay participants and were, to them, more compelling than arguments based on reproductive autonomy or the moral status of the embryo. Furthermore, our participants did not use a logical, step-by-step propositional argument to arrive at their position (Banks *et al.* 2006) but relied on something closer to a coherence argument. In the example we have explored here, the metaphor of gift was a condensed articulation of a set of interlocking intuitions that were given high priority in our participants' evaluations. Our participants' position on SSS draws on a background of moral understandings that formed the basis for their judgements. We are not suggesting that 'ordinary ethics' provides *better* ethical arguments than professional bioethics, or that both use the *same kind* of argument. We conclude, however, that the divide between professional and lay bioethics has less to do with the 'good arguments' of philosophy versus the 'poor arguments' of the public, than the difference between two styles of reasoning.

If it is also true that secular-liberal bioethics generally draws on a limited range of experience, as well as a narrow repertoire of arguments, then the input of lay people is especially needed to illuminate areas of moral importance that this style of bioethics is likely to miss. For example, Tizzard

(2004: 64) refers to the public's 'deep-seated belief that children are gifts and not consumer commodities' and goes on to question the belief by asking whether children born as the result of sex selection are likely to be psychologically harmed – apparently missing the point that the lay belief is *not* in fact about consequentialist harms. Additionally, some lay experiences and moral perceptions may simply lie outside the experience of experts. Many of the life experiences of the women in the educational group in our study, for example, might fit into this category. Here, empirical data on moral life or lay moral opinions can be taken as not in themselves normative, but as extending our knowledge of the moral values that lay people find salient and the rationales they find compelling as they go through their ethical deliberations. This extended database can challenge what secular-liberal, or indeed other forms of bioethics, assume to be normative values, goals or acts.

Forms of public input

The commonly used approaches to accessing public opinion all have drawbacks. For instance, public consultation exercises are likely to be dominated by vested interests: professional bodies and campaigning organisations (such as 'Pro-Life' groups) will usually respond to invitations to give opinions, whereas lay people may not be aware of the opportunity, or may not consider their ideas worthy of consideration (Irwin 2001). More carefully designed ways of giving people a voice need to be well planned in order to be inclusive of a range of perspectives among different groups in society. Where statistical representativeness is achieved by reaching large numbers of people, the form of enquiry is often shallow: opinion polls or other forms of survey may be successful in quantifying stances, but are less helpful in understanding respondents' more considered rationales. With an issue of moral or technical complexity, where some familiarity with the background and context may be desirable, 'thin' forms of engagement can be particularly misleading.

Deliberative methodologies – such as the consensus conference or the citizens' jury – entail a more sustained discussion of issues, with participants having the opportunity to hear from expert witnesses (Joss and Durant 1995). Arguably, the group interviews conducted for this study begin to approach this deliberative ideal, because information was provided on request, and space provided for extensive discussion (Wakeford 2002, Glasner 2001). We suggest that more engaged forms of democratic input like these are less likely to generate superficial and unreflected lay responses, of which the critics mentioned earlier are so wary. Regulatory and advisory public bodies could, for instance, commission a citizens' jury to deliberate on specific questions, the results of which could then be fed into the final decision-making process. We note that the UK National Institute for Health and Clinical Excellence (NICE) has a Citizens Council that meets several times a year to advise on questions of overall values and priorities. This approach could be emulated more widely (but see Davies *et al.* 2005, Barnett *et al.* 2006). The result might be a greater legitimacy for the resulting decisions, as well as a more democratic and less elitist style of policy-making.

But even when supported by considered reasons such as those gathered in our research, public opinion (just like expert opinion) can be flawed, and philosophy provides an invaluable scrutiny of intuitions, arguments and claims. As we see it, the issue here is not about whether professional or lay ethical evaluation provides the best arguments, but about how to avoid the excessive use of a limited kind of philosophical analysis and mode of argumentation in public bioethical debate and policy discussions (Holm 2005). This is one reason why joint input by both expert and lay reasoning is necessary to inform policy and, we would argue, why more research is needed to explore how this input can be achieved. One conclusion of this study is that some of the reasons given by lay participants are akin to those used in the professional ethical analyses – for instance, where the ethical impermissibility of social sex selection derives from a claim about the intrinsic value of the human individual, or that SSS would not be the act of a virtuous parent. This is important for the practice of joint public and professional bioethical consultations, because it means that the insights of lay bioethics *can* be articulated in ways that make them compatible with those of professional ethics in a joint discourse (without saying that the two are the same). But in order for this to happen, the lay arguments first need to be excavated and articulated, in the way we have illustrated here; a more diverse range of bioethical approaches needs to become firmly established in public debate; and bioethics itself needs to become more knowledgeable about the concerns, values and forms of reasoning that lay people bring to their ethical deliberations.

Acknowledgements

The authors would like to thank all those who volunteered to take part in this study, two anonymous referees for their helpful comments, and Tom Wakeford for some invaluable input. The financial support of the Wellcome Trust project grant number 068439/Z/02/Z is gratefully acknowledged.

Note

1   See Banks *et al.* 2006 for a fuller discussion.

References

Baldwin, T. (2005) Reproductive liberty and elitist contempt, *Journal of Medical Ethics*, 31, 288–90.

Banks, S., Scully, J.L. and Shakespeare, T.W. (2006) Ordinary ethics: the ethical evaluation of the new genetics by lay people, *New Genetics and Society*, in press.

Barnett, E., Davies, C. and Wetherell, M.S. (2006) *Citizens at the Centre: Deliberative Participation in Healthcare Decisions*. London: The Policy Press.

Bazeley, P. and Richards, L. (2000) *The NvIvo Qualitative Project Book*. London: Sage.

Borry, P., Schotsman, P. and Dierickx, K. (2005) The birth of the empirical turn in bioethics, *Bioethics*, 19, 49–71.

Braude, P., Pickering, S., Flinter, F. and Ogilvie, C.M. (2002) Preimplantation genetic diagnosis, *Nature Reviews Genetics*, 3, 941–53.

Buber, M. (1937) *I and Thou*. Trans Gregor Smith, R. Edinburgh: T. and T. Clark.

Buchanan, A., Brock, D.W., Daniels, N. and Wikler, D. (2000) *From Chance to Choice: Genetics and Justice*. Harvard: Cambridge University Press.

Callon, M. and Rabeharisoa, V. (2003) Research 'in the wild' and the mapping of new social identities, *Technology in Society*, 25, 193–204.

Capps, B. (2005) Bioethics and misrepresentation in the stem cell debate, *Cardiff Centre for Ethics, Law and Society*. http://www.ccels.cf.ac.uk/literature/publications/2005/Capspaper.html

Cheal, D. (1988) *The Gift Economy*. London: Routledge.

Davies, C., Wetherell, M., Barnett, E. and Seymour-Smith, S. (2005) *Opening the Box: Evaluating the Citizens Council of NICE*. Milton Keynes: Open University Press. http://pcpoh.bham.ac.uk/publichealth/nccrm/PDFs%20and%20documents/Publications/Citizens%20council%20Mar05.pdf

De Vries, R. (2004) How can we help? From 'sociology in' bioethics to 'sociology of' bioethics', *Journal of Law, Medicine and Ethics*, 32, 279–92.

De Vries, R. and Subedi, J. (eds) (1998) *Bioethics and Society. Constructing the Ethical Enterprise*. Englewood, New Jersey: Prentice Hall.

Dickens, B.M. (2002) Can sex selection be ethically tolerated? *Journal of Medical Ethics*, 28, 335–6.

Dworkin, R. (1993) *Life's Dominion: An Argument about Abortion, Euthanasia and Individual Freedom*. New York: Knopf.

Gibbs, G. (2002) *Qualitative Data Analysis: Explorations with NVivo*. Buckingham: Open University Press.

Glasner, P. (2001) Rights or rituals? Why juries can do more harm than good. In Pimbert, M.P. and Wakeford, T. (eds) *Deliberative Democracy and Citizen Empowerment*. Special issue of *PLA Notes 40*, IIED. Co-published by The Commonwealth Foundation, ActionAid, DFID, Sida and IIED (download from http://www.iied.org/NR/agbioliv/pla_notes/pla_backissues/40.html)

Haidt, J. (2001) The emotional dog and its rational tail: a social intuitionist approch to moral judgement, *Psychological Review*, 108, 814–34.

Handyside, A.H., Kontogianni, E.H., Hardy, K. and Winston, R.M. (1990) Pregnancies from biopsied human preimplantation embryos sexed by Y-specific DNA amplification, *Nature*, 344, 768–70.

Harris, J. (2005a) No sex selection please, we're British, *Journal of Medical Ethics*, 31, 286–88.

Harris, J. (2005b) Sex selection and regulated hatred, *Journal of Medical Ethics*, 31, 291–4.

Hedgecoe, A.M. (2004) Critical bioethics: beyond the social science critique of applied ethics, *Bioethics*, 18, 120–43.

Holland, S. (2003) *Bioethics: a Philosophical Introduction*. Cambridge: Polity.

Holm, S. (2004) Like a frog in boiling water: the public, the HFEA and sex selection, *Health Care Analysis*, 12, 27–39.

Holm, S. (2005) Bioethics down under-medical ethics engages with political philosophy, *Journal of Medical Ethics*, 31, 1.

House of Commons Committee on Science and Technology (2005) *Report on Human Technologies and the Law*. London: The Stationery Office.

Human Fertilisation and Embryology Authority (2002) *Sex Selection: Choice and Responsibility in Human Reproduction*. London: HFEA.

Human Fertilisation and Embryology Authority (2003) *Sex Selection: Options for Regulation*. London: HFEA.

Irwin, A. (2001) Constructing the scientific citizen: science and democracy in the biosciences, *Public Understanding of Science*, 10, 1–18.

Irwin, A. and Michael, M. (2003) *Science, Social Theory and Public Knowledge*. Maidenhead, Berks: Open University Press/McGraw Hill.

Jonsen, A. (1998) *The Birth of Bioethics*. Oxford: Oxford University Press.

Joss, S. and Durant, J. (eds) (1995) *Public Participation in Science: the Role of Consensus Conferences in Europe*. London: Science Museum.

Kass, L. (1997) The wisdom of repugnance, *The New Republic*, 2 June 1997, 17–26.

Kass, L. (2002) *Life, Liberty, and the Defense of Dignity: the Challenge for Bioethics*. Milwaukee: Encounter Books.

Kerr, A., Cunningham-Burley, S. and Amos, A. (1998) Drawing the line: an analysis of lay people's discussions about the new genetics, *Public Understanding of Science*, 7, 113–33.

Lakoff, G. and Johnson, M. (1980) *Metaphors We Live By*. Chicago: University of Chicago Press.

Levitt, M. (2003) Public consultation in bioethics. What's the point of asking the public when they have neither scientific nor ethical expertise? *Health Care Analysis*, 11, 15–25.

Light, D.W. and McGee, G. (1998) On the social embeddedness of bioethics. In De Vries, R. and Subedi, J. (eds) *Bioethics and Society. Constructing the Ethical Enterprise*. New Jersey: Prentice Hall.

Mahowald, M.B. (2001) Cultural differences and sex selection. In Tong, R. (ed.) *Globalizing Feminist Bioethics: Crosscultural Perspectives*. Boulder, Colorado: Westview Press.

Mauss, M. (1960) *The Gift: Forms and Functions of Exchange in Archaic Societies*. New York: Norton.

McCarthy, D. (2001) Why sex selection should be legal, *Journal of Medical Ethics*, 27, 302–07.

Michael, M. and Brown, N. (2005) Scientific citizenships: self-representations of xenotransplantation's Publics, *Science as Culture*, 14, 39–57.

Moazam, F. (2004) Feminist discourse on sex screening and selective abortion of female foetuses, *Bioethics*, 18, 205–20.

Nelson, H.L. (1997) *Stories and their Limits: Narrative Approaches to Bioethics*. New York: Routledge.

Nowotny, H., Scott, P. and Gibbons, M. (2001) *Re-thinking Science: Knowledge and the Public in an Age of Uncertainty*. Cambridge: Polity.

Osteen, M. (ed.) (2003) *The Question of the Gift*. London: Routledge.

Pembrey, M. (2002) Social sex selection by preimplantation genetic diagnosis, *Reproductive BioMedicine Online*, 4, 157–9, http://www.rbmonline.com/Article/418

Rawlinson, M.C. (2001) The concept of a feminist bioethics, *Journal of Medicine and Philosophy*, 26, 405–16.

Robertson, J.A. (2003) Extending preimplantation genetic diagnosis: medical and non-medical uses, *Journal of Medical Ethics*, 29, 213–16.

Salter, B. and Jones, M. (2005) Biobanks and bioethics: the politics of legitimation, *Journal of European Public Policy*, 12, 710–32.

Savulescu, J. (1999) Sex selection: the case for, *Medical Journal of Australia*, 171, 373–5.

Savulescu, J. and Dahl, E. (2000) Sex selection and preimplantation diagnosis. A response to the Ethics Committee of the American Society of Reproductive Medicine, *Human Reproduction*, 15, 1879–80.

Scully, J.L. (2002) *Quaker Approaches to Moral Issues in Genetics*. Lampeter: Mellen.

Scully, J.L., Banks, S. and Shakespeare, T.W. (2006) Chance, choice and control: lay debate on prenatal social sex selection, *Social Science and Medicine*, 63, 21–31.

Solomon, M.Z. (2005) Realizing bioethics' goals in practice: ten ways 'is' can help 'ought', *Hastings Center Report*, 35, 40–7.

Tizzard, J. (2004) Sex selection, child welfare and risk: a critique of the HFEA's recommendations on sex selection, *Health Care Analysis*, 12, 61–8.

Tong, R. (1998) The ethics of care. A feminist virtue ethics of care for healthcare practitioners, *Journal of Medicine and Philosophy*, 23, 131–52.

Wakeford, T. (2002) Citizens Juries: a radical alternative for social research, *Social Research Update*, 37, http://www.soc.surrey.ac.uk/sru/SRU37.html

Walker, M.U. (1998) *Moral Understandings: A Feminist Study in Ethics*. New York: Routledge.

Weed, D.L. and McKeown, R.E. (1998) Epidemiology and virtue ethics, *International Journal of Epidemiology*, 27, 343–9.

Wolf, S. (1996) *Feminism and Bioethics: Beyond Reproduction*. New York: Oxford University Press.

Zussman, R. (2000) The contribution of sociology to medical ethics, *The Hastings Center Report*, 30, 7–11.

7

It's money that matters: the financial context of ethical decision-making in modern biomedicine
Adam M. Hedgecoe

Introduction

The issue of autonomy has long been a site of tension between bioethics and the social sciences. A wealth of studies suggest that informed consent, so vital to respect patients' and research participants' autonomy, is extremely hard to obtain in a meaningful sense (Gray 1975, Lidz *et al.* 1983, Fox and Sawzey 1984, Harth and Thong 1995, Corrigan 2003). Yet the chronological and topical range of these studies has done little to persuade bioethicists to alter the central role autonomy plays in modern Western ethical thinking. These data lead sociological sceptics about bioethics to ask: Does autonomy, in fact, exist? Or is it a construct created by philosophically-oriented bioethicists and used by researchers and clinicians to get their work done?

Yet while bioethics has traditionally, and correctly, focused on patient autonomy and the protection of the vulnerable, an equally important but less studied topic involves the autonomy of doctors (and other caregivers) and their freedom to make clinical decisions. Traditionally, bioethics conceptualises the clinical encounter in terms of *clinical* autonomy, 'the classical fiduciary ideal' that 'Physicians should do whatever is in the best interests of their *individual* patient' (Khushf 1999: 43). Such autonomy depends upon 'the discretionary space normally afforded professionals' since 'the nature of professional judgement and making right and good decisions requires a degree of responsible freedom in clinical matters' (Pellegrino and Thomasma 1981: xii). I use a case study of the breast cancer drug Herceptin to propose that economic pressures in modern healthcare mean that this 'discretionary space', so vital for clinical autonomy, has ceased to exist. As a consequence, the current bioethics model of clinical decision-making is out of step with social reality.

The bioethics model has much in common with 'prescriptive' approaches to medical decision-making that explain 'how medicine ought to be practiced' (McKinlay, Potter and Feldman 1996: 769) as opposed to a 'descriptive' approach that highlights the way clinical decisions are influenced by 'a range of social factors that are logically unrelated to the etiology or course of illness' (1996: 769). Both bioethics and the prescriptive approach tend to assume:

that physicians are autonomous decision makers practising in socially insular clinical settings . . . [But in reality] . . . Clinical decision making invariably takes place in a social relationship that is penetrated and shaped by patients' age, gender, socio-economic status, and race, physicians' professional training and clinical experience, and bureaucratic features of the organized settings of clinical transactions (Clark, Potter and McKinlay 1991: 861).

The 'bureaucratic features of the organized setting of the clinical transaction' that I focus on in this chapter are rationing decisions about a drug called Herceptin. Thus I am less interested in rationing in the sense of the social and political reasons underlying exactly which patients are allowed specific treatments, and more focused on the impact particular rationing decisions have on clinician decision-making. More specifically, I explore the way in which rationing impacts on clinical autonomy by following a particular rationing decision, made at a national level, and showing how it impacts on clinical decision-making in breast oncology in the UK. Thus I use rationing as a tool to explore the problems and limits of current bioethical thinking about medical decision-making.

My intent here is not to weigh in on traditional bioethical debates over the rights and wrongs of rationing healthcare and the particular mechanisms by which this should be done (*e.g.* Daniels, Light and Caplan 1996, Harris 1987, Rawles 1989, Mooney 1989, Singer *et al.* 1995). These discussions tend to be 'top down'. There is little bioethical discussion of how rationing decisions get *implemented* and their effect on how clinicians treat patients. The assumption seems to be that either a particular treatment is funded or it is not. As Samia Hurst and colleagues, among the few bioethicists to address these issues, note in their recent survey of this area, 'Two commonly held assumptions seem to be . . . : first, physicians are making these decisions on their own, and second, the decisions to ration are simple dichotomous choices' (Hurst *et al.* 2005: 643). As they go on to note, 'physicians' experiences in situations of resource constraints appear to be more complex than the normative literature assumes' (2005: 644).

My point is not that there is no discussion of the effect of rationing on clinical autonomy in the literature, but rather that it occurs almost exclusively among medics, and in medical journals, and is largely missing from bioethics debates[1]. Thus despite ethical discussion of 'just' healthcare and the roles of rationing and economics, there is a blind spot in bioethical discussion in this area, a failure to note, in Lindsay Prior's elegant phrase, that 'Rationing principles . . . are woven like a fine thread through the broad tapestry of [clinical] action' (Prior 2001: 571). In this case Prior is referring to the oncological genetics unit, yet as the remainder of this chapter shows, the 'fine thread' of rationing also binds the hands of clinicians dealing with more conventional breast cancers, and in turn raises questions about the bioethical model of medical decision-making[2].

A case study in clinical rationing: Herceptin

Trastuzumab is a monoclonal antibody marketed under the brand name Herceptin developed for the treatment of the around 30 per cent of breast cancers that produce too much of a particular protein, HER2. Before a woman receives Herceptin, a series of diagnostic tests are run on her tumour tissue, one of which is to determine the levels of HER2. Because too much HER2 protein ('over-expression') is deemed to be the result of a genetic fault in the tumour tissue, many commentators present Herceptin as one of the first widespread examples of 'pharmacogenetics', the use of genetics to help develop and prescribe drugs. The research presented below was carried out as part of a Wellcome Trust funded study of the clinical development of pharmacogenetics (Hedgecoe 2004). But since the focus of this chapter is the relationship between clinical decision-making around Herceptin and rationing, the novel, pharmacogenetic aspects of this drug will remain in the background, except when they are directly relevant to these narrower concerns.

My case study is based on qualitative semi-structured interviews carried out between January 2002 and July 2003 with 25 UK-based breast cancer specialists (two Clinicians, 20 Clinician Researchers, one Researcher and two Oncological Pharmacists, self-selected categories), identified through publications in this area, lists of those involved in clinical trials and snowball sampling. In addition, interviews were carried out with two policy-makers at a local healthcare level, one representative of the National Institute for Clinical Excellence (NICE, the central body that approves drugs for the NHS), one representative from Roche (the company that markets Herceptin in Europe), and two people from breast cancer charities[3].

A second round of interviews was carried out in Spring 2005 as part of a European Commission-funded project comparing, among other things, Herceptin use in different EU member states. These interviews covered six clinician researchers (three oncologists and three histopathologists) and a re-interview with one of the previously interviewed oncological pharmacists. These interviewees were chosen to complement the first round of interviews and update information on clinical practice, economic issues and testing issues.

The institutional context

Although Herceptin was approved for use in the UK in 2000, this did not guarantee that the drug would be made available on the National Health Service (NHS). One of New Labour's first decisions upon coming to power in May 1997 was the creation of NICE (the National Institute for Clinical Excellence), which opened in April 1999[4]. NICE issues guidance on new and established technologies and interventions, and whether they should be funded by the NHS (Birch and Gafni 2002). NICE is a 'fourth hurdle' to drug regulation; after the traditional three hurdles of safety, efficacy and quality of manufacture comes the fourth hurdle of clinical and cost effectiveness (Paul and Trueman 2001).

The exact mechanism by which NICE reaches its decisions is largely irrelevant to the concerns of this chapter as are the details of the controversy that surrounded the NICE guidance on Herceptin (see Hedgecoe 2004: 131–9). The main point of interest is that the NICE approval took an unexpectedly long time. Although the NICE appraisal process for Herceptin began in September 2000, when the drug got its EU licence, the Institute's guidance was not published until March 2002. This 18-month delay, perhaps half as long again as most other NICE decisions, meant that while it was legal to prescribe Herceptin in the UK, there was no obligation on the part of NHS healthcare providers such as Primary Care Trusts (PCTs), which oversee primary care services in a given area and can commission services from NHS acute trusts (hospitals), to actually pay for the drug, or for the testing. A partial solution to this latter problem was provided by the company Roche which, through three 'reference centres', funded HER2 testing in the UK between October 1999 and March 2003: any clinician who wanted to could send a tissue sample to one of the three labs and Roche would cover the cost of the testing.

'As good as I possibly can be': clinical decision-making before the NICE decision
This still left the issue of how to fund Herceptin, with the essential clinical decision being, is Herceptin even an option? Obviously, this is only a problem for patients seeking treatment on the NHS. As one of my interviewees put it, 'Here it's a funding issue; if patients are privately covered, insured, they receive it' (CR3). But for the NHS, prior to the publication of NICE's appraisal of Herceptin, whether a clinician could prescribe the drug depended on local factors determined by their hospital or health authority. As one of my interviewees put it:

> a number of my colleagues in other major centres around the country who have been using Herceptin for maybe a year prior to NICE Guidance . . . somehow they persuaded their purchasers to pay for it . . . and that has not happened in [city name]. I would estimate that probably about 50 per cent of the country are like us and unable to fund it – prior to NICE Guidance (CR16).

This figure of around 50 per cent coverage was supported by other interviewees, and thus raises the issue of why some healthcare providers decided to fund Herceptin and some did not. Clinician Researcher 13, who *was* allowed to prescribe Herceptin at this time, suggested that it was, in part, on the basis of a scientific case made by clinicians:

> Based on the evidence, we sped ahead of NICE and thought we can't deny our patients this and it was very strict in terms of the evidence, we used it

well before. But that's the postcode prescribing – we happened to be able to do it, eked money out of our health authority[5].

Yet even this decision was partly based on idiosyncratic, local factors, since the hospital concerned 'had a very forward thinking clinical director who recognised that this was a drug that was going to be approved and we shouldn't get into these situations and having some patients catch up' (CR13).

But beyond individual hospitals, clinicians attempted to allow some Herceptin use at a regional level, often running into structural problems within the NHS. For example, one interviewee described the attempt by:

> our own network . . . [where] . . . we have a new drug group . . . [which] . . . came down using the same format as NICE effectively but we came down and decided that we felt it was justified to use Herceptin for a limited number of people . . . and what's happened is that within our own cancer network, patients who lived within [one] Health Authority can get it, the ones in [a neighbouring Health Authority] can't. So we've got postcode prescribing within our own network (CR2).

The exact mechanism by which the cancer network managed to get some Herceptin funded revolved around certain clinicians having greater expertise than others, manifesting itself in the form of a 'named prescriber' system, where only a limited number of clinicians were regarded as 'expert' enough to indicate HER2 testing and prescribe Herceptin. The need for this was highlighted by Clinician Researcher 6, who talked about running a clinic in another location, where 'there's somebody else up there who's . . . been sending people he thought were HER2 positive, sending samples for testing'. Such decisions would be based on severity of the disease, age of the patient and various other features of the cancer that would lead one to think that the tumour was HER2 overexpressing. But in this case, of the samples sent to the lab, 'he's had about a 15 per cent hit rate which goes to show that actually the prediction of who is positive and who is not positive is not that good on the basis of other histological features' (CR6). The implication is that working out which patients' samples to send for HER2 testing is a skilled job, not to be undertaken by just any oncologist.

Although Roche was underwriting testing costs in the UK when this policy got off the ground, Herceptin was funded by individual healthcare providers[6]. Therefore: 'Within the network, we've actually said that the only two people who should instigate prescribing are [CR2] and [CR6]. So, we're actually trying to control the initiation of Herceptin so that we make sure that people are actually FISH 3 positive [*i.e.* clearly over-expressing HER2], have been properly tested, have been through the other options' (Pharmacist 1). The clear aim of this named prescriber system is to ensure that Herceptin is 'not being prescribed willy-nilly' (Policy 2). Set up as a means of responsibly using the limited budget provided for Herceptin use prior to the NICE guidance, this sort of mechanism underlines clinicians' practical response to rationing decisions. As Hurst and colleagues note in their recent work, such decisions are not made by individual clinicians, nor are they dichotomous 'fund' or 'do not fund' decisions. But rather it is about trying to provide care to as many patients as possible, given the financial restrictions imposed from above, and the consequent impact on clinical autonomy.

The point about these attempts by individual Trusts and cancer networks to pre-empt NICE's decision is, of course, that the decision-makers at NICE were not the only people with access to data on Herceptin and its cost. Oncologists were just as capable of reading the clinical reports and drawing their own conclusions, yet their expertise in oncology was often of little importance in a situation where decisions about prescribing practice were being made at a level higher than that of the individual doctor. While some clinicians managed, through various mechanisms, to prescribe Herceptin, others could not, with a consequent impact on their clinical autonomy. As one oncologist said: 'I'm being seen to be as good as I possibly can be by our Trust people, by not using drugs in advance of NICE approval when they're expensive drugs but I know that I'm flying in the face of the increasing body of evidence because I can read the papers just as well as NICE can' (CR8).

'A much stickier wicket legally': clinical decision making after the NICE decision

When the NICE guidance was published in March 2002, the guidance document was presented to a professional community frustrated by the patchy availability of Herceptin over the previous 18 months, and showing signs of considerable antipathy towards NICE due to its perceived lack of expertise and susceptibility to political pressure. The NICE guidance document states that Herceptin is recommended as an option to treat women whose tumours express high levels of the HER2 protein measured by a test called Immunohistochemistry (IHC). It should be used in combination with a chemotherapy (paclitaxel) in patients who have not received chemotherapy for their metastatic breast cancer or on its own, in women who have received at least two courses of chemotherapy, without effect (National Institute for Clinical Excellence 2002). A number of features of this guidance are open to question, including the reliance on IHC testing rather than the more advanced FISH test and the tight restrictions on who should get Herceptin as a monotherapy. Yet in terms of clinical decisions, none of this matters, since once NICE issues its guidance on a particular piece of technology, healthcare providers in the UK are legally obliged to make that treatment available, whatever the feelings of individual clinicians might be. One effect of such a requirement is to erode clinical autonomy:

> if NICE say it's okay, we've got to give it even though we actually would rather spend a bit more money on the dialysis machines than not be

restricted ourselves because the patient can say: 'Look, if NICE says that I can have Herceptin, why aren't you giving it to me?' *There may be reasonable clinical judgement against it [*i.e. *prescribing Herceptin] but you're on a much stickier wicket legally as a doctor to then deny the patient Herceptin* (CR7; emphasis added).

And the NICE rules do not just require clinicians to prescribe Herceptin to women who, in clinical terms, might not be good candidates, they also force delays on the use of Herceptin on women who are suitable. One interviewee suggested that the health care providers were 'being advised by people who are reading the NICE Guidance to the letter of the law . . . [*i.e.* that] . . . you cannot give Herceptin until post three lines of metastatic chemotherapy which, from a clinical point of view, doesn't make sense' (CR16). For this clinician, the NICE rules make no sense since Herceptin would presumably also be of benefit to these women at an earlier stage in their treatment.

Another example of the restrictions the NICE guidance puts on the autonomy of clinical decision-making mentioned by this interviewee is the way in which managers required the strictest definition of HER2 over-expression before allowing the prescription of Herceptin. The NICE guidance requires only that patients who score highly (3+) on IHC testing should necessarily be treated, although research has shown that some people who score lower (2+) may benefit from Herceptin and that further (FISH) testing can identify them. But a strict reading of the NICE guidance excludes this group of patients, and allows these guidelines to serve as a means of controlling clinical decision-making regarding this drug. This means that, whatever an individual's clinical opinion may be, they may not be able to exercise it when prescribing Herceptin.

It should not come as a surprise to find that even within the tight constraints placed on practice by NICE guidance, clinicians attempt to exercise some kind of control over clinical decision-making. Yet what is clear is that the kinds of clinical decisions that are made are phrased in terms of further rationing. Clinician Researcher 16 noted that:

all of us have been very conscious about the resource issue . . . we're still at the point of requesting the test individually when the number of at-risk features make us feel that we would want to offer the patient either the HERA Trial[7] or the drug in the metastatic setting. . . . So we have looked at ways . . . of not introducing HER-2 as an across-the-board test, but rationing it . . . and I would definitely use age, myself, as a rationing tool . . . and I don't have a big problem in saying that the 75-year-old with 20 Node positive, ER negative, grade three disease, needs anything, except lots of alcohol and morphine. I don't have a problem with that. . . .

Although this kind of decision is phrased in terms of 'clinical judgement', it is, explicitly, a rationing decision, a choice focused on the costs incurred rather than the clinical outcome for a specific patient. This becomes clearer when one thinks about Herceptin's very usefulness as a treatment, its low toxicity and limited side effects, which can make choices harder than they might be with a 'conventional' chemotherapy: 'the major issue with them is going to be cost, and I think that unlike conventional chemotherapy where you get a lot of side-effects from the treatment, then it can limit their use by the toxicity and here you cannot use that. And the spectrum of ages you can use it in is wide' (CR3). Thus, when thinking about the possibility of Herceptin in the case of the hypothetical 75-year-old woman, the clinician cannot 'ration by toxicity' as they might with a conventional chemotherapy. A decision not to treat becomes explicitly about 'rationing'. In the context of broader discussions this is clearly an example of 'bedside rationing' (Hall 1994), the 'withholding by a physician of a medically beneficial service because of that service's cost to someone other than the patient' (Ubel and Goold 1997: 74). In the context of US healthcare, such behaviour on the part of clinicians generates much discussion, up to and including debates about the Supreme Court's view of its legality (Bloche and Jacobson 2000). In the UK, with its socialised system of medicine, however, doctors have always been aware of the wider financial impact of their choices.

Moreover, oncologists' use of age as a key factor in making these decisions is not exceptional. Social scientists have explored clinical rationing on the basis of age in a number of other conditions such as end-stage renal dialysis (Varekamp, Krol and Danse 1998) and myocardial infarction (Elder and Fox 1992). So ubiquitous are clinical rationing decisions based on age, that it is described as 'the factor most often invoked to deny treatment. It provides an automatic pilot for doctors, so simplifying the perplexities and avoiding the agonies, of choosing between different lives' (Klein, Day and Redmayne 1996: 87).

When age is not an option, other solutions present themselves. The following case illustrates the way access to testing is used as a means of restricting access to the drug:

> One case that had prolonged discussion associated with it was this particular girl, 30 years old, who was severely mentally impaired, with a huge breast tumour which had obviously been ignored because she didn't talk about breast lumps, having a mental age of five, as she did, and she turned up with anaemia, and the bone marrow showed almost complete replacement with tumour cells. We couldn't give her a cytotoxic; the question is, is it the appropriate use of Herceptin to treat her, and we said if it is an appropriate use, then test her. If it's not an appropriate use, then we won't test her, or test the tumour. That's the one real debate we've had (CR8).

As suggested above, the decision is phrased as being about rationing. The context for the interviewee introducing this case was the suggestion that: 'I think our Trust takes a positive approach to funding issues saying things that are approved by NICE must be funded *but there has to be proper case selection'* (CR8; emphasis added). Thus the decision whether to treat the 30-year-old mentally impaired patient is not to do with the safety of the treatment concerned[8] but whether this is an appropriate use of resources. The second point to notice is that the discussion here is not over whether to prescribe Herceptin or not, but whether to test this patient's tumour for HER2 status. While the reason for this might be to do with the cost of HER2 testing, in fact this test is not expensive and can be carried out at almost any pathology lab. A more likely explanation is that NICE rules specifically require health providers to prescribe Herceptin to those women whose tumours overexpress HER2; but if a HER2 test is not run on a patient's tumour, then no obligation is incurred by the healthcare provider.

This sort of situation was described in an early (pre-NICE decision) interview by Clinician Researcher 1 who faced:

> An interesting dilemma here . . . although the Trust has given us funding for the drug, they haven't given us any funding for the HER-2 testing so they don't seem to have taken a global view of this and so we're struggling at the moment to try and get some funding for our pathology department to go on to do the HER-2 testing.

This situation was presented as an example of bureaucratic mismanagement, with the healthcare provider willing to pay for the expensive drug, but not for the (comparatively) cheap testing. This may be too generous an interpretation. Given that restricting access to HER testing has become the main way healthcare providers avoid the NICE requirement to provide Herceptin to women who over-express HER2, this looks like an early indication for how things have developed. Controlling access to HER2 testing serves as a way of rationing the total number of patients who might be eligible for Herceptin. Surveys carried out by breast cancer charities (Breast Cancer Care 2004) and follow-up interviews with other clinicians conducted 18 months later suggest that the restriction of HER2 testing as a form of rationing has become more widespread and seems to have become informal policy for a number of healthcare providers in the UK, reinforcing the idea that clinical autonomy is constrained by rationing systems.

The NICE guidance impacts on clinical autonomy in two ways. First, and most obviously, it clearly restricts the kinds of decisions open to clinicians, the patients they can and cannot treat. Second, when clinicians do exercise their autonomy, the 'discretionary space' within which they make their decisions is structured in terms of further rationing, rather than other clinical features.

'Our inability, as doctors, to give the therapy that we believe is right'
It is commonly assumed that there is a tension for clinicians in modern healthcare systems, between their duty to do the best for an individual patient, and a

broader concern towards society, as articulated in terms of cost containment. Yet for many of my interviewees, this dilemma was not an issue. As some economists have noted (*e.g.* Weinstein 2001), a central problem for the individual clinician weighing up the ethical aspects of rationing healthcare is that, for all their expertise, they lack the kind of bird's-eye view required to assess the consequences of their decisions. As one interviewee suggested:

> If the money is [from] a new source of money you take it and you give that treatment. But if someone said to you, 'oh you can have this treatment but you can't have your radiotherapy machines', obviously you wouldn't do that. But there is no central way of actually seeing that if you were to get this extra money, that if somebody else is going to lose are you robbing Peter to pay Paul. The budget which these things come from are so vast, and so inaccessible to us, we don't know where they will have come from (CR3).

To some extent, oncologists' views about budget limits, which tend to be sceptical, are shaped by their experience with a series of expensive drugs; 'in the beginning when we started using Taxol it was extremely expensive, carboplatin was extremely expensive, it's less expensive now but it's still kind of expensive. These drugs will continue to be expensive' (CR11). Yet these drugs are still used. When it comes to the family of drugs known as taxanes (of which Taxol is one), 'we spend hundreds of thousands now on taxanes which five years ago we couldn't spend because we were told the money doesn't exist for that. And we were told, if you have the money for taxanes somebody has to do without . . . I mean have some beds been closed because of that? I don't know' (CR3).

Thus, in the case of Herceptin at least, clinicians do not face an ethical dilemma since a dilemma implies choice: two or more possible courses of action. Yet, partly because of their experience of using expensive drugs, and partly because their actions are so financially restricted anyway, these clinicians are not ethically troubled by the need to constrain costs for the sake of wider society. Rather, rationing serves as part of the structure, a 'fine thread' in the tapestry of clinical decision-making. This limits ethical debates in Herceptin use to issues around informed consent and whether patients are told about HER2 testing prior to it taking place (Hedgecoe 2005).

But more than this, such rationing is in keeping with the broader culture within the UK's NHS, which acknowledges that 'decisions to treat one patient . . . may mean that others are denied care' – even if one is not in a position to know if this is the case or not (Newdick 1995: 21). While the origins of such beliefs may lie partly in economics, they also have strong cultural foundations, based on the postwar origins of the NHS, and its link to the welfare state. De Vries is correct in saying that medical sociologists need to pay greater attention to broader cultural themes if they are to provide a full explanation for why healthcare practices and system differ between states. He convincingly shows how the Dutch preference for midwife-led home births has its roots in Dutch cultural features including the role of women in the family and home, thriftiness, solidarity and Dutch dislike of heroics (De Vries 2004). We might speculate about US clinicians' resistance to rationing by reference to the primacy of the individual in US public life, a feature of American culture that has been the subject of discussion since at least Alexis de Tocqueville.

In the case of the UK, understanding the cultural roots of NHS rationing is necessarily reflexive, given the iconic role the NHS plays in British public life. It is hard to overestimate the cultural impact of this 'anomaly, not to say . . . anachronism' whose 'overall architecture and method of funding have remained largely unchanged in a rapidly changing society', an institution whose popularity derives from its anomalous status, its position as 'an exercise in institutionalised nostalgia' symbolising 'a simpler warmer world of camaraderie, solidarity and national success' (Klein 2001: vii). How we in the UK view healthcare rationing has its cultural roots in wartime Britain, where rationing of food and clothes 'became a symbol of social solidarity and of shared commitment to a national enterprise' and where the 'black market was synonymous with spivvery' (Klein, Day and Redman 1996: 7–8). But this is not to say rationing is always acceptable. Its acceptability 'seems to depend on its perceived reasonableness, which, in turn, appears to depend on the form it takes' (Klein, Day and Redman 1996: 8). Thus clinicians' willingness to ration Herceptin use beyond the restrictions placed by NICE depends on the (culturally mediated) view of what counts as reasonable grounds.

At the broadest level, clinicians' tales about the use of this new drug should alert us to a very simple state of affairs: if a hospital or healthcare funder does not allow the prescription of Herceptin, then the ethical issues surrounding clinical decision-making about this drug are rather limited. And this is in keeping with the binary model of rationing that bioethics uses when it considers the effects of economics on healthcare provision: either a treatment gets funded or it does not (Harris 2005).

My research has exposed the inadequacy of thinking in such simple, dichotomous terms. But even when bioethics engages with these issues in a more complex way, something is missing. This is highlighted by the Nuffield Council on Bioethics' report on the ethical issues involved in the clinical use of pharmacogenetics, which provides one of the few discussions of Herceptin and rationing available. They admit that 'bodies such as NICE may provide guidance about the circumstances in which medicines may be provided . . . as in the case of Herceptin'. But they imply that 'Although not formally binding on health professionals . . . physicians may feel obligated to restrict prescription to those individuals who . . . meet the necessary criteria . . . and indeed, health providers may impose such requirements' (Nuffield Council on Bioethics 2003: 66). This picture is not wrong so much as incomplete. There is no *legal* requirement for clinicians to only prescribe in accordance with NICE; they could offer the drug 'off label' to women at an earlier stage of breast cancer[9]. It is just that for most clinicians that sort of autonomy in their clinical decision-making is simply not available; 'may feel obligated' and 'may impose such requirements' do not do justice to the relationship between clinicians and the restrictions imposed on their autonomy by healthcare providers.

As I noted at the outset, bioethical discussions of autonomy typically focus on the choices patients have to make, the information provided to them, and their ability to make a free, informed decision. My data show the need for a broader conception, which includes clinicians' autonomy, the freedom of doctors to choose the best treatment for the patient. It is clear that, in the case of Herceptin in this particular health system, such autonomy is in short supply. As Clinician Researcher 16 put it: 'It's very difficult, I think, if we work within a system that has an enormous amount of regulation and an enormous amount of rationing, and there's no getting away from our inability, as doctors, to give the therapy that we believe is right'.

Conclusion: towards an ethics of decision-making at the margins

In the light of the Herceptin story I am led to ask: are bioethicists asking the wrong questions, or asking the right questions wrongly? If they are asking the wrong questions then, by focusing on autonomy, bioethicists are relying upon a concept so sociologically complex that the solution is to abandon autonomy as a useful way of thinking about clinical decisions. The problem with such a point of view is that it does not offer an alternative, a way forward for discussing the clinical encounter. 'Bioethics knocking' is great sport for social scientists, yet perhaps the time has come to offer more constructive criticism. If we suggest that the problem with bioethics is that it asks the right question wrongly, we see a way to proceed: if we don't just throw out autonomy, but rather use the insights of sociology to appreciate what it means and how it *really* functions, we have a way forward. Because at the same time as this story undermines the myth of clinician autonomy, and hence the bioethical model of medical decision-making, it also suggests productive areas for bioethical inquiry. These are at the margins of clinical practice, and centre on the ways in which clinicians try to 'get round' the restrictions imposed on them. While there is some discussion of the legal issues surrounding such practices in US medicine (for example, underbilling in the case of uninsured patients, Weiner 2001), the range of clinicians' ingenuity and the ethical aspects of the strategies remain underexplored.

Two examples from the case of Herceptin may prove useful. In the first case, in one of the follow-up interviews conducted in early 2005, one clinician claimed that because his local healthcare provider would not supply Herceptin while NICE was deliberating: 'We had to go through the process where one of my patients had to go to the media and eventually the health authority did give us the money to give people Herceptin. After a lot of publicity . . . This is the normal route in view of the way NICE behaves, and I think we can expect more of that in the future'. This prediction has proved accurate, with recent controversy over the NHS's willingness to pay for Herceptin to treat early stage breast cancer (Meikle 2005)[10]. Supporting or even organising these sorts of actions allows clinicians to exercise their autonomy in order to get individual patients the best possible treatment. But clearly there are ethical elements to such 'guerilla' healthcare that need to be thought through. What are a clinician's duties regarding his or her employer, and how do these relate to their responsibility towards patients? Do clinicians have a moral obligation to wage these sorts of campaigns, or are they beyond what we can reasonably expect? Social scientists in turn might seek to show how these issues fit within the broader culture of the NHS, which traditionally has steered away from the kind of Hippocratic individualism that characterises the US healthcare system (Zussman 1997).

The second example is the interviewee who told me that because 'With the new drugs, it's a lot harder [to get access]. My approach is to put patients into clinical trials wherever possible' (CR8). The point is that the control arm in such trials are not given placebos but often receive a standard of treatment which exceeds that normally agreed by the healthcare provider, perhaps because the drugs concerned have not yet received NICE approval. By entering patients into trial, this clinician is ensuring that they receive the best drugs available, thus circumventing financial restrictions on their clinical use. Obviously a number of interesting ethical issues are raised by this practice including what counts as research and what counts as treatment, whether this behaviour counts as deception (and if so, is this wrong?), and whether there are obligations on clinicians to seek out and use such tactics to ensure their patients get the best treatment.

I stated at the beginning that this chapter was not about rationing but rather about what rationing tells us about the limits of the bioethical model of clinical decision-making. This model, which requires a 'discretionary space' for the clinician to act in a patient's best interest, is undermined by the way rationing decisions permeate the clinic, and restrict clinicians' autonomy. At the same time, this case provides an opportunity for bioethics to explore the margins of clinical decision-making, where there is space for autonomy. It is beyond the remit of a single case study to prove whether this is an isolated case or indicative of modern medicine as a whole, but should clinical autonomy be restricted by rationing on a wider basis, then the challenges presented to bioethics and the way it tackles clinical decisions need a vigorous and comprehensive response.

Notes

1   For example, while Povar and Moreno's (1988) article 'Hippocrates and the health maintenance organization' is a classic contribution to debates in this area,

it is largely ignored by bioethicists. It has been cited 51 times in the ISI database, only three of which are published in bioethics journals (based on a list of top nine bioethics journal by impact factor) and the large majority of the remaining 48 articles were not written by bioethicists (based on affiliation). The assumption, that ethical discussions among medics, in medical journals, are not the same thing as 'bioethics', cannot be defended in full here (see Cooter 2000). It rests upon a view of bioethics as a very specific ideology rooted in time and place, rejecting the potentially anachronistic position that counts all medical ethical debates as 'bioethics'.

2   For an excellent introduction to the emerging sociology of rationing, see Light and Hughes 2001.

3   In the UK there are a number of breast cancer charities (which in the US might be termed activist groups), non-governmental organisations largely supported by public donations which provide support and information for women with breast cancer. They also, to varying degrees, combine these roles with political lobbying and the funding of scientific research.

4   In April 2005 NICE joined with the Health Development Agency to become the new National Institute for Health and Clinical Excellence, also called NICE.

5   'Post-code rationing' is the controversial situation whereby different regions have access to different medical services and treatments. The idea that people in another part of the country, or even in the next street, could get access to drugs denied you by your local health provider 'offended against the equity principle' at the core of the NHS (Klein 2001: 200–01). One of the apparent aims in setting up NICE was to reduce this kind of variability.

6   I deliberately use this vague, broad term because of the complex nature of healthcare funding in the UK. Depending on the situation, the organisation responsible for ensuring Herceptin is made available in any one case might be a Strategic Health Authority (responsible for strategic planning within regions), a Primary Care Trust (PCT, which provides primary care services in local areas), a Hospital trust (these are commissioned by PCTs to provide acute services – such as oncology) or a cancer network (Kewell, Hawkins and Ferlie 2002), 34 of which were set up in 2001 to provide cancer services in England (James 2002).

7   The HERA trial is testing Herceptin's suitability in the adjuvant (post-operative) setting, and thus makes the drug available to women far earlier than the metastatic stage. Since the trial is industry funded, patients entered into it do not cost healthcare providers money.

8   Most professionals regard Herceptin as far less toxic than standard chemotherapies.

9   From my follow-up interviews it is clear that a small number of clinicians have convinced healthcare providers to fund this.

10   The research for this chapter was carried out before the 2006 controversy over access to Herceptin for pre-metastatic patients blew up.

References

Birch, S. and Gafni, A. (2002) On being NICE in the UK: guidelines for technology appraisal for the NHS in England and Wales, *Health Economics*, 11, 185–91.

Bloche, M.G. and Jacobson, P.D. (2000) The Supreme Court and bedside rationing, *Journal of the American Medical Association*, 284, 21, 2776–9.

Breast Cancer Care (2004) Press Statement: on HER2 testing and Herceptin.

Clark, J.A., Potter, D.A. and McKinlay, J.B. (1991) Bringing social structure back into clinical decision-making, *Social Science and Medicine*, 32, 8, 853–66.

Cooter, R. (2000) The ethical body. In Cooter, R. and Pickstone, J. (eds) *Medicine in the Twentieth Century*. Amsterdam: Harwood Academic Publishers.

Corrigan, O. (2003) Empty ethics: the problem with informed consent, *Sociology Of Health and Illness*, 25, 7, 768–92.

Daniels, N., Light, D. and Caplan, R.L. (1996) *Benchmarks of fairness for health care reform*. New York: Oxford University Press.

De Vries, R. (2004) *A Pleasing Birth: Midwives and Maternity Care in the Netherlands*. Philadelphia: Temple University Press.

Elder, A.T. and Fox, K.A.A. (1992) Thrombolytic treatment for elderly patients, *British Medical Journal*, 305, 846–7.

Fox, R.C. and Swazey, J.P. (1984) Medical morality is not bioethics – medical ethics in China and the United States, *Perspective in Biology and Medicine*, 27, 336–60.

Gray, B.H. (1975) *Human Subjects in Medical Experimentation: a Sociological Study of the Conduct and Regulation of Clinical Research*. New York: Wiley Intersci.

Hall, M.A. (1994) Rationing health care at the bedside, *New York Unviersity Law Review*, 69, 4–5, 693–780.

Harris, J. (1987) QALY fying the value of life, *Journal of Medical Ethics*, 13, 117–23.

Harris, J. (2005) It's not NICE to discriminate, *Journal of Medical Ethics*, 31, 373–5.

Harth, S.C. and Thong, Y.H. (1995) Parental perceptions and attitudes about informed consent in clinical research involving children, *Social Science and Medicine*, 41, 12, 1647–51.

Hedgecoe, A.M. (2004) *The Politics of Personalised Medicine – Pharmacogenetics in the Clinic*. Cambridge: Cambridge University Press.

Hedgecoe, A.M. (2005) 'At the point at which you can do something about it, then it becomes more relevant': informed consent in the pharmacogenetic clinic, *Social Science and Medicine*, 61, 6, 1201–10.

Hurst, S.A., Chandros Hull, S., DuVal, G. and Danis, M. (2005) Physicians' responses to resource constraints, *Archives of Internal Medicine*, 165, 639–44.

James, R.J. (2002) Commentary on Kewell, B., Hawkins, C. and Ferlie, E. (2002) Calman-Hine reassessed, *Journal of Evaluation in Clinical Practice*, 8, 3, 299–301.

Kewell, B., Hawkins, C. and Ferlie, E. (2002) Calman-Hine reassessed: a survey of cancer network development in England, 1999–2000, *Journal of Evaluation in Clinical Practice*, 8, 3, 303–11.

Khushf, G. (1999) The aesthetics of clinical judgement: exploring the link between diagnostic elegance and effective resource utilization, *Medicine, Health Care and Philosophy*, 2, 141–59.

Klein, R. (2001) *The New Politics of the National Health Service*, 4th Edition. Harlow: Prentice Hall.

Klein, R., Day, P. and Redmayne, S. (1996) *Managing Scarcity: Priority Setting and Rationing in the National Health Service*. Buckingham: Open University Press.

Lidz, C.W., Meisel, A., Osterweis, M., Holden, J.L., Marx, J.H. and Munetz, M. (1983) Barriers to informed consent, *Annals of Internal Medicine*, 99, 539–43.

Light, D.W. and Hughes, D. (2001) Introduction: A sociological perspective on rationing: power, rhetoric and situated practices, *Sociology of Health and Illness*, 23, 5, 551–69.

McKinlay, J.B., Potter, D.A. and Feldman, H.A. (1996) Non-medical influences on medical decision-making, *Social Science and Medicine*, 42, 5, 769–76.

Meikle, J. (2005) Minister forces Herceptin U-turn, *The Guardian*, Thursday 10 November.

Mooney, G. (1989) QALYs: are they enough? A health economist's perspective, *Journal of Medical Ethics*, 15, 148–52.

National Institute for Clinical Excellence (2002) *Guidance on the Use of Trastuzumab for the Treatment of Advanced Breast Cancer*. London: National Institute for Clinical Excellence.

Newdick, C. (1995) *Who Should We Treat?: Law, Patients and Resources in the NHS*. Oxford: Clarendon Press.

Nuffield Council on Bioethics (2003) *Pharmacogenetics: ethical issues*. Report of Working Party. London: Nuffield Council on Bioethics.

Paul, J.E. and Trueman, P. (2001) Fourth hurdle reviews, NICE, and database applications, *Pharmacoepidemiology and Drug Safety*, 10, 429–38.

Pellegrino, E.D. and Thomasma, D. (1981) *A Philosophical Basis of Medical Practice: Towards a Philosophy and Ethic of the Healing Professions*. New York and Oxford: Oxford University Press.

Povar, G. and Moreno, J. (1988) Hippocrates and the health maintenance organization: a discussion of ethical issues, *Annals of Internal Medicine*, 109, 5, 419–24.

Prior, L. (2001) Rationing through risk assessment in clinical genetics: all categories have wheels, *Sociology of Health and Illness*, 23, 5, 570–93.

Rawles, J. (1989) Castigating QALYs, *Journal of Medical Ethics*, 15, 143–7.

Seedhouse, D.F. (1995) Why bioethicists have nothing useful to say about health care rationing, *Journal of Medical Ethics*, 21, 288–91.

Singer, P., McKie, J., Kuhse, H. and Richardson, J. (1995) Double jeopardy and the use of QALYs in health care allocation, *Journal of Medical Ethics*, 21, 144–150.

Ubel, P.A. and Goold, S. (1997) Recognizing bedside rationing: clear cases and tough calls, *Annals of Internal Medicine*, 126, 1, 74–80.

Varekamp, I., Krol, L.J. and Danse, J.A.C. (1998) Age rationing for renal transplantation? The role of age in decisions regarding scarce life extending medical resources, *Social Science and Medicine*, 47, 1, 113–20.

Weiner, S. (2001) 'I can't afford that!' Dilemmas in the care of the uninsured and underinsured, *Journal of General Internal Medicine*, 16, 6, 412–8.

Weinstein, M.C. (2001) Should physicians be the gatekeepers of resources? *Journal of Medical Ethics*, 27, 268–74.

Zussman, R. (1997) Sociological perspectives on medical ethics and decision-making, *Annual Review of Sociology*, 23, 171–89.

8

The power of ethics: a case study from Sweden on the social life of moral concerns in policy processes
Klaus Hoeyer

Introduction

Today the concept of ethics is much more widely in use in policymaking circles than just 20 or 30 years ago. In particular, those providing health services seem attracted to the idea of developing ethics policies for a range of issues. The use and storage of human tissue in so-called biobanks is a particularly apt example of this ethics policymaking tendency. Though part of normal routines in all European welfare states for almost a century, it was not until the 1990s that biobanking became subject to 'ethical regulation'. By ethical regulation I mean policymaking explicitly presenting itself as motivated by ethical or moral concern. 'More ethical regulation' sounds almost irresistibly benevolent, but it is not obvious what it is that the health sector is getting more of in the name of ethics. Is 'more ethics' the same as 'more ethical'? And how can this issue be explored empirically?

José López (2004) identifies two broad forms of sociological engagement with bioethics: one inspired by political analysis focusing on 'the wider historical, political, cultural and economic conditions of the possibility of bioethics as a discourse and an institutionalised practice' (2004: 877); the other inspired by ethnography focusing on 'how moral values and ethical behaviours are embodied and lived by social agents' (2004: 878). Bioethics lives a double life: it is both organisational practice and moral dilemma, both politics and morality. Nevertheless, few studies combine power analytics with ethnographic sensitivity towards the dilemmas and values of social agents; thus bioethics is represented as either an expression of power or of morality, but rarely both. In this chapter I seek to bring these two dimensions of bioethics together by exploring the social life of moral concerns in a concrete policy process in northern Sweden.

My research is focused on an ethics policy developed by a start-up genomics company, UmanGenomics, at the time it gained all commercial rights to a population-based biobank in the town of Umeå in northern Sweden. The ethics policy had at its core an increased emphasis on the use of informed consent in relation to tissue-based research, and in several prestigious journals it was favourably compared with that of a more widely known Icelandic counterpart, deCODE Genetics (Abott 1999, Nilsson and Rose 1999). To explore the local context, rather than its international reputation, my study describes the concerns articulated and acted on by policymakers, nurses – who implement the consent requirement – and donors, for whom and *on* whom the policy was supposed to work. I begin with some general reflections on how to study ethics as policymaking, before describing the concrete policy process in Sweden. In particular, I explore the way three topics, namely *trust*, *protection* and *fairness*, are problematised differently by policymakers, nurses and donors. In conclusion, I suggest contemplating the power of ethics with increased awareness of the ways in which it potentially acts as a double-edged sword both serving as leverage for the discursive regulation of moral concern, and as a forceful restraint on potentially exploitive power structures.

Studying power *and* morality

In line with the distinction introduced by López, anthropological ethnographers working with bioethics tend to portray ethics as a particular form of power (based on universal knowledge claims), which impinges on local moral worlds (*cf.* Kleinman 1999). From this perspective, ethics policies are related to the ethical only by name: they are essentially an execution of power[1]. However, for the social scientist wanting to understand both the type of regulation executed in the name of ethics and the organisational change it produces in the health services, it is not enough to see ethics solely as an imposition of power. Rather, ethics is a form of power that works only when it manages to present itself as morally relevant.

As we know, moral concerns differ according to one's social location. My study takes this sociological evidence one step further by showing how moral concerns emerge during, and are defined through, the very process of problematising particular aspects of life in particular social institutions[2]. Seen in this light, an ethics policy is a product of connected concerns rather than an attack on local moral worlds, as those working in the critical ethnographic tradition often suggest.

As we will see, the ethics policy that I studied emerged through wider social institutions and networks of obligation (Powell and DiMaggio 1991), in which nurses responded to the initiatives of county officials and health consumers responded to nurses, with an unanticipated outcome (Lindblom 1959). Important aspects of the wider historical and institutional context for the ethics policy I studied include perceptions of medical progress and the welfare state. Ethnographic literature often emphasises how the construction of the Swedish welfare state is intertwined with popular social movements, namely the temperance movement, the workers movement and the free churches (Ambjörnsson 1998, Frykman and Löfgren 1987). Self-discipline, solidarity and trust in science were central concerns in these movements, and even today, northern Sweden is characterised by solidarity and egalitarianism (Bondeson 2003: 50). The institutional context reflects both power and morality.

It is through ethics policy that moral concerns get a social life (*cf.* Appadurai 1986). The policy relates people to the concerns of others, and the analytical task is to unravel the ways in which some moral positions are respected and entrenched in organisational structure, while other concerns become marginalised and excluded from organisational influence. This implies, among other things, studying a series of 'productive misunderstandings' (*cf.* Löwy 1992) where the same words are imbued with different meaning, and some taken-for-granted positions avoid confrontation with other taken-for-granted positions by way of tacit misunderstanding.

Identifying policy problems

UmanGenomics, the company that initiated the ethics policy I analyse, was created by Umeå University in collaboration with Västerbotten County Council. The policy was produced at the time UmanGenomics was assigned 'all commercial rights' to a biobank containing blood samples and questionnaire data from the greater part of the adult population in the county. The company management hoped that the policy would pre-empt public criticism of the new usages. Samples had been collected since 1985, as people at the age of 40, 50 and 60 attended a preventive medical examination conducted by publicly employed nurses at the county healthcare centres. While various, similar versions circulated, the policy was never written down in an official, certified version. It was described orally and in different articles and leaflets as a 'model' focusing on public oversight and control in three forms: a) public majority ownership of the company; b) approval by a regional research ethics committee; c) individual consent from all donors. Sometimes, separation of the company and the biobank was also described as part of the ethical model (and was presented as a safeguard against commodification of human tissue), and sometimes community benefit-sharing was emphasised. Local establishment of the company, in contrast to facilitating access for foreign companies, was emphasised at press conferences and during interviews, but not explicitly fitted into the public descriptions of 'the model'. The role of individual consent was emphasised the most.

Three types of actors were central to this policy process: 1) policymakers, 2) policy workers (namely nurses obtaining informed consent for blood collection during the medical examinations) and 3) members of the policy target group (potential donors). These three levels are distinguished by different means of influence on the policy. Policymakers respond to their assumptions about what donors would prefer and then name and frame the consent requirement as a particular object for organisational intervention.

In turn, the consent requirement creates a space for action, which can be used by nurses. Through the (often unintended) ways of using this space, nurses are part of shaping the conditions of possibility for potential donors, who in turn give their own meaning and content to the procedures set in motion. In my analysis I examine both what people say and the concerns and values embedded in acts, *e.g.* the act of donation.

Fieldwork was conducted intermittently from June 2000 to February 2004. I interviewed and interacted with the central policy makers and read their contracts, letters and other official documents; made observations at five healthcare centres and interviewed nurses conducting the preventive medical examinations; observed 57 potential donors as they donated blood (or declined) during this examination, and subsequently interviewed them. My data come from observation, participant observation, document analysis, semi-structured interviews and various forms of informal interchanges, and from two surveys of public attitudes to biobanking and informed consent. Policymakers were identified by way of 'snowballing', *i.e.* every interviewee was invited to help identify other persons who in their view had influenced the policy process. Nurses were encountered at the healthcare centres, and the centres were selected to ensure representation of the rural region in the interior, smaller towns in the interior, the periphery of Umeå, and the centre of Umeå[3]. Potential donors were offered written information by the nurse about my study in which I stated my interest in their attitudes to new forms of medical research, and were asked by the nurse to confirm their willingness to participate prior to the examination, at which I would then be present. In this way, the informed consent procedure for my study might have contributed to a selection of informants, primarily including those most willing to participate in research in general, *i.e.* those people most willing to view themselves as being obliged to help the progress of science.

The problematisations encountered through this form of fieldwork changed over time, not least in response to changing relations among various actors at the policymaking level. At the outset of the fieldwork and during the initial presentation of the ethics policy, central actors behind the biobank (in the company, the university, politicians, and public servants in the county and the university hospital where storage facilities were provided) seemed to agree on the arrangements made for the biobank, including the content of the ethics policy. Substantial disagreement on the dispositional rights in the biobank, however, slowly surfaced; this produced an intense and pernicious conflict between decision-makers – including those in university management, the company and the county council – and the researchers working in the biobank. Basically, a group of researchers who played a part in founding the biobank wanted to retain some control over the stored tissue, despite the contracts written with UmanGenomics. Analysis of the conflict is not the aim of this chapter, and can be found elsewhere (Hoeyer 2004, Laage-Hellman 2003, Rose 2003). Nevertheless, the conflict introduced a bifurcation among the group of actors originally identified as being in a position to influence the naming and framing of policy issues by way of the organisational network.

My analysis of the different modes of problematising found among the three types of actors reveals three issues common to all groups: trust, protection and fairness. Policymakers repeatedly mentioned *trust* as the main objective of the consent requirement, and trust was analytically significant for understanding donors' willingness to participate in the biobank collection. With regard to *protection*, everybody seems to believe that something, 'X', is in potential danger of being infringed by commercial genetic research, but each group has a different idea of *what* needs protection. Finally, notions of *fairness* are articulated independently by donors, nurses and policymakers.

Trust

At the time of the formation of UmanGenomics, people at the policymaking level were concerned that commercial genetic research might cause an erosion of trust and during the policy process most policymakers came to agree that people would be requesting more information to protect their sense of integrity. Consequently, more elaborate information sheets were produced. From this perspective, informed consent is an organisational requirement for establishing a trustworthy relationship between biobank research and individual donor. In contrast to this logic, nurses tended to think about trust from a more concrete and personal perspective reflecting their professional position. As policy workers they did not simply implement the policy: they saw consent as mostly an issue of responsibility. Some, for example, argued that the strengthened consent requirement was a relief to them, as 'the donor now writes a contract with the county council'[4], as one nurse put it, implying that they as nurses were less personally responsible than previously. Accordingly, some began providing less oral information than they had formerly done. Others felt an increasing sense of responsibility and simply stopped asking for blood. Two such nurses explained to me how they thought of themselves as 'mothers' asking their 'children' to donate for purposes they knew nothing about, which violated the maternal care their patients expected from them. This very personal sense of responsibility was articulated most in rural areas, where nurses tended to know their patients. In both cases, however, trust has not so much to do with the provision of information as with the notion of a responsible agent: somebody (themselves or the authorities) worthy of trust.

Trust is also very important for potential donors, the policy's target group. Though few people read, remember or recall the information provided, most sign the consent form and thus donate both blood and questionnaire data. Hence, the biobank rests on an act (donation), which can be interpreted as an expression of trust. During interviews, people often articulated this trust as hinging specifically on public oversight and control. One man said: 'I have great trust in the health services and research (. . .) So if [the blood] can be of use for somebody else, please let it . . . Because I'm not worried about abuse, and all that'. He had the feeling that he was first and foremost donating to a *public* biobank (though realising that a private company would have access to the samples), and he explains why he thinks he can trust the county:

> It stems, kind of, from society, which means . . . it isn't created for the sake of profit. But with a commercial company it appears a little more precarious – what their objectives are. Still, if there's some kind of overseeing from the authorities in relation to what they do, it feels quite alright.

Interestingly, the Swedish word for oversee is *in-sight* [insyn], as in seeing into something otherwise hidden. This metaphor relates to a sense of the public domain as a place where 'we' are 'sharing'. Implicitly, this domain tends to correlate with some sense of bounded locality. Hence, the following statement was not unusual in its association between unanticipated uses and foreign places:

> . . . It's this worry about where it's going to end up. What it'll be used for – if it's just these things mentioned in the letter or if it's . . . well, if it is passed on, is sold on, sent along to something, perhaps . . . That's what I felt.

Importantly, this woman could not remember the content of the information sheet, and, like the majority of her fellow donors, she could mention no specific uses that she would not approve of, only illegitimate *purposes* and *motives*. Donor trust seems to include a notion that not only will the local authorities ensure overseeing and control – they will also figure out what to control. If donor trust were to be broken, it appears that it would be on the grounds that the biobank was being used for objectives other than those motivating the donations: interest in furthering science and healthcare.

It is important to remember that donors are asked to donate at *public* healthcare centres. As citizens taking part in a shared welfare state project, they feel obliged to respond to public demands; 'to do their share' as it was often phrased. The donors want to pre-empt potential moral criticism for selfishness by performing their duty as citizens and contributing to public health efforts with blood and data, much like county politicians and university researchers use informed consent procedures to pre-empt moral criticism and ensure trust in the authorities. Even if a consensus seemed to prevail among donors that public health should not be sidestepped by profit interests, there is no agreement among donors regarding commercial involvement in research in general (some expected it would speed up the research process positively, others were strongly opposed to any form of commercial involvement).

During the development of the conflict concerning the dispositional rights in Medical Biobank, which gave rise to some unfortunate publicity, most policymakers began worrying that public trust was endangered. This, however, did not influence the number of issues addressed by the ethics policy, though it did influence the *interpretation* of informed consent. The emphasis on information was increased and more information was sent to encourage donors' approval for the activities of each party of the conflict. From the perspective of the policymaking level, it became essential *who* provided and defined the content of information sheets, but adequate information was still seen as the key to public trust. Perhaps this signals a lack of feasible alternatives, rather than a wholehearted belief in information as a tool for building trust.

Protection

The ethics model presumably aims to protect the individual through the requirement of informed consent, a statement often made by policymakers and common also in the international literature on biobank ethics. Closer analysis, however, shows that this is not the perception held by the donors that the policy is designed to protect. Policy discourse centres on protection of blood as a physical substance from commercial trade. Trade in genetic codes is perceived as legitimate by policymakers, however, once genetic codes are transformed into de-personalised, patented information. Few donors agree with this distinction between genes and knowledge-about-genes and most strongly oppose patenting of DNA. Policymakers and donors thus hold divergent understandings of what it means to infringe the integrity of the donating person. Also, while policymakers never mentioned ethical problems associated with the questionnaires collected along with the blood, some donors saw the use of questionnaires and health records as more sensitive than blood samples (Hoeyer 2002). When nurses were identifying problems, they focused on the structures responsible for what happened to the blood. From the perspective of the nurse, these structures determine whether donors were wise to donate a blood sample. Hence, nurses most often mentioned organisational integrity and transparency as the problem that needed to be addressed.

Though some donors wonder where their material will 'end up', most of them focus on the *consequences* of research using their material, rather than use of the material per se. In general, they express optimism that research will contribute to alleviation of human suffering. However, the commercial element, though welcomed by some, was generally seen as a potential threat to the integrity of research. For example, one man explained that, in his view, commercial research was inevitable, but it was acceptable as long as it was good research. Most donors felt that research into drugs that would not treat serious health problems, or that would be unavailable to those in need, was pointless. Health is perceived as ideally beyond economic interests, as this man, among others, pointed out:

[Money] shouldn't need to affect the health services – they [the health services] must be able to bear the costs whatever the costs are without any other limitations than the help it is possible to offer (. . .) . . . really, if it were to be proper . . . common sense.

From the perspective of most donors, what is perceived as in need of protection is the integrity of research and values of solidarity with those afflicted by medical problems. It is, of course, difficult to define medical needs, as exemplified in the debates about lifestyle drugs versus treatment of serious illness, which have surrounded genetic medicine. The point is, however, that the majority of my respondents donated for the sake of ill people. Along similar lines, it is reasonable to see the resentment expressed against patenting of human genes as a protest against breaches of solidarity: genes and genetic knowledge should not be monopolised by individual property holders. Accordingly, it seems safe to conclude that the main worry for most donors is that the research agenda will be controlled by interests other than those reflecting public health concerns.

Interestingly, the evolving conflict makes various policymakers who are deeply engaged in the struggle to define dispositional rights in the biobank increasingly eager to defend not only the biobank, but also the public image of science. Like donors, policymakers now find it relevant to protect the integrity of science. Members of the staff in the biobank, for example, write complaints opposing, on *ethical* grounds, the current university and county management, claiming that scientific freedom is under threat from short-sighted profit objectives. Though in this sense, sharing values and concerns with donors, there is no agreement among policymakers concerning how science should be protected, and because of the organisational conflict these issues cannot be transformed into a new ethics policy. When inter-organisational alliances cannot be formed, the voice of ethics seems to represent opposition, rather than co-ordinated regulation. And rather than harmonising inter-organisational relationships, the original policy now serves to delineate battlegrounds, *e.g.* 'what should be the content of the information sheet?'.

Fairness

Questions of fairness draw heavily on a vocabulary of ethics and morality. Reflections on fairness surrounded the ethics policy of UmanGenomics throughout the studied period, and were articulated independently by most actors at some point[5]. If we distinguish between issues perceived as fair (to be promoted) and not-fair (to be avoided), the fair type of issue tends to revolve around benefit-sharing and the not-fair around what, in a local concept, is called *baggböleri*.

In the 19th century, the Baggböle manor house, 12 kilometres west of Umeå, acquired an unsavoury reputation for buying up the main local resource, the forest wood, too cheaply and selling it off to companies abroad. The profit left the region impoverished (except for a few wealthy traders concentrated at Baggböle), and such callous exploitation of local resources came to be known as 'baggböleri'. At the time of the establishment of UmanGenomics, the university, the county and the company made it clear that they wanted to avoid *baggböleri* and instead keep the jobs and profit in the region. Public majority ownership of UmanGenomics was one measure to achieve this objective. As the company began facing problems raising venture capital, however, it was attributed to the dangers of political control of private enterprise. In 2002, the most influential actors therefore re-wrote the contract between the county, the university and UmanGenomics. The new contract excluded the clause on public majority ownership and replaced it with a clause stating that the company could not leave the area without losing its rights to the biobank. This was explained as a way of ensuring continued public involvement, but it implicitly reduced the previously accepted idea that public ownership was a way to ensure both overseeing and direct community benefit-sharing. Benefit-sharing was still an issue, but rather than relying on public ownership, it was now perceived as relying on regional development through provision of a viable *commercial* environment; without a viable company, it was sensibly argued, there would be nothing to share.

In contrast to the broad notion of regional development, most nurses were concerned with specific ways of ensuring what they perceived to be fair. In the rural areas, unfair 'baggböleri' was related to criticism of those posh people in the main town, Umeå, who disrespected local work and interests. Many nurses worried that the powerful interests surrounding UmanGenomics would deter the attention otherwise paid to the preventive healthcare programme. Some wanted the company to return part of the profit to the *preventive programme* and at least eliminate the standard charge for the physical examination, and perhaps offer participants a sandwich or a soft drink. Hence, when it comes to ideas about the sharing of profit, the nurses have a much more concrete notion of fairness than the modified policy suggests. It is important to note, however, that there is also no consensus among people operating at the policymaking level. Indeed the research group associated with Medical Biobank has strongly advocated a concrete return of profit; but unlike nurses, they believe the money should be used for a research foundation under the control of researchers. This idea has not received support from the founders of UmanGenomics, the university management, or the county, who wanted the company to control its own assets.

Donors, conversely, often raise concerns about what is sometimes called the rule of the Money-Devil, *i.e.* when profit overrules other considerations. Several donors associated private companies with international capital and saw the problem of 'baggböleri' mainly as a question of lack of local control and of the rich deceiving the poor. Benefit-sharing, on the other hand, was articulated in various ways often emphasising that any profit should be used for the objectives associated with their donation. One woman, who had never before contemplated the fact that medical research could be undertaken commercially, said: 'It is important that the money circulate back where it comes from. That it will be used for research'. Others emphasised the importance of not letting one area of interest prevail over others, as this man explains: 'I guess it's important with research breadth [a wide agenda of medical problems]. And to ensure that there's an even level for everything'. Others wanted profits to go straight to the authorities and the delivery of healthcare. Even more dominant was the view, also expressed above, that everybody should have equal access to the health benefits emanating from research. In addition to this aspiration, one woman reflected on the changed ownership structure of the company by saying:

> If it benefits your purposes, I don't think you should pin yourself down to something being 'owned by the county' [stressed in an ironic tone], or not. As long as it won't result in only those with money enjoying the benefits of the products. It has to be on equal terms for all, I think that's important. But then how the ownership issue is handled, that doesn't matter, does it?

Asked whether people would have liked to receive money for their donation as part of the profit, only a handful even considered the idea (Hoeyer 2005). One man, who had just said that the offer of money would make him doubt the purposes of the project, went on to say:

> If they should develop some absolutely revolutionary drug and some researcher would call and say, 'we found a new drug for cancer thanks to your blood sample and here's 5,000 kronor' – yeah, but then I'd be really happy! But I would probably send it on to some child in Brazil or something. Because I'd like the profit they make, that they spend a good part on . . . the developing countries and all that.

On the whole, these people do not want personal gain. They want to further the alleviation of suffering, and their donations seem motivated by a sense of obligation to participate in a shared project to achieve this objective. Their donations express trust that the authorities will work towards this end. However, at the policymaking level, only more manageable issues become entrenched in the ethics policy. Indeed, no policy would ever be able to address all worries mentioned by potential donors. Nevertheless the patterns in the divergences between the levels are interesting and are summarised and discussed below.

Contested ethics or emergent ethics?

Bearing in mind that it leaves out a number of minor variations, Table 1 is presented to help illustrate the tendencies described in the preceding three

Table 1 *Tendencies in different problematisations at the three analytical levels*

	Policymaking level	Policy workers (nurses)	Target group (potential donors)
Trust	Adequate information is essential	Responsibility is essential	Local overseeing and control to ensure usefulness for those in need is essential
Protection	The individual's biological body needs to be protected	Institutional integrity and transparency need to be protected	Science and solidarity need to be protected
Fairness	– Baggböleri is when money leaves the county. – Benefit-sharing is regional development.	– Baggböleri is when posh people in Umeå disrespect local work and interests. – Benefit-sharing is when profit returns to the preventive healthcare programme.	– Baggböleri is when the 'Money-Devil' rules, *i.e.* when profit overrules moral considerations, and the rich deceive the poor. – Benefit-sharing is when all population groups get equal access to research results; securing more research; securing local interests; securing the public part of the profit.

paragraphs. The form of power produced in this policy process is not simply trickling down from 'higher' to 'lower' levels; from left to right side of the table. Rather, actors at the policymaking level are subject to various forms of pressures such as anticipated reactions from donors, and they are often unable to address the issues they personally find most compelling, as illustrated by the aforementioned letters of complaint from Medical Biobank. Potential donors find themselves in situations where they are expected to exercise a personal choice through informed consent, though they tend to prefer trusting the logic of mutual obligations embedded in the state-citizen relationship to make the authorities take responsibility for scientific enterprises. Hence, the policy is a product of many actors, of volatile alliances and unintended re-interpretations between people with different frames of reference. Nevertheless, the features that can be acted on and become part of the policy constitute a form of power, which structures social relations: the policy creates space for action for nurses and donors by naming informed consent as a central moral concern. It is a form of power which needs to present itself as morally relevant and it does so partly by way of open concepts such as 'baggböleri', which leaves room for productive misunderstandings. In this sense, the policy is a product of a complex ethico-political process, rather than the result of somebody's intention or authority.

A question we need to consider is whether the table represents *contested ethics* or *emergent ethics*. In the first view, people in different subject positions can be assumed to hold particular moral values which are then contested in the process. Alternatively, the policy process and the differences in problematisation can be viewed as the social basis from which moral values and positions emerge. In this view, the institutionally framed strife is the very stuff that 'ethics' is made of. Whereas the choice between the two inter-pretations will rely on definition and theoretical framework rather than empirical evidence, it is relevant to clarify how my study propagates the latter view. From the perspective of emergent ethics, moral positions emerge in institutional contexts where people relate to each other in particular ways and occupy particular positions. The policy process produces reflections on responsibility; it makes people engage in morally obliging interaction and it produces new discourses on ethics. It is likely that my interviews engaged donors further in such a process of what might be called 'responsibilisation'. Organisational power and moral life are not different entities colliding with each other; they are co-produced[6]. The objects of moral thought, and the action which is experienced as legitimate, are shaped in an institutional context, while notions of moral legitimacy simultaneously shape the boundaries of feasible organisational action.

The idea of emergent ethics, however, is subject to one important qualifi-cation: most people involved in the policy process I studied experienced it as a contestation of ethics: they felt their moral values threatened by a power play. In fact, they would often use the language of ethics to produce the most effective weapon in the struggle against the organisational features they considered most unfair or immoral. For these people ethics is the antithesis of power. Accordingly, for them the language of ethics serves to challenge institutional structures and oppose forms of power deemed illegitimate. If we propagate the emergent ethics perspective we implicitly undermine the rhetorical strength of the people here described as a 'target group'; those people least able to directly influence the naming and framing of moral concerns at the policymaking level. The perspective of emergent ethics rests on a moral relativism, which is a theoretical and methodological choice, not a statement of definite truth.

The perspective of emergent ethics makes visible unacknowledged variations in the moral understandings of different people. These will always exist, and productive misunderstandings can facilitate interconnections and action, as argued above (*cf.* Löwy 1992). Indeed, the reintegration of the moral understandings of policymakers and donors is an important first step toward moral accountability. Benefit-sharing is one area where dialogue between different parties can ensure accountability. As Alan Petersen noted in relation to UK Biobank, citizens were offered strong assurances 'about the potential scientific value and public health benefits', but were given 'few details about the nature of these benefits' (Petersen 2005: 281). The direct involvement of private companies in the construction of a research infrastructure, as described in this case, raises important questions about the distribution of profit and the objectives of the research agenda; and yet, few analysts offer advice on organisational structures with in-built mechanisms for benefit-sharing. A notable exception is Haddow *et al.* (forthcoming), who describe procedures designed to ensure democratic representation, overseeing and benefit-sharing according to the judgement of these democratically elected organisations. Where implemented, such a procedure constitutes an example of ethics embedded in the very organisational structure. It will then define the future spaces for action for people with different agendas. We will therefore continue to need several modes of enquiry (Rabinow 2003), some providing solutions, others identifying problems.

Conclusion

The introduction of ethics as a form of regulation has important implications for the healthcare system, not least in relation to its research obligation. As we have seen, it operates through both organisational mechanisms (as when nurses respond to their superiors' demands) and the moral life of the individual. This regulation encourages particular forms of personalised responsibility for both nurses and donors. During the conflict on dispositional rights, even policymakers began to use the vocabulary of ethics in ways representing an individualised response to the organisation. The arguments posed in the name of ethics tend to revolve around notions of altruism and therefore explorations of such moral notions are crucial to comprehend organisational behaviour.

My study also makes clear two distinct meanings of *the power of ethics*. On the one hand, we have seen ethics as a form of power that marginalises and excludes some moral positions while allowing others to become entrenched in the organisation structure. On the other hand, we have seen ethics used as a vocabulary for critique of power structures.

With regard to the first meaning of the power of ethics, my research shows how the elites determined the boundaries of legitimate moral concern with regard to consent, justice and ethical issues raised by nurses and donors. The ethics policy I studied used informed consent as a way of generating trust – the focus on 'informed choice' was less about ensuring that participants understood all dimensions of the research than it was about gaining co-operation. The ethics policy also defined blood and genes as physical substances (in contrast to knowledge about genes, which is perceived as patentable information), and, as a result, justice came to be understood by the local elite as one anticipated product of *regional development*, not as the fair distribution of health improvements generated by research. Finally, the ethics policy addressed only 'manageable' issues. Moral positions highlighting themes other than these were marginalised and excluded from organisational impact. The emphasis of nurses and donors, on the need for a responsible agent to protect community solidarity and to ensure the fair use of donated blood for those in need, did contribute to the shaping of everyday practice, but their moral concerns had minimum impact on the organisation and on decisions made for the biobank.

The self-interested use of ethics by the elite should not, however, cause us to overlook how the moral power of ethics can be used as a force for change. As social scientists we are quite familiar with the way bioethics is co-opted by the powerful – including politicians, corporations, funding agencies and the media – but we must not ignore the way ethics is used as a tool to challenge social power and to give shape to visions for a better life. When we sociologists *of* bioethics (De Vries 2004) attack moral discourse as nothing more than the expression of power, we give greater weight to the social power of ethics than we do to its moral power, diminishing important meanings of ethics and reducing ethical critique to just one moral position among many. My research shows the power of ethics to be a double-edged sword: yes, bioethics is used by the powerful to promote their interests, but it is also mobilised to challenge those with power. Those who study the social dimensions of bioethics must understand the value of ethics to the powerful *and* to the vulnerable.

Acknowledgement

This study was supported financially by a grant from the Swedish Ethics in Healthcare Programme (no. 2000/056) and the Danish Social Science Research Council (no. 24-03-0219). I would like to thank Gill Haddow, University of Edinburgh, and my colleagues at the Department of Health Services Research for constructive comments on an earlier version.

Notes

1 Three notions of 'the ethical' seem to prevail, namely: 1) one's personal sense of right and wrong, 2) a notion of what most people (society) think is right or wrong, 3) what is *'really'* right or wrong, *i.e.* the idea that it is possible to move beyond one's personal or society's views and contemplate what *ought to be*, rather than what is. In relation to the ethnographic criticism it is important to note how an ethics policy is typically described as representing a 'personal' or 'societal view', while the criticism of its impact implies a notion of 'really right or wrong': the policies are described as circumventing morality; they are seen as 'unethical'.
2 In my approach to problematisations I am inspired by Foucault (1986, 1992, 1997).
3 The few people declining participation in the study all came from central Umeå and had either practical reasons to decline (one was deaf-mute, another had various psychiatric diagnoses and thought observations would stress her), or simply stated that they wanted the examination to be a personal 'treat' and not a contribution to research: 'I do this for my own sake', as one woman explained.
4 All quotes have been translated from Swedish into English by the author.
5 In response to the commercial element of most large-scale biobank activities, the international sociological literature has similarly begun focusing on fair distribution of potential benefits (Busby and Martin forthcoming, Haddow, Laurie, Cunningham-Burley and Hunter forthcoming, Petersen 2005).
6 In its emphasis on the co-production of morality and power, the study is closely affiliated with the Durkheimian tradition in the sociological study of bioethics, exemplified in the work of, for example, Anspach (1993), Bosk (1979, 1992), Chambliss (1996) and Zussman (1992). However, this study focuses on policies on ethics (rather than the organisation to which these policies respond) as a form of power, and accordingly seeks to explore the *moral shaping* of organisational power as well as the organisational conditions for moral problems.

References

Abott, A. (1999) Sweden sets ethical standards for use of genetic 'biobanks', *Nature*, 400, 3.

Ambjörnsson, R. (1998) *Den skötsamme arbetaren*. Stockholm: Carlsson Bokförlag.

Anspach, R.R. (1993) *Deciding Who Lives. Fateful Choices in the Intensive-Care Nursery*. Berkeley: University of California Press.

Appadurai, A. (1986) Introduction: Commodities and the politics of value. In Appadurai A. (ed.) *The Social Life of Things. Commodities in Cultural Perspective*. Cambridge: Cambridge University Press.

Bondesen, U.V. (2003) *Nordic Moral Climates. Value Continuities and Discontinuities in Denmark, Finland, Norway, and Sweden*. New Brunswick: Translation Publishers.

Bosk, C. (1979) *Forgive and Remember. Managing Medical Failure*. London: University of Chicago Press, London.

Bosk, C. (1992) *All God's Mistakes. Genetic Counseling in a Pediatric Hospital*. London: University of Chicago Press.

Busby, H. and Martin, P. (2006) National biobanks and imagined communities: UK Biobank and the appeal to national identity, *Science as Culture*, 15, 3, 237–51.

Chambliss, D.F. (1996) *Beyond Caring. Hospitals, Nurses and the Social Organization of Ethics*. Chicago: Chicago University Press.

De Vries, R. (2004) How can we help? From 'sociology in' bioethics to 'sociology of' bioethics, *Journal of Law, Medicine and Ethics* 32, 2, 279–92.

Foucault, M. (1986) *The Care of the Self*. London: Penguin Books.

Foucault, M. (1992) *The Use of Pleasure*. London: Penguin Books.

Foucault, M. (1997) Polemics, politics, and problematizations: an interview with Michel Foucault. In Rabinow, P. (ed.) *Ethics. Essential Works of Michel Foucault 1954–1984*. London: Penguin Books.

Frykman, J. and Löfgren, O. (1987) *Culture Builders – a Historical Anthropology of Middle-Class Life*. New Brunswick and London: Rutgers University Press.

Haddow, G. and Laurie, G. (2006) Tacking Community Concerns regarding commercialisation in Genetic Research: A Modest Interdisciplinary Proposal. ESRC Genetics Forum, Workshop on Genomics and Intellectual Property, Cdinburgh.

Hoeyer, K. (2002) Conflicting notions of personhood in genetic research, *Anthropology Today* 18, 5, 9–13.

Hoeyer, K. (2004) The emergence of an entitlement framework for stored tissue – elements and implications of an escalating conflict in Sweden, *Science Studies*, 17, 2, 63–82.

Hoeyer, K. (2005) The role of ethics in commercial genetic research: notes on the notion of commodification, *Medical Anthropology*, 24, 1, 45–70.

Kleinman, A. (1999) Moral experience and ethical reflection: can ethnography reconcile them? A quandary for 'the new bioethics', *Dædalus*, 128, 4, 69–98.

Laage-Hellman, J. (2003) Clinical genomics companies and biobanks – the use of biosamples and commercial research on the genetics of common diseases. In Hansson, M.G. and Levin, M. (eds) *Biobanks as Resources for Health*. Uppsala: Research Programme Ethics in Biomedicine.

Lindblom, C.E. (1959) The science of 'muddling through', *Public Administration Review*, 19, 79–88.

López, J. (2004) How sociology can save bioethics . . . maybe, *Sociology of Health and Illness* 26, 7, 875–96.

Löwy, I. (1992) The strength of loose concepts – boundary concepts, federative strategies and disciplinary growth: the case of immunology, *History of Science*, 30, 371–96.

Nilsson, A. and Rose, J. (1999) Sweden takes steps to protect tissue banks, *Science*, 286, 894.

Petersen, A. (2005) Securing our genetic health: engendering trust in UK Biobank, *Sociology of Health and Illness* 27, 2, 271–92.

Powell, W.W. and DiMaggio, P.J. (1991) Introduction. In Powell, W.W. and DiMaggio, P.J. (eds) *The New Institutionalism in Organizational Analysis*. Chicago: The University of Chicago Press.

Rabinow, P. (2003) *Anthropos Today. Reflections on Modern Equipment*. Princeton: Princeton University Press.

Rose, H. (2003) An ethical dilemma. The rise and fall of UmanGenomics – The model Biotech Company? *Nature*, 425, 123–24.

Zussman, R. (1992) *Intensive Care. Medical Ethics and the Medical Profession*. Chicago: University of Chicago Press.

9

Explaining the emergence of euthanasia law in the Netherlands: how the sociology of law can help the sociology of bioethics

Heleen Weyers

Introduction

In 2001 the Dutch Parliament gave legislative ratification to the long-standing practice of legal euthanasia[1]. The *Law on Termination of Life on Request (Review Procedure)* stipulates that the behaviour penalised in Articles 293 and 294 of the Criminal Code[2] – killing on request and assistance with suicide – is not punishable if committed by a doctor who has complied with two conditions. The *first* condition is that the doctor must act in accordance with the 'requirements of careful practice' set forth in Article 2 of the law. The requirements state: 1) the doctor must be convinced that the patient had made a voluntary and well considered request; 2) the doctor must be convinced that the patient's suffering is hopeless and unbearable; 3) the doctor must have informed the patient about the situation; 4) both doctor and patient must be convinced that there is no reasonable alternative solution to the situation; 5) the doctor must have consulted at least one other independent doctor; and 6) the ending of life must be carried out with due medical care. The *second* condition is that the doctor must report the behaviour to the coroner in accordance with a form that is specified in Article 7 of the *Law on the Disposal of Corpses*. The report is then sent to an 'assessment committee', which judges whether the doctor has fulfilled the requirements of careful practice. Should the committee conclude that the doctor had satisfied all the requirements, he or she will not be punishable. If the assessment committee finds that the doctor had been 'not careful', the file is sent to the prosecutorial authorities and the Medical Inspectorate[3].

Ethicists, healthcare workers and members of advocacy groups have watched closely the way the Dutch have approached the practice of euthanasia. In spite of extensive documentation of the process of legal change that resulted in the ratification of the *Law on Termination of Life on Request* (Otlowski 1997, Griffiths, Bood and Weyers 1998, Kennedy 2002, Weyers 2004) no one has offered a convincing explanation for why euthanasia was legally permitted in the Netherlands (Weyers 2002). Analysis of this topic – the social and cultural sources of ethical ideas and practices – is central to a bioethics that seeks to ground its moral insights in sociological reality, but can we social scientists deliver such an analysis? As Babbie (1986) noted, sociology is the 'most difficult science': given the huge number of variables involved in the creation of this law it is impossible to provide a complete explanation of its evolution and adoption. However, the contrast provided by the uniqueness of the Dutch approach makes it possible to identify critical features that led the Dutch to create and implement the *Law on Termination of Life on Request*.

My analysis of events in the Netherlands begins in the sociology of law. It is surprising that social scientific studies of bioethics have only rarely called on ideas drawn from the sociology of law. From Marx, Durkheim and Weber on through to contemporary scholars, sociological studies of legal systems offer theoretical approaches that can be tested with, if not directly applied to, developments in bioethics. My starting place is with two contemporary, and opposed, theories of the emergence of law. The first theory, proposed by, among others, Richard Schwartz (1954) and Donald Black (1976), states that *law varies inversely with other forms of social control*. According to Black (1976: 107), there is more law, defined as 'governmental social control', when other forms of social control are weak. The second theory, developed by Philip Selznick, claims that law emerges in social systems with *strong* social control. Selznick believes that social systems with strong social control are characterised by informal norms and vague litigation procedures. This situation creates pressure for the formalisation of norms in order to protect vulnerable persons. Law, then, liberates from a regime of strong unofficial norms, of great social pressure, of too much arbitrariness (Selznick 1968: 52).

Both theories pay close attention to social control. Social control includes 'all those social processes and methods through which society ensures that its members conform to expectations' (Cohen 1985: 2–3), or in the words of Lon Fuller (paraphrased by Griffiths 2006): 'Social control is the enterprise of subjecting human behaviour to the governance of rules'. There are several different agents of social control (Ellickson 1991: 131): first-party controllers (*i.e.* self-control), second-party controllers (*e.g.* friends, family, clients) and third-party controllers (*e.g.* professional associations, the government). Law and ethics are thereby defined by reference to those who ensure conformity with expectations, and it is a characteristic of law that specifically-appointed experts – police officers, prosecutorial authorities, judges, etc. – are in charge of upholding compliance with rules.

In order to test these two theories (and thereby show the value of the sociology of law for the sociology of bioethics) I review the social and cultural conditions associated with the debate and policy-making on euthanasia in the Netherlands in the second half of the 20th century. But I begin with a description of the background and process of legal change regarding euthanasia in the Netherlands.

The Dutch process of legal change regarding euthanasia

The Law on Medical Practice, passed in 1865, reserved the practice of medicine for those who had proven to be sufficiently trained by passing a state exam. From that time on, the training of doctors was limited to academic settings and subject to governmental inspection. A *Medical Disciplinary Law* was enacted in 1928[4].

The enactment of *The Law on Medical Practice* began a process of professionalisation of doctors which replaced heterogeneity with organisation, standardisation and the enhancing of expediency. The Medical Association, which in 1850 included only a modest minority of doctors, developed into an extraordinarily strong organisation which unites almost all Dutch doctors. The medical domain expanded rapidly, with an increase in the number of doctors, the number of patients and the number of symptoms per patient (Jaspers 1985: 18).

The doctor-patient relationship was at first a hierarchic, paternalistic one. Most doctors were in solo practice and when they worked together this was almost always with respect to shared material facilities. Formal social control was rare. For a long time the state operated as a 'night watchman' acting only when the protection of society was at stake[5].

The supervision of doctors' behaviour in relation to end-of-life decisions fitted (and to a large extent still fits) into this general outline. *The Burial Act* states that a burial – and after 1955, also a cremation – can only take place after the written permission of a municipal Registrar of Births, Deaths and Marriages has been given. Such permission is granted if the doctor responsible for treatment files a death certificate expressing the conviction that the patient died from a 'natural cause'. If, on the other hand, the doctor has doubts concerning the cause of death, filling the form is not allowed. In that case, permission for the disposal of the corpse has to be obtained from the prosecutorial authorities. In this way doctors play a role in the investigation of potential crimes. However, if it is the doctor who has committed the crime, the system tends to fail[6].

From small-scale studies done in the early 1980s, we know that in the 1970s Dutch doctors sometimes terminated a life on request. There are, however, no known cases of a doctor who did not fill in the death certificate because he or she believed that medical behaviour had led to a non-natural death. Moreover, no authority ever suggested that this failure to report presented a problem. In 1980 the Prosecutorial Authorities became active, both on the national and the local level. On the local level, some prosecutors tried to encourage doctors to be more open about their life-shortening behaviour; they co-operated with doctors in their jurisdiction in designing reporting and investigation procedures. At a national level, the Committee of Procurators-General decided that every case of euthanasia that came to the attention of a prosecutor must be referred to the Committee for a decision whether or not to prosecute, the objective being to achieve national uniformity in prosecutorial policy. After this policy decision, a small succession of court cases took place. The Supreme Court's decisions that followed clarified the grounds on which euthanasia could be justified and the conditions doctors must fulfil in order to act lawfully. Doctors who complied with what, after 1984, came to be called the 'requirements of careful practice', could invoke the so-called justification of necessity which provides that a doctor who, when faced with a conflict of duties – the duty to relieve the suffering of the patient and the duty not to kill – makes a decision that is legitimate according to medical knowledge and current medical ethics, is not guilty of the offence.

At the same time as these court cases were beginning to take place, the Dutch Medical Association took an affirmative position on the legalisation of euthanasia. An important contribution of the Medical Association was the reframing of the requirements of careful practice, developed in case law, into a professional standard. The Medical Association also made clear that Dutch society could trust doctors to make themselves accountable in cases of euthanasia, a position that made it easier for the Supreme Court to hold that euthanasia could be justified (Remmelink 1992).

Until 1994 the rulings of the Supreme Court – allowing termination of life on request to go unpunished if the requirements of careful practice were met – resulted in a political deadlock. Formal ratification of the verdict was unacceptable to the Christian Democrats – the majority party of the coalition governments since early in the 20th century – and a government bill to overrule the Supreme Court's decision was unacceptable to their coalition partners, liberals or social-democrats (Van Hees and Steunenberg 2000).

After the first court cases, both the government and the Medical Association tried to improve the formal social control of euthanasia by means of active attempts to increase the reporting rate. They did so by instigating research dealing with the prevalence of physician assisted dying, by developing a national reporting procedure, by organising a system for consultation and information for doctors contemplating participating in euthanasia, and by setting up regional assessment committees to create a buffer between the reporting doctor and the prosecutorial authorities. Although the formal social control of euthanasia is far from perfect, the reporting rate has risen from ±18 per cent in 1991, to ±41 per cent in 1995, to ±54 per cent in 2002 (Van der Wal et al. 2003)[7]. This reporting rate makes the Netherlands the country in which governmental social control on physician-assisted death is the most comprehensive in the world.

After two decades of policy interventions – in which public opinion on euthanasia changed from 49 per cent opposition to euthanasia in 1966 to nine per cent in 1991 (Griffiths et al. 1998: 198) – and with a shift in the composition of the governing coalition (the Christian-Democrat party was now excluded), the government ruled in 2001 that euthanasia should be legalised.

To conclude, the Dutch process of legal change with respect to euthanasia is special in four respects. First, prosecuting authorities used the prosecution of doctors to explore the boundaries of the law. Second, judges were receptive to legalisation. Third, the Dutch Medical Association broke ranks with other medical associations by taking a positive view toward euthanasia. And fourth, Dutch political parties kept looking for a common ground a long time before the 'purple coalition' government[8] ratified the legal practice of euthanasia (Weyers 2005).

The social and cultural sources of the regulation of euthanasia

This brief history of legal change with regard to euthanasia does not answer the fundamental question about the regulation of the termination of the life in the Netherlands: Why did the Dutch – unlike nearly every other developed nation – choose this approach? In order to understand the Dutch difference as summarised in the four points of the preceding paragraph, we must take a close look at some features of society and culture in the Netherlands, including Dutch views of death, medical technology and individualism, factors which are supposed to have influenced the debate on euthanasia.

The taboo on death

In the second half of the 20th century, taboos regulating several spheres of private life – including birth, sexuality and death – were loosened. Ariès distinguished two parts of the taboo related to death: 'the big lie' and 'the dirty death' (Ariès 1981). 'The big lie' is the idea that the dying patient should not be told about his or her diagnosis and prognosis. Telling the truth about a forthcoming death was seen as cruel and likely to worsen the patient's condition. Furthermore, medical knowledge was so primitive that confident diagnosis and prognosis were difficult. The 'dirtiness' refers to seeing death as indecent: death was to be kept out of sight just like many other bodily processes, for example, excretion. The growing importance of cancer as the main cause of death, and thereby the growing frequency of a protracted and painful deathbed, contributed to the 'dirtiness' of dying (Sontag 1978). Access to a dying person was restricted to a few intimates and those who were indispensable for the nursing of the patient. After World War II the loneliness of the dying deepened further as dying at home decreased in favour of dying in an institution.

It is widely agreed that in most western countries the taboo on death largely disappeared in the 1960s (Ariès 1981). Wouters (1990) examined the diminishing of the taboo on death in the Netherlands by looking at, among other things, changes in the ways dying persons were treated. Until 1955 his sources did not reveal any interest in emotions; it was only through rituals that emotions were allowed to be expressed. Beginning in the mid-1950s the dominant codes of behaviour allowed for greater directness and openness. This new attitude toward emotions resulted in a far-reaching curiosity about everything connected with death and dying (1990: 229). In this context, new rituals for burial ceremonies were developed and discussions about medical treatment at the end of life began.

Kennedy (2002) argues that the diminishing of the taboos on death (and sex) occurred more rapidly in the Netherlands than in the rest of the Western world. He explains this by pointing to Dutch culture, in which candour is highly valued, and to the important changes which took place in the Netherlands in the 1960s and 1970s. With the advent of internationalisation, increased prosperity and secularisation, the once very traditional Dutch society was thrown into flux. The Dutch saw no reason to hold to 'old-fashioned' ideas and convictions which seemed arbitrary and repressive (2002: 28–29).

The disappearance of the taboo on death created an opportunity for patients to play a more active role. The awareness of an approaching death offers the opportunity to think about one's preferences for that moment and about desired and undesired medical treatments. Thus, the weakening of the taboo shifts control of the event prompting a reconsideration of the proper role of caregivers both medical and religious.

Development of medical technology and the Dutch healthcare system
After World War II, medical technology flourished. Antibiotics were increasingly available and techniques for anaesthesia, and thus for surgical treatment, improved considerably. Techniques for resuscitation were also substantially expanded. Moreover, the refined surgical techniques and increased knowledge about the problems of rejection brought organ-transplantation within the doctors' reach. Medicine appeared to be a domain without limits. In the 1960s, however, feelings of discomfort arose, discomfort which was provoked by medical embarrassments like the thalidomide affair. These affairs showed the need for the regulation and supervision of medicine. As a result, the state began to take a more active role in healthcare. At the same time criticism was heaped on the power medicine had come to exercise in society (in the Netherlands by Van den Berg 1978, among others). Patients were urged to challenge the almost autonomous growth of medical technology and its range of application. This movement also caused doctors to reflect on the limits of their profession.

Part of the response to developments in medical technology was public discussion of medical-ethical questions. The ability of doctors to postpone death, even when recovery was impossible, created questions about when life should be preserved and the permissibility of relieving pain when such relief would hasten death. Caregivers and ethicists also pondered the difference between acting and refraining from action. If abstention is allowed when the result is the patient's death, why should actively ending the life of a patient who suffers unbearably and hopelessly be prohibited? The role of the patient was another contested issue: should the patient participate in decisions concerning prolonging or shortening his or her life?

In the Netherlands, consensus on most of these issues was reached in a relatively short time. Pain relief with a life-shortening side effect was considered permissible if the relief of pain, and not death, was the aim of treatment. Continuation of futile medical treatment came to be seen as a form of maltreatment and, consequently, stopping it became a duty. Today pain relief with a life-shortening side-effect and the cessation of futile medical treatment are considered 'normal medical practice' – 'behaviour that doctors are generally authorised to perform based on medical indications and according to professional (technical and ethical) norms' (Griffiths *et al.* 1998: 91).

Debate over the doctor-patient relationship resulted in a strengthening of the patient's position. In the new Constitution of 1982, an article safeguarding the right to physical integrity was included. Thereafter, informed consent and the right to refuse treatment were elaborated in the Civil Code (*Law on Contracts for Medical Treatment*).

Characteristics of the Dutch healthcare system – which reflect societal attitudes – can account, to some extent, for the rapid and rather uncomplicated process of change. Traditionally, social politics in the Netherlands has reflected broad support for equity and solidarity in sharing financial burdens. The Netherlands is a well-developed welfare state. In healthcare, the country's cultural commitment to social equity and solidarity translates into a dominant role for income-related payments, and limited use of co-payments. Healthcare insurance companies levy contributions based on income, and offer entitlements according to need. Virtually everyone in the Netherlands is covered by health insurance.

Home care has a prominent position in the Dutch healthcare system and general practitioners (GPs)[9] play an important role in the healthcare system. GP care has three major system characteristics: 'listing', 'gatekeeping' and 'family orientation'. Listing means that, in principle, every Dutch inhabitant is registered with a GP. Gatekeeping refers to the fact that patients generally do not have direct access to specialists or hospital care but must be referred by their GP. The impact of gatekeeping is reflected in the low referral rate: more than 90 per cent of all complaints are treated by GPs. The third characteristic, family orientation, refers to the fact that a Dutch GP generally serves as the personal physician for a patient's entire family. Moreover, GPs make many home visits: 17 per cent of all contacts are visits to the patient's home (De Melker and Verhey 2002: 69–70).

The Netherlands is further distinguished by rates of death and birth at home. De Vries (2005) points out that birth and death at home fit well with Dutch ideas about medicine and science, and Dutch notions of 'thriftiness'. In his sociological analysis of the high rate of home birth in the Netherlands, De Vries also notes that 'The Dutch are disinclined to celebrate the heroic' (2005: 163–166). With respect to end-of-life decisions this can be illustrated by the frequency of deaths with a GP as the doctor in attendance: 40 per cent of all deaths take place at home or in a residential home. As an explanation of the role of GPs in the healthcare system, De Vries notices that the Dutch view of the 'family' is distinctive. In the late 17th and early 18th centuries, the Dutch were the first among modern nations to experience the 'nuclearisation' of the family. In other European countries the nuclearisation of the family occurred simultaneously with industrialisation and was marked by the increasing use of professional help for events once attended by family members: birth, sickness and death. Having nuclearised earlier, the Dutch family resisted the institutionalisation of birth and death (De Vries 2005).

What conclusion can be drawn with respect to changes in the social control of medical practice at the end of life? In the Netherlands as elsewhere, developments in medical technology have provoked a change in the norm regarding the sanctity of life. Although life is still seen as something very important, it has come to be acknowledged that respect for life is not unlimited. In the Netherlands, when discussions emerged concerning who should participate in the decision whether or not to stop treatment, or whether or not to relieve pain with a possible life-shortening effect, it became clear that medical considerations alone could not determine the issue. Opinions about quality of life became part of the discussion. The patient's opinion was, therefore, more important. In this way, self-control based on the personal ethics of the doctor was combined with second-party control. The extent of second-party control in the Netherlands is shown by the high percentage of physicians who report discussions with patients in end-of-life decision-making (Van der Heide *et al.* 2003). With respect to euthanasia second-party control is a necessary condition – otherwise the termination of life is not an option.

The data of Van der Heide *et al.* point to another change: the existence of non-governmental third-party control. Third-party control by other doctors and other caregivers is possible if doctors discuss their decision with them. It is not clear whether developments in medical technology caused this change but it seems obvious that more technical complexity goes together with more collegial consultation. The Netherlands is among the countries in which professional discussions on end-of-life decisions occur frequently. Apart from the required consultation with another doctor, which took place in 91 per cent of the cases, doctors also consult nursing personnel frequently: specialists consulted nursing personnel in 78 per cent of the cases of eutha-nasia and GPs, who normally work without nursing personnel, consulted a nurse in 16 per cent of the cases of euthanasia (Van der Wal *et al.* 2003).

With respect to 'normal medical practice' at the end of life, therefore, we see self-control supplemented by second-party control and informal third-party control, but not with *governmental* social control. With respect to euthanasia we not only see self-control supplemented by second-party control (by definition) but also officially regulated third-party control. Consultation with an inde-pendent colleague is one of the requirements of careful practice, whereas the reporting procedure offers the opportunity for governmental social control.

Individualisation
Individualisation refers to the process by which social relations change from collectivism – a situation in which people are bound to each other and the place they live with strong, multiple ties – to individualism. International comparative research shows that the Netherlands is among those countries

in which individual choice – for example with respect to divorce and soft drugs consumption – is widely accepted. This research also shows that in the Netherlands the 'post-materialistic value-orientation' is stronger than in most other countries (Inglehart 1997: 139). Preferences fitting into this value-orientation can be seen in the answers Dutch people give to questions regarding 'self-determination with respect to one's body' (Elchardus *et al.* 2000: 154–5): suicide, abortion, homosexuality, 'euthanasia' (defined as 'terminating the life of an incurably sick person') and divorce. Over the years, the Dutch have always scored high on the acceptance of homosexuality, suicide and 'euthanasia'.

The consequences of this change for social control, however, are not clear in advance. Is individualisation connected with more or less informal social control? Did individualisation in the Netherlands lead to isolation and less sensitivity to one another's opinions? Whether or not the Dutch look after each other can be ascertained by research on trust and participation. In this research, the hypothesis is that a society of people who trust each other and where many people participate in civil society needs less regulation and less governmental social control (Fukuyama 1995). A comparison of 54 regions in seven European countries – Belgium, France, Germany, Italy, Spain, the Netherlands and the United Kingdom – shows that the Netherlands as a whole scores high on trust and participation (Beugelsdijk and Van Schaik 2003: 128). It can therefore be concluded that, although the Netherlands is an individualistic society, it is not a society of atomistic individualism. Hofstede (1997), who studied cultural differences in business, also sees the Dutch as non-atomistic individualists. In his research the Dutch appear as 'feminine' individualists, a combination the Dutch share with Nordic countries. Individualism makes them appreciate personal time, freedom and challenge, and 'femininity' makes them value good working relationships and co-operating (1997: 81–82).

How has this non-atomistic individualism influenced the public debate on euthanasia? How is self-determination discussed with respect to the end of life in the Netherlands? In the early years of the debate on medical behaviour that potentially shortens life, the issue of self-determination, or 'having a say in one's own life' as it was then called, was hardly ever mentioned. Beneficence was the most often invoked principle for legitimising life-shortening by doctors. In the 1970s consensus grew on a more restricted meaning of the word euthanasia: termination of life on request. At the same time, proponents of euthanasia connected beneficence with self-determination. The conjunction of these two principles is reflected in the 'requirements of careful practice', which require both a voluntary, well-considered request and unbearable and hopeless suffering. It is thus not self-determination as such but the combination of the request and the suffering that constitutes the situation in which termination of life is considered justifiable. In 2002 the Supreme Court ruled that only suffering based on a 'disease' leads to a doctor having a conflict of duties (*Nederlandse Jurisprudentie* 2003, no. 167). A consequence of legalisation via the justification of necessity is also that termination of life without a request can be, and sometimes is, considered justifiable. Therefore, although the position of Dutch patients has been strengthened, it is wrong to conclude that the *Law on Termination of Life on Request* rests only on self-determination[10].

The Dutch are seen – correctly, I believe – as people who put a high value on their personal judgement. In the slipstream of the process of individualisation, opinions regarding the sanctity of life have changed. The vast majority of the Dutch think that euthanasia can be legitimate. The legalisation of euthanasia and assistance with suicide, which came into effect in 2002, reflects this belief. Much of the regulation surrounding euthanasia practice, however, seeks to guarantee that the choice for euthanasia and its implementation is not done in isolation by the patient and his or her physician. In 2001, consultation with relatives took place in 96 per cent of the cases of termination of life on request. There is circumstantial evidence that isolated persons hardly ever manage to convince their doctor to perform euthanasia.

The legalisation of euthanasia: a shift in social control

A common denominator of the disappearance of the taboo on death, developments in medical technology and individualisation, is altered attitudes toward death. The loosening of the prohibition of ending a life in a medical context, however, does not mean that anything goes. Rather, this loosening goes together with new forms of social control. Self-control of doctors is coupled with second-party control, with professional third-party control, and with governmental social control.

Since 1970 the position of the patient with respect to dying has changed: today it is widely believed that a patient ought to be told of his or her impending death and to be given a say in how death will be managed. Patients are no longer totally dependent on their doctors.

Euthanasia, however, is not covered by the *Law on Contracts for Medical Treatment*. Unlike withholding and withdrawing treatment, ending a life at the patient's request is not seen as 'normal medical practice'. A doctor, therefore, is never obliged to perform euthanasia. He or she can refuse a patient's request. Nevertheless, asking to die is no longer seen as problematic behaviour (Norwood 2005) and if a patient finds a doctor willing to help them, euthanasia is an option. More generally, legal euthanasia seems to go together with a lower frequency of actively ending life without a request (Kuhse *et al.* 1997, Deliens *et al.* 2000[11]) and an increase in the rate of consulting patients regarding all kinds of medical end-of-life decision-making (Van der Heide *et al.* 2003). Therefore, and somewhat ironically, the patient who is against actively ending life is perhaps in a better position in the Netherlands than in countries in which euthanasia is prohibited.

The euthanasia law has also changed the way doctors relate to each other. The Medical Association played an important role in the debate on euthanasia and complemented that role with protocols and guidelines. Currently, it organises meetings and courses in which doctors can learn about the requirements of careful practice and can talk to each other about the problems they experience in medical end-of-life care. With respect to euthanasia, professional social control is formalised in the required consultation of an independent doctor.

In the Netherlands there is now much more governmental control regarding euthanasia than there was in the past. Before 1980 governmental social control only existed in theory. As in many other countries, prosecutorial authorities never actively looked for doctors who broke the law. Nowadays, although far from perfect, Dutch governmental social control regarding euthanasia is fairly comprehensive. Nowhere else have so many cases concerning ending of life on request been investigated by prosecutorial authorities and so many doctors prosecuted and brought to trial. Active control has continued after the enactment of the law in 2002, and although not perfect, the current reporting procedure produces a level of public control of euthanasia practice that has no comparable example in the rest of the world.

From sociology of law to sociology of bioethics

My research sheds light on the factors associated with the set of regulations governing euthanasia in the Netherlands. What we have seen is: a well-developed welfare state, social relations characterised by a high level of trust, a country with permissive attitudes regarding 'self-determination with respect to one's body', that values candour highly, that has been successful in finding a common ground on which euthanasia is acceptable for almost all inhabitants. These features account for the fact that important organisations – like the Medical Association and the prosecutorial authorities – were willing to contribute to the process of change. In turn, their contribution helped to enlarge formal and informal social control of euthanasia. The Dutch appeared to be unafraid of the prospect of abuse; to welcome openness with respect to end-of-life decision making (Kennedy 2002); to value consensus on such a sensitive issue (Weyers 2004); and to be willing to enlarge social control on medical behaviour at the end of life.

Where does this leave us with respect to the theories of the emergence of law put forward by Black and Selznick? In the case of the law regulating the practice of euthanasia in the Netherlands, it is clear that law does *not* vary inversely with other forms of social control. Furthermore, although the position of patients is strengthened in many ways, the law on euthanasia did not liberate the patient from a doctor reluctant to perform euthanasia.

Why should a sociologist of bioethics care about these theories of law? My work lifts the gaze of those who work in bioethics by calling attention to the fact that bioethics, and the regulatory regimes associated with it, are part of larger systems of formal and informal social control. A rigorous sociology of bioethics must explore how this relatively new profession and new mode of regulation fits with the rise and fall of other means of controlling the behaviour of professionals and their clients.

Notes

1   I use the term euthanasia to refer to termination of life on request and physician-assisted suicide.
2   Article 293: A person who takes the life of another person at that other person's express and earnest request is liable to a term of imprisonment of not more than twelve years or a fine of the fifth category.
    Article 294: A person who intentionally incites another to commit suicide, assists in the suicide of another, or procures for that other person the means to commit suicide, is liable to a term of imprisonment of not more than three years or a fine of the fourth category, where the suicide ensues (Rayar and Wadworth 1997).
3   *Staatsblad van het Koninkrijk der Nederlanden*, 2001, no 194.
4   The former disciplinary law governed by the Dutch Medical Association was thought deficient because not all physicians were members of the organisation and because the most serious sanction was expulsion from the association. Dutch Medical Disciplinary Law changed considerably in the 1990s. The aims of these changes included improvement of patients' opportunity to complain and increased transparency of disciplinary procedures.
5   Healthcare institutions in the Netherlands derive historically from the activities of churches, later taken over by private organisations.
6   See the British case of Harold Shipman, a doctor who probably killed more than a hundred of his patients.
7   The other cases are reported as a 'natural death' and are unknown by authorities, like all the cases of physician-assisted death in other countries.
8   This was the nickname given to the government that excluded the Christian Democrats.
9   The Dutch word for GP is 'huisarts', literally 'house doctor'.
10 The debate, however, did not stop with the enactment of the Law on Termination of Life on Request. Nowadays, the Dutch Euthanasia Society, which for many years worked together with the Medical Association and political parties, is championing the so-called 'last-will-pill', which would ensure that a patient has access to assistance in dying. This idea might be a step towards a more individualistic form of self-determination but it can also be considered an attempt to prevent ill-considered and lonesome suicides.
11 In the research of Van der Heide *et al.* 2003, Belgium and Denmark have a higher percentage on this subject than Switzerland and the Netherlands; however, Italy and Sweden have a lower percentage.

References

Ariès, P. (1981) *The Hour of our Death*. New York: Knopf.
Babbie, E. (1986) *Observing Ourselves: Essays in Social Research*. Belmont, California: Wadsworth Publishing Co.

Berg, J.H. van den (1978) *Medical Power and Medical Ethics*. New York: W.W. Norton (translation of *Medische Macht en Medische Ethiek*. Nijkerk: Callenbach).

Beugelsdijk, S. and van Schaik, T. (2003) Participation in civil society and European regional economic growth. In Arts, W. *et al.* (eds) *The Cultural Diversity of European Unity: Findings, Explanations and Reflections from the European Values Study*. Leiden: Brill.

Black, D. (1976) *The Behavior of Law*. San Diego: Academic Press.

Cohen, S. (1985) *Visions of Social Control. Crime, Punishment and Classification*. Cambridge: Polity Press.

Deliens, L. *et al.* (2000) End-of-life decisions in medical practice in Flanders, Belgium: a nationwide survey, *The Lancet*, 356, 1806–11.

De Vries, R. (2004) Making maternity care. The consequences of culture for health care systems. In Vinken, H., Soeters, J. and Ester, P. (eds) *Comparing Cultures. Dimensions of Culture in a Comparative Perspective*. Leiden and Boston: Brill.

De Vries, R. (2005) *A Pleasing Birth. Midwives and Maternity Care in the Netherlands*. Amsterdam: Amsterdam University Press.

Elchardus, M., Chaumont, J.-M. and Lauwers, S. (2000) Morele onzekerheid en nieuwe degelijkheid. In Dobbelaere, K. (eds), *Verloren Zekerheid. De Belgen en hun Waarden, Overtuigingen en Houdingen*. [Moral uncertainties and the new respectability. In Dobbelaere, K. (eds) *The Belgians and their Values, Convinctions and Attitudes*] Tielt: Lannoo.

Elias, N. (1978) *The Civilizing Process. The History of Manner* (translated by Edmund Jephcott). Oxford: Basil Blackwell.

Ellickson, R. (1991) *Order without Law. How Neighbors Settle Disputes*. Cambridge/ London: Harvard University Press.

Fukuyama, F. (1995) *Trust: the Social Virtues and the Creation of Prosperity*. New York: Free Press.

Griffiths, J. (2006) The idea of sociology of law and its relation to law and to sociology. In Freeman, M. (ed.) *Law and Sociology*. Oxford: Oxford University Press, 49–68.

Griffiths, J., Bood, A. and Weyers, H. (1998) *Euthanasia and Law in the Netherlands*. Amsterdam: Amsterdam University Press.

Halman, L. (2001) *The European Values Study: a Third Wave. Source Book of the 1999/2000 European Values Surveys*. Tilburg: WORC, Tilburg University.

Hees, M. van and Steunenberg, B. (2000) The choices judges make. Court rulings, personal values, and legal constraints, *Journal of Theoretical Politics*, 12, 305–24.

Heide, A. van der (2003) End-of-life decision-making in six European countries: descriptive study, *The Lancet*, 362, 345–50.

Hofstede, G. (1997) *Cultures and Organizations. Software of the Mind*. 2nd Revised Edition. New York: McGraw-Hill.

Inglehart, R. (1997) *Modernization and Postmodernization. Cultural, Economic and Political Changes in 43 Societies*. Princeton: Princeton University Press.

Jaspers, J.B. (1985) *Het Medische Circuit. Een Sociologische Studie van de Ontwikkeling van het Netwerk van Afhankelijkheid tussen Cliënten, Artsen, Centrale Overheid, Ziekenfondsen en Ziekenhuizen in Nederland (1865–1980)*. [*The Medical Circuit. A Sociological Study of the Development of the Dependency Network of Clients, Doctors And Government* (1865–1989)] Utrecht/Antwerpen: Bohn, Scheltema and Holkema.

Kapteyn, P. (1980) *Taboe, Ontwikkelingen in Macht en Moraal Speciaal in Nederland*. [*Taboo. Developments in Power and Morals, Especially in the Netherlands*] Amsterdam: Synopsis.

Kennedy, J. (2002) *Een Weloverwogen dood. Euthanasie in Nederland*. [*A Well-considered Death. Euthanasia in the Netherlands*] Amsterdam: Uitgeverij Bert Bakker.

Kuhse, H. (1997) End-of-life decisions in Australian medical practice, *Medical Journal of Australia*, 166, 191–8.

Melker, R.A. de and Verweij, T. (2002) The family doctor – central pillar of the Dutch health system. In van Rooij, E. (eds) *Health and Health Care in the Netherlands. A Critical Self-assessment of Dutch Experts in Medical and Health Sciences.* Maarsen: Elsevier Gezondheidszorg.

Norwood, F. (2005) *Euthanasia Talk. Euthanasia Discourse, General Practice and End-of-Life Care in the Netherlands.* Berkeley.

Otlowski, M. (1997) *Voluntary Euthanasia and the Common Law*. Oxford: Oxford University Press.

Rayar, L. and Wadsworth, S. (1997) *The American Series of Foreign Penal Codes. Volume 30. The Dutch Penal Code.* Littleton: Fred B. Rothman and Co.

Remmelink, J. (1992) *Spanningen tussen Recht en Strafwet. Rede Gehouden door Prof. mr. J. Remmelink ter Gelegenheid van Zijn Afscheid als Procureur-Generaal bij de Hoge Raad der Nederlanden op de Buitengewone Zitting van het College op Woensdag 29 april 1992. [Tension between Law and Criminal Code. Valedictory Lecture of Professor J. Remmelink as Procurator-General of the Supreme Court of the Netherlands, delivered at the extraordinary session of the Court on Wednesday, 29 April 1992*] Den Haag: Ministerie van Justitie.

Schwartz, R.D. (1954) Social factors in the development of legal control: a case study of two Israeli settlements, *Yale Law Journal*, 63, 471–91.

Selznick, P. (1968) Law: the sociology of law. In Sills, D.L. (ed.), *International Encyclopedia of the Social Sciences. Volume 9.* New York and London: Macmillan.

Sontag, S. (1978) *Illness as Metaphor.* New York: Farrar, Straus and Giroux.

Wal, G. van der (2003) *Medische Besluitvorming aan het Einde van het Leven. De Praktijk en de Toetsingsprocedure Euthanasie. [Medical Decision-making at the End of Life. Euthanasia Practice and the Review Procedure*] Utrecht: De Tijdstroom.

Weyers, H. (2002) De weloverwogen dood volgens Kennedy [The well-considered death according to Kennedy], *Facta*, 10, 2, 8–11.

Weyers, H. (2004) *Euthanasie. Het Proces van Rechtsverandering. [Euthanasia. The process of legal change*] Amsterdam: Amsterdam University Press.

Weyers, H. (2005) Legal recognition of the right to die. In Garwood-Gowers, A., Tingle, J. and Wheat, K. (eds) *Contemporary Issues in Healthcare Law and Ethics.* Edinburgh. Elsevier.

Wouters, C. (1990) Changing regimes of power and emotions at the end of life. The Netherlands 1930–1990, *Netherlands' Journal of Social Sciences: a Publication of the Netherlands' Anthropological Society*, 26, 151–67.

10

From biopolitics to bioethics: church, state, medicine and assisted reproductive technology in Ireland
Orla McDonnell and Jill Allison

Introduction

Ireland, relative to other European countries, has been exceptionally slow to address issues of contemporary bioethics, particularly in the areas of molecular biology and genetic technologies, and assisted reproductive technologies (ART). Ireland, for example, remains one of the few EU states that has not ratified the European Convention on Human Rights and Biomedicine (1997). ART in Ireland is currently unregulated by legislative statute; medical practice in the field of infertility and human embryology has been loosely governed by the ethical guidelines of the Irish Medical Council since 1989. The plurality of modern societies along with the complexity of the moral, social and ethical questions raised by technological developments, which radically alter the way in which biomedicine can intervene in biological life processes, has meant that moral challenges are increasingly becoming a question of legal code (Habermas 1996). It is widely presumed, however, that Ireland's constitutional ban on abortion and the constitutional reference to the 'right to life of the unborn' (Article 40.3.3) serves as an explicit prohibition on embryo research and pre-empts many of the ethical and legal dilemmas faced by other states in relation to developments in ART. The conditions by which this presumption may hold firm against any analysis, however, depends on the absence of public debate and conflict over competing social and ethical values. The apparent reticence of policy makers to engage in the emerging international bioethical discourse on advances in biomedical science and biotechnology reflects, in large part, the legacy of what Inglis (1998) describes as the 'moral monopoly' of the Catholic Church over questions of identity, ethics and public morality in Ireland.

Until relatively recently Ireland was viewed as a homogenous society dominated by the ideologies of Catholicism, familism and communitarianism (O'Carroll 1991). The sense of a unified moral community was essentially maintained by the institutional apparatus of the Catholic Church, whose moral authority extended across the institutions of family, education, health and the provision of welfare. This institutional authority has had a chequered history since Independence in 1922, marked by periods of conflict and consensus in church-state relations. The influence of the church over civil society has been mediated by a strong Catholic social movement from the 1920s, which was to become the main conduit for Catholic social teaching (Whyte 1980, Fuller 2002). This moral authority has been, arguably, inscribed most indelibly in the symbolic meaning of women's reproductive bodies as an ethically contested terrain, particularly in the ideological lines that symbolically tie motherhood to a quintessentially Irish definition of woman-hood. This observation is an important marker of the analysis developed in this chapter of the longstanding and complex relations of power between church, state and the institution of medicine in conflicts that have primarily centred on reproduction, sexuality and the family.

While Ireland emerged from the experience of social change in the 1970s as a conservative society marked by considerable consensus between the state and the Catholic Church (Whyte 1980), the acceleration of social change in the 1990s towards a modern, pluralist society has seen a considerable shift in church-state relations. Most certainly, the ideal of a post-Catholic, pluralist republic has growing currency within mainstream cultural and political discourse. The moral authority of the Catholic Church in Ireland, as in many other European countries, has been weakened by the values of individualism, consumerism and materialism (Inglis 2003) and the Irish Catholic hierarchy's handling of clerical child abuse and sexual scandals within the church has created a serious institutional crisis for the church, weakening the power it once held over matters of personal and sexual morality (Inglis 1998, Fuller 2002, Smyth 2005). In historical terms, the institutionalisation of Catholic social teaching in Ireland has been one of prescription and proscription rather than negotiation and dialogue. In the face of the current escalation of child abuse scandals, various commentators from within the church itself have begun to reflect on the institutional culture of the Irish Catholic Church as one of clericalism, anti-intellectualism and authoritarianism (Lane 2004, Twomey 2003). The apparently strong adherence to a Catholic identity in Ireland, even in the face of the decline in the moral authority of the hierarchy, can be explained by the stronghold of social convention and conformity (Fahey 1994). Inglis (1998) describes this phenomenon in terms of the role that 'religious capital', as generated and controlled by the Church, has played in shaping the lives, dispositions and mindsets of Irish people. In the early 1980s, as the church's influence over social policy was apparently receding, any moral vacuum in social values was quickly filled by a more fundamentalist Catholic social movement and the birth of the ideal of a 'pro-life nation' enshrined in the 8th Amendment (1983) of the Irish constitution on the 'right to life of the unborn' (Smyth 2005).

It is only since the late-1990s that the state has been willing to open up a regulatory debate on ART through the establishment of a Commission on Assisted Human Reproduction in 2000 (CAHR 2005). Drawing on documentary and media evidence, our case study seeks to explain the absence of a sustained public debate on bioethics in relation to ART and the exceedingly slow pace of the institutionalisation of bioethics in Ireland. In our analysis we show how the intersecting interests of the church as well as the state and the institution of medicine are served by a 'semantic subterfuge' that maintains a status quo in the emerging regulatory ART debate and preserves the ideal of a 'pro-life nation'. In that sense, bioethics in Ireland remains strongly tied to questions of national identity while elsewhere it evolves more around diversity and cultural pluralism.

Situating the debate: the Catholic Church and the politics of moral authority

For complex historical reasons, Catholicism became the primary badge of national identity in Ireland (Whyte 1980, Lee 1989). In the 1930s, the prohibition on divorce, the banning of the importation and sale of contraceptives, and state-operated cultural censorship reflected the importance of Catholic morality in the nation-building project. These measures were framed by Catholic social principles as protecting Ireland's newfound sovereignty against external cultural influences, particularly in terms of safeguarding traditional moral values (Whyte 1980). The infusion of faith-based social values into a nationalist political vision, reflected in particular in the 1937 Constitution, served to make gender a key component of Irish citizenship from the outset. Article 41, which gives constitutional recognition to the family as the natural and fundamental unit of society, ties women's identity and status as citizens to motherhood[1].

This became the key framework through which public policy could direct the private relations of individuals and establish that the common good take precedence over the individual aspirations of women as citizens. The ideal of domesticity, marshalled into the politics of Catholic nationalism, was reinforced by both church and state as a form of 'bio-power' (Foucault 1978) in an attempt to control women's fertility and sexuality in lockstep with a narrowly defined public morality. From the perspective of the Catholic Church, control over the family, sexuality and fertility was crucial to the continuing success of the church as a moral authority. Any challenge to Catholic orthodoxy in these areas was seen not only as contrary to church teaching but also had deep implications for the traditional values of cultural identity and, therefore, was seen as potentially corrosive of the social cohesion of Irish society. To speak about the power of the Catholic Church in Ireland refers not only to the role of religion and faith-based values as a cultural resource for everyday meaning, but to the institutional power that it has exercised through its direct and indirect influence on the state and its institutions, including the medical profession and healthcare provision.

Church and state: the biopolitics of reproduction

A significant test of church-state relations occurred, not surprisingly, in relation to women's reproductive health. The expansion of public health in the 1940s and 1950s brought the state into direct conflict with the church and provided the occasion for a strategic political alliance between the Catholic hierarchy and the medical establishment. The conflict concerned a proposal within the 1947 Health Act, which subsequently came to be known as the 'Mother and Child' scheme, to extend free medical care to all mothers and their children under the age of 16[2]. Emphasising the constitutional primacy of the family as the appropriate institution to provide for the needs of children and the right of the church to educate on sexual morality, the hierarchy forewarned that state provision of healthcare for women would lead to access to information on contraception and abortion (Wren 2003). It cannot be overstated that the Catholic hierarchy perceived such incursions into the realm of family values and sexual health as a threat to their domain of moral authority[3]. The Catholic medical elite, on the other hand, was mindful of its own material interests in protecting the income-generating potential of private medicine and the status it accrued from its association with the Catholic voluntary hospitals. The 'Mother and Child' controversy highlighted the capacity of both church and medical institutions to strategise around the issues of reproductive ethics and morality for their own ends. While the medical establishment protected its economic autonomy against the state, the controversy became an occasion for the Catholic hierarchy to assert its self-identity as the rightful interpreter and arbiter of public and private morality.

The legalisation of restricted access to contraception in 1979 captures the nature of the consensus between church and state over the sensitively guarded area of family, sexuality and fertility. Following a landmark Supreme Court ruling in the McGee case in 1973, the ban on the sale and importation of contraceptives was deemed unconstitutional on the basis of a personal right to privacy and an interpretation of family rights to include marital privacy. In light of the apparent void created by the McGee case allowing for unrestricted access to contraception, the Catholic Church, whilst pronouncing on the morality of contraception, now paradoxically relied on the state to introduce regulatory restrictions. Most significantly in terms of biopolitics, the McGee case was seen as setting a new and 'distinctly American' precedent in Irish legal practice by introducing the privacy concept (Whyte 1980). The McGee case came to represent present the threat of 'legal activism' to traditional, Catholic social values and parallels were drawn by the Pro-life Amendment Campaign in the early 1980s with the Roe v. Wade Supreme Court ruling legalising abortion in the US (Hesketh 1990, Hug 1999). In the absence of any political demand for abortion services in Ireland, this became the pre-emptive political rationale behind a concerted campaign by a strong conservative alliance demanding a referendum to secure a constitutional prohibition on abortion, which incidentally was already illegal under statute law.

Reflecting a return to traditional, Catholic social values, the abortion amendment of 1983 endorsed the constitutional 'right to life of the unborn'. O'Carroll (1991) describes the emergence of the campaign for a pro-life constitutional amendment as representing the desire for continuity of 'the core values of Irish identity – Catholicism, family, patriarchal domination, fear of sex and opposition to "alien" ideas' (1991: 67). In the 20-year history of abortion politics involving no less than three referenda (1983, 1992 and 2002) and numerous court rulings, the issue of reproductive rights has been subsumed by a distinct nationalist discourse. Smyth (2005) argues that the dominant discursive framing of abortion politics through all of these debates involves numerous recastings of the nation state as 'pro-life' in appeals to the 'common good' and the 'familial nation' (2005: 145). A sign of Ireland's determination to distinguish its national pro-life identity was the move by the state to negotiate the inclusion of a Protocol maintaining its constitutional protection of the 'unborn' prior to its ratification of the Maastricht Treaty on EU integration in 1992 (Smyth 2005). The 'right to life of the unborn' is now being debated and redefined in light of ART, drawing the abortion debate into a rapidly changing bio-technological context.

The declining authority of the Catholic Church

The declining social power of the Catholic Church in Ireland is seen as part of a gradual and incremental process of social change since the 1970s, reflected in a more general shift in the belief system of practising Catholics (Fahey et al. 2005). Hug (1999) argues that the diminished authority of the Catholic Church represents a trend in which Irish Catholics have 'reclaimed' morality as a question of personal choice. She argues that 'a widening of the ethical dissensus' is evident as representatives of staunchly conservative Catholic and pro-life values are becoming part of a heterogenous multitude of social minorities rather than a homogenous 'moral majority' (1999: 242). In the moral vacuum opened up by the demise of its authority, the Catholic Church now has to navigate a difficult terrain between catholic relativism, which has unhinged the institutional church from its social power base, and catholic fundamentalism that can hardly conceal its own sense of moralism[4].

The demise of Catholic orthodoxy is clearly illustrated by the ethical dissensus opened up by the debate on ART in Ireland. When the then Archbishop of Dublin, Dr. Desmond Connell, chose to make ART the theme of his speech to the Life Society of St. Patrick's College, Maynooth, to mark the 30th anniversary of the Papal encyclical, *Humanae Vitae* (2 March 1999), it became a test of the church's ability to engage in bioethical issues within an increasingly secularised public domain. What might have passed as an uncontentious event quickly escalated into public criticism, challenging the cultural authority of the hierarchy to proscribe on social ethics and personal morality in relation to reproductive decision-making and sexuality. The main controversy, played out in the media, centred on the following extract from the Archbishop's speech:

> The wanted child is the child that is planned; the child produced by the decision of the parents begins to look more and more like a technological product. This is clear in the case of in-vitro fertilisation, surrogate motherhood, genetic engineering, cloning; but it may not be altogether absent in the practice of family planning. [. . .] A profound alteration in the relationship between parent and child may result when the child is no longer welcomed as a gift but produced as it were to order. Parental attitudes would thereby be affected, creating a sense of consumer ownership as well as a new anxiety to win and retain the child's affection. The child no longer belongs to the family in a personal sense if it is radically a product rather than a person (Extract from the full text of the Archbishop's speech published in the *Irish Times*, 8 March 1999).

The 'wanted child' as a construct of family planning discourse on responsible parenting is inverted here. The idea of the 'planned child' as a 'technological product' made 'to order' is analogous in moral terms to the church's position on birth control and women's sexuality. In radio and newspaper discussions, many women were critical of the Archbishop's questioning of their motives as responsible parents in choosing to limit or space their children or in undergoing infertility treatments.

The problem that Dr. Connell sets out to illuminate in his speech is the context in which the infinite choices that science and technology open up have become increasingly defined by the modern imperative of consumerism and decoupled from a moral duty of responsibility. The sub-text of his speech, however, was perceived as framed by the church's concern with the demise of a traditional value consensus based on the ideology of Catholic sexual morality. Much of the public reaction, therefore, was to the historical role of Catholic morality as a means of controlling women's sexuality. One media commentator recalled the history of the Magdalene laundries to show how in the recent past childbearing was a punishment for some women, while for others it was one of the few means of moral status in a society in which identity was morally regimented by the Catholic Church (*Irish Times* 6 March 1999). In radio discussions, this was echoed by the voices of women who recounted the emotional, physical and economic burden of pregnancies over which they had little or no control under unflagging moral prescription and surveillance, while others recounted the feelings of shame irrevocably etched into their biographies as 'fallen women' who had 'unwanted children'. If the speech was intended to open up public debate about the power of medical technology and science to alter radically moral and cultural belief systems, its moral insistence, instead, became an occasion for the public to question the relevance of religious discourse on sexual morality in public life. This media outburst highlights a widening dissensus and the shift in which morality is no longer public and under the church's jurisdiction. Moral matters have evolved into private, intimate and personal choices even as the Catholic Church remains, in the Irish context, strongly tied to the public domain at an institutional level.

Some contextual comments are warranted here, given the current crisis within the church and widespread public speculation that religious discourse, if not the institution of the church itself, has become redundant in public debate. One could argue that the public response to Archbishop Connell's speech was predictable on the very basis that it was an historical replay of the debate that ensued over *Humanae Vitae*. That debate had been less concerned with the morality of family planning than with the unquestionable authority of the Catholic hierarchy to prescribe over sexual and reproductive practice (Lane 2004, Twomey 2003)[5]. However, in the context of the sexual and child abuse scandals that had been breaking since the early 1990s, the 'sensory antennae' (to borrow a construct from Habermas 1996) of an increasingly secularised public were attuned to the social power of the Catholic hierarchy as an institutional actor in public debate. Therefore, what the public and media reacted to was not the opportunity to engage with bioethical discourse but to the tone of chastisement and the apparently intransigent position of the Catholic hierarchy embedded in the argument that the 'wanted child' is a radical commodification of the gift relationship. By appealing to doctrinal claims as absolute truths in a speech that apparently was about opening up public discussion on broad bioethical issues, the hierarchy's public posture was seen as defensive in the face of the Catholic Church's declining moral and institutional power. After all, doctrinal claims to universal truths have the effect of foreclosing debate while giving the hierarchy the last word.

The emergent debate on ART

The institutionalisation of bioethics has been slow to occur in Ireland compared to America and many European states. The term 'bioethics' has had little if no currency in the Irish context; for example, it is absent from the text of the substantive discussion in the Report of the Commission on Assisted Human Reproduction (CAHR April 2005). Indeed, as the discussion below shows, both the state and the medical establishment show considerable political scepticism and apprehension about the opening up of bioethical debate. While the Irish Council for Bioethics was only formed in 2002, it has focused its attention primarily on issues around clinical research and the development of standardised guidelines for research ethics committees in Ireland. This level of institutionalisation is increasingly required in the context of recent EU directives on the regulation of drug trial protocols and on the preservation and storage of human tissue and cells. In fact, the Council has avoided addressing the bioethical issues around medical practices like ART and has been conspicuously silent in the emergent bioethical debate.

In the European Union context, bioethics is framed by a human rights discourse, and the overarching moral question concerns the relationship between society and science. While many European states were moving towards the institutionalisation of bioethics through the formalisation of national debates on regulatory issues (Le Bris 1993), the Irish state was otherwise preoccupied in securing its 'pro-life' agenda against any external point of reference in European institutions and a rights discourse (Conrad 2001, Smyth 2005). This became obvious, not only in the securing of the Protocol in the Maastricht Treaty as mentioned above, but in the highly charged 1992 abortion referendum issue on whether women's right to travel abroad for an abortion should be restricted by law based on the 8th Amendment of the constitution. This may also explain the complete absence of any public debate on the reasons why the Irish state has not ratified the EU Convention on Human Rights and Biomedicine.

Within the space of a decade, in vitro fertilisation (IVF) moved from being a potentially controversial issue to a clinically valuable technology in infertility therapeutics in Ireland. As the clinical repertoire of infertility therapeutics was extended from 'conventional'[6] IVF involving married couples only to IVF involving donor gametes and embryo freezing, a political mandate for bioethical regulation began to emerge in Ireland in the mid-1990s. The debate initially occurred around the ethical prohibitions surrounding IVF treatment and this was framed by the public testimonies of infertility patients who travelled to private clinics outside Ireland. The 'export script', a legacy of the silent export of thousands of Irish women who travel to Britain for abortions, was a key motif to emerge in media reportage of infertility patients who, weighed down by the silence surrounding their experience, had been forced by ethical restrictions to seek treatment elsewhere (McDonnell 2001). As the private market for ART began to expand in Ireland in the late 1990s, the export script gave way to a counter-narrative of the vulnerability of infertility patients to the possibility of 'maverick' and 'unscrupulous' practitioners and 'outside charlatans' operating in an unregulated context. This was the dominant framing on both sides of the Senate debate on Dr. Mary Henry's Private Member's Bill to regulate ART[7]. Although this Bill was defeated, the government had accepted a clear political mandate to introduce regulatory legislation.

By now, the main hospital-based IVF clinic had introduced embryo freezing, which had been the central issue before the Assisted Reproduction Sub-Committee of the Institute of Obstetricians and Gynaecologists, which published its report in May 1999[8]. Mindful of how embryo freezing could publicly provoke a re-animation of anti-abortion rhetoric, the issue was potentially contentious for the medical profession. While the Reproductive Sub-Committee reported a consensus on the therapeutic value of embryo freezing, the term 'embryo' is not to be found in a single clause on cyropreservation. Reflecting competing moral positions on the status of the embryo, the sub-committee focused on technical, scientific distinctions between 'pro-nuclear' and 'zygote' stages of embryonic development from the embryo *proper*. This facilitated a pre-legislative consensus amongst the medical profession on changing medical practice that could also be supported by a clear therapeutic rationale. While the revised ethical guidelines of the Medical Council (1998 and 2004) have effectively removed an earlier prohibition on embryo freezing, the guidelines themselves make no direct reference to the practice, and the term embryo does not appear. What is, perhaps, most striking about the Medical Council's guidelines is the extent to which political subterfuge and moral ambiguity operate where we would most expect to find clarity in ascribing ethical principles to practices deemed therapeutically valuable and legitimate.

The Green Paper on Abortion (September 1999) points out that the legal ambiguity as regards the use of the term 'unborn' in the Constitutional ban on abortion posed legislative difficulties for the whole area of infertility treatment and, in particular, embryo freezing. From the point of view of the state, the effect of a consensus within the medical profession is strategically important in avoiding the re-igniting of the abortion controversy in terms of framing a public debate on the need for legislation to regulate ART. This is particularly important since the medical profession itself was deeply implicated and divided on the abortion issue (Hesketh 1990). Bioethical regulation inevitably requires the opening up of a bioethical debate, which could prove contentious for IVF practice since moral subterfuge had become the operational face of the dominant Catholic medical ethos. The potential for such a conflict had already been played out in a *Prime Time* current affairs documentary programme (*RTE*, 1 October 1996), which exposed the practice of placing 'surplus' embryos into a woman's cervix rather than her womb in an effort by clinicians to comply with Medical Council guidelines while attempting to reduce the risk of multiple pregnancy. The programme framed the restrictive medical guidelines, which at the time required that all embryos created in IVF be placed in the woman's body, as part of a politics of appeasement to the Catholic Church and pro-life opposition. However, it also highlighted that there is sufficient symbolic latitude within a 'pro-life' rhetoric for the construction of a moral counter-argument: in the case of embryo freezing, the argument was made that embryos should *not* be allowed to perish in a woman's cervix, rather they *should* be frozen for use by infertile couples (McDonnell 2001).

The emergence of an unequivocal mandate for bioethical regulation of ART came about because of the intersecting and, sometimes, conflicting interests of clinicians, the regulatory bodies of the medical profession, the state and patient advocacy. Within the medical profession, amongst both supporters and dissenters on the need for legislative regulation, there is a concern that restrictive legislation could encroach upon clinical autonomy and jeopardise future technological and scientific developments. On the other hand, those who hold to a strong Catholic medical ethos fear that legislation will liberalise access to fertility treatments. Interestingly, the most vocal advocates of the need for legislative regulation have been the private clinics that have been set up in Ireland – perhaps because they are less steeped in the cultural politics of subterfuge and, at the same time, are politically more vulnerable to the moral spectre raised by the image of the 'unscrupulous predator' (McDonnell 2001). The establishment of the CAHR in February 2000 by the Minister for Health and Children was intended to frame public debate on future legislation concerning the ethical, social and legal implications of ART through expert deliberation and public consultation. While the Commission received over 1,700 public responses and held a public conference in February 2003, its attempt at public consultation amounted to the Commission becoming a key pressure point for the pro-life lobby. The Commission itself sought little in the way of a public profile, and other than sporadic references to its much-anticipated report there was little media coverage of its activities. The most contentious issue facing the Commission was again the 8th Amendment to the Constitution. In terms of bioethical legislation protecting current medical practice in the field of infertility and embryology – and not foreclosing the possibility of future scientific developments in relation to embryo and genetic research – the problem is clearly one of lending legal clarity to the definition of the 'unborn'[9]. However, the more difficult task faced by the Commission was disentangling bioethical deliberation from the emotively and morally charged rhetoric of abortion.

While the state and the medical profession have, at least publicly, shied away from bioethical discourse, the procedural aspect of bioethics has been semi-institutionalised through the work of the CAHR and the current 'hearings' on its report by the Joint Government Committee on Health and Children. Indeed, it would appear from the initial discussions of the committee that the only substantive bioethical issue is the question of when human life begins, and there is considerable political apprehension about opening up bioethical debate for fear of re-igniting a polarised debate on abortion. This latent conflict is captured by politicians referring to the issues involved as a 'minefield' and the need for the hearings to be guided by expert medical, scientific and legal constitutional advice that can be assimilated into the policy and regulatory technologies of the state. Despite rhetorical gestures to public transparency and open deliberation in the proceedings of the joint committee, much of the emphasis of the initial discussions of the committee are on containing public controversy illustrated in the words of the chairman: '[. . .]. We are not here to make earth-shattering recommendations or to cause controversy. We must try to assist this very delicate debate, which creates huge emotional outbursts from both sides. I want to avoid the use of the word "argument" ' (Parliamentary Debates 21 July 2005). Here we see how public debate is already prefigured as polarised, and political decision-making burdened by the abortion issue.

In the initial hearings, the committee referenced the situation in Italy in which a recent referendum upheld restrictive legislation introduced in 2004 with regard to ART practices. Before legislation, the situation in Italy was described as the 'Wild West of assisted reproduction' (*The Scientist*, 12 December 2003). In contrast, infertility practitioners in Ireland took a conservative and apparently conciliatory approach to the ethos of the Catholic Church, despite the absence of legislation. Restrictive legislation in Italy now bans embryo freezing, limits the number of eggs fertilised in treatment and requires that all embryos be placed in the womb. This situation is not unlike the restrictive medical ethical guidelines implemented by the Irish Medical Council in 1989. The Italian situation is discussed in the committee hearings from the perspective of medical risk and the need for therapeutic efficacy, illustrating how moral questions linked to a Catholic medical ethos have been superseded by a therapeutic and clinical rationale, which favours a more liberal legislative framework in Ireland.

The Catholic Church and bioethics

In terms of understanding how the Catholic Church positions itself in the emergent bioethical debate, primarily in relation to the status of the embryo and the meaning of personhood, it is important to understand the role that the 8th Amendment plays for those wishing to maintain the status quo. Smyth (2005) shows that the framing of the abortion debate has moved from a moral discourse to a medico-legal framing, which shifts the power of definition from the Catholic Church to the jurisdiction of medicine *proper*. Medical ethics no longer strictly reflect a Catholic ethos in relation to abortion. From the point of view of the institution of medicine (and the state) a politico-ethical compromise has been reached, for now, in the distinction between abortion as therapeutically and morally legitimate where the life of a mother is at risk and abortion as a 'social' response to crisis pregnancy. This is seen as outside of the jurisdiction of Irish medicine[10]. In line with this shift, the report published by the CAHR is explicitly framed in medico-legal terms. Given that the 8th Amendment on the 'right to life of the unborn' presents a burdensome challenge to the legislature in the context of the bioethical issues raised by ART, both the state and the medical profession instrumentalise bioethics in a way that Tong (1996: 86) aptly describes as 'another rule, regulation and policy generating enterprise'. This circum-scribes the emergent debate narrowly in terms of a medico-legal framework, which defines bioethics as a professional discourse and experts as the definers of the terms of public debate.

The Catholic Church has responded to the emergent debate on bioethics through its own institutional innovation. A Bishop's Committee for Bioethics was established in 1996 at the point when the need for bioethical regulation was being animated by the embryo-freezing debate that had emerged from within the medical profession itself. The mandate of the Bishop's Committee is to 'contribute to the development and understanding of an ethos, consistent with the values of the Gospel, in relation to issues of healthcare and bio-medical research' (Bishops' Committee on Bioethics 2003). In the context of the current legislative vacuum, the Bishops' Committee has also lent its voice to the need for a regulatory framework as a means of legislatively encoding Catholic morality on 'the right to life of the unborn and the unique status of the family founded on marriage' (2001).

In 2003, the Bishops' Committee, assuming its privilege as an institutional actor close to the centre of political decision-making, addressed the Irish government directly in order to press its case for a uniquely Irish position with regard to EU research proposals for embryonic stem cell research. No longer assured of any special status to exert influence over public policy, the Catholic Church is reduced to appeals to the 8th Amendment, which symbolically enshrines the ideal of Ireland as a Catholic nation. Moreover, the Bishops' Committee appropriates a bioethics platform to recast its position as one of consensus with, rather than opposition to, an already formulated ethos that lies embedded in the construction of Ireland as a pro-life nation. The Bishops' Committee raises the moral stakes by asserting Ireland's responsibility within the EU to uphold the pro-life values enshrined in the Constitution as a sign of this consistency and commitment.

The Catholic Church continues to exert indirect influence over healthcare delivery and medical ethics through its control of the ethos of voluntary hospitals that are publicly funded. Catholic voluntary hospitals that came under direct state control during the 1990s retain an overarching Catholic ethos, continuing to require physicians to sign what has become known as the 'Bishops' Clause'[11] (Manning and Smith 2002, Wren 2004). The institutionalisation and professionalisation of bioethics within the domain of the hospital ethics committees presents another opportunity for the Catholic Church to retain control over the moral framework of medical ethics. This is evident in recent events in which hospital ethics committees in several key Dublin hospitals refused to sanction cancer drug trial protocols, that required the use of contraceptives in conjunction with treatment, on the grounds that it was contrary to a Catholic ethos. There is considerable ambivalence within the medical profession and the state about the continuing influence of a Catholic ethos on healthcare practices.

The Medical Council, however, continues to defend contractual relationships that bind doctors to the ethos of the institution in which they work (*Irish Examiner*, 6 August 2005), while the state continues to endorse the right of individual hospitals to determine the ethos of healthcare practices (*Irish Times*, 4 October 2005). This illustrates how the debate on bioethics is more broadly constrained by institutional arrangements without a wider reference point in public debate and public policy. This ambivalence towards the residual influence of the Catholic Church is reflected in the way in which the medical profession engages in a semantic of subterfuge, avoiding potentially contentious terminology as a means of maintaining professional autonomy, accommodating divergent moral views regarding the status of the embryo, and positioning itself in line with the social norms and traditional values constituted by a Catholic ethos. Counter to the ambiguity and lack of clarity in medical constructions that blur the distinction between the embryo, pre-embryo, zygote or foetus, the Catholic Church refers to the doctrinal teaching of *Donum Vitae*[12] to establish that all such terms are deemed to have 'an identical ethical relevance' (Congregation for the Doctrine of the Faith 1987). However, as the Church negotiates from a position of moral absolutes to engage publicly with bioethics, it adopts a rhetorical strategy of scientific discourse to lend biological facticity to the moral status and personhood of the human embryo.

The Bishop's Committee on Bioethics uses its faith-based theological arguments, drawn from *Donum Vitae*, to side-step rather than engage with the philosophical frameworks of bioethical debate. This does not preclude the Church's participation in bioethics debate, however, its position of moral absolutes eclipses the philosophical debate inherent in what Beauchamp and Childress (1994) describe as a 'common morality' inclusive of multiple moral and ethical frames (1994: 6). As Smith (1996) – a Jesuit and academic theologian – points out, there is dissention even among Catholic theologians as to the biblical basis of absolute claims to truth put forward in *Donum Vitae* to support the personhood of the embryo. He notes that '*Donum Vitae* makes remarks which are tantamount to foreclosure on the issue', the purpose of the document being to confirm a Catholic ethos in terms of moral absolutes rather than contributing to an analytical and thoughtful debate on reproductive technology (Smith 1996: 103). Twomey (2003), another theologian, laments the eroding of the power of such an ideal by the growing social acceptance in Ireland of what he refers to as 'a pluralism not only of various cultural traditions but even a pluralism of what are misleadingly referred to as "moral values"' (2003: 117). In July 2004, the Irish Bishops' Conference released a document that engages directly with the challenges of a pluralist society to moral and ethical decision-making and, indeed, the influence of secularising philosophies on Catholic thinking. The Bishops challenge directly 'the explicit denial of moral absolutes' by liberal theologians in justifying IVF, contraception, abortion and homosexuality. Further, they argue that moral relativism, increasingly present in contemporary society, is eroding the concept of an 'objective' and certain 'truth' for understanding the intrinsic wrongness or evilness of such acts. Hence, while the Catholic Church in Ireland seeks to participate in a bioethical debate, it would appear to do so from an intransigent, doctrinaire position.

In spite of its apparent absolutist position and reliance on the universal applicability of a natural law the Catholic Church in Ireland finds itself in a somewhat ambivalent position as it attempts to appeal to an increasingly secularised Catholic population, while publicly distancing itself from the more fundamentalist 'pro-life' movement. Referring to the disruption of proceedings by pro-life protesters at the public conference organised by CAHR in 2003, Fr. Kevin Doran of the Bishops' Committee for Bioethics publicly dismissed such tactics, arguing that 'the case for protecting human embryos and for defending the integrity of the family was compelling, but it must be made through rational dialogue' (*Irish Times*, 19 February 2003). The appeal to 'rational dialogue' is a lever for the institutional church in a context where fundamentalist-sounding rhetoric threatens to undermine the move towards a bioethical regulatory framework. Not only has the church been involved in calling for bioethical regulation, it has been far more attuned to the symbolic leverage afforded by the currency of bioethics from the point of view of asserting Catholic ethics in a context where there is much political scepticism and fear about the opening up of bioethical debate. Such fear may again afford the Catholic hierarchy, through the Bishops' Committee on Bioethics, a greater purchase on the official voice of Catholic moral values in Ireland as their call for dialogue represents a less threatening and divisive participation in the public hearings currently underway.

Discussion and conclusion

We discuss the three key institutional players in the emerging bioethical regulatory debate on ART in Ireland – the Catholic Church, the state and medicine. Our analysis focuses on this nexus of institutional power relations and how it serves to circumscribe bioethical debate to one that occurs within and between institutions, rather than being informed by wider public participation. Our analysis of the emerging debate on bioethical regulation highlights contradictions and ambivalence in the positions and arguments articulated by key institutional players, not the least of which is the Catholic Church itself. We draw particular attention to the legacy of the social power of the Catholic Church in defining the social values that underscore the meanings of sexuality, reproduction and the family and their historical significance in the social formation of national identity. We trace the history of relations of power through which the church held a moral monopoly in exerting significant influence in the policy areas of education, healthcare and family life in Ireland for most of the last century. Equally significant in the context of our chapter is the recent and dramatic decline in social trust in the church in the wake of revelations of sexual abuse by members of the clergy and the cover-up of such scandals by the Catholic hierarchy. This brings to the forefront of public debate the latent conflict between the church as an institutional player and the state in a secularised and plural society in which the ideal of a post-Catholic, liberal Republic is increasingly embraced within mainstream politics and culture. We also highlight questions around the somewhat ambivalent role of the medical profession for whom much would seem to be at stake in the outcome of bioethical debate about and regulation of 'cutting-edge' medical technologies.

The paper highlights a number of contradictions in the way that the Catholic Church positions itself in the debate on bioethical regulation in light of its historical, institutional position as a moral authority. First, while the church seeks an engagement with bioethics, it is critical of liberal and secularising values that are fundamental to the development of a bioethical discourse. Secondly, while the operational imperative of bioethics is to facilitate deliberative politics or dialogue amongst contested values and perspectives and, hence, facilitates religious viewpoints, bioethics cannot be conducted solely by a religious discourse or appeals to moral absolutes that inevitably seek to have the last word. A key thesis of our analysis is that the 8th Amendment on abortion symbolises the most enduring aspect of Catholic conservative political control over social values both within the health field and more broadly in terms of national identity. As Garvin (2005: 269–70) argues '[. . .] despite dramatic cultural change [. . .] the moral basis of Irish society has not changed beyond recognition, and Catholic-derived moral imperatives, particularly with regard to abortion, still have a considerable power over people's minds'. Hence, the Catholic hierarchy embraces bioethics as a meta-frame or code for refocusing questions of nation identity within the political logic of the 8th Amendment. At the same time, the political scepticism and professional apprehension about bioethics can be explained by the reticence of the state and the institution of medicine to face challenges to background cultural assumptions by competing values and post-conventional identities. We have described the shift in discourse employed by legislators and representatives of the state that moves the bioethics debate from a moral-ethical issue to a medico-legal one that can be contained within a regulatory context of 'expert' opinion. But how do we explain these positions from the point of view of institutional dynamics and intersecting interests?

While the church seeks an engagement in bioethical debate, it relies on its hierarchical and authoritarian structures to contain diverse voices within Catholicism. We have, for example, shown that the Catholic hierarchy has not so much formulated a bioethics policy as absorbed bioethics into its position of universal truth values for doctrinaire teaching. The opening up of bioethical issues to democratic debate and more democratic institutional arrangements is deeply antithetical to the Catholic Church's own modus operandi. We speculate that the residual social power of the Catholic Church in Ireland is less and less to do with a way of life or an identity of 'Irishness' and more to do with the remnants of its institutional power base bolstered by other institutional interests. As Inglis (1998: 220) points out, the successes of the abortion and divorce referenda in the 1980s, at a time when the Catholic Church would have appeared to have been losing its institutional foothold in the political sphere, suggested that the church 'still represented the moral conscience of Irish society'. This role has been undermined throughout the 1990s, not so much by secularising influences within Irish society, but by the institutional crisis within the church itself in relation to child sexual abuse and sex scandals in what Garvin (2005) emphasises as a more significant shift towards 'declericalism'. He claims Ireland, however, is not unique in this respect, noting a general declining influence in traditional clerical and Episcopal authority on Catholics elsewhere in Europe and America.

The institution of medicine has proved adept at employing a semantic of subterfuge to appease the church, which continues to control a large number of public and private hospitals. At the same time, a politics of subterfuge accommodates potentially divergent moral perspectives on ART within the medical profession, albeit still within an overall Catholic ethos, giving it considerable power to determine its own regulatory course. The state, by keeping the church on board, neutralises a more fundamentalist Catholic lay movement, which has the potential to be a more direct and hostile threat. In legal terms, the 8th Amendment poses particular technical problems for resolving bioethical issues in the Irish case. However, the conservatism that underlies the intersecting interests of the key institutional actors relates as much to unease with opening up the fractious debates that have accompanied subsequent abortion referenda as with maintaining the status quo of conservative social values encoded by the 8th Amendment.

The political agility that both the state and the medical profession have shown in negotiating the regulatory debate on ART through a semantic of subterfuge reveals the conservatism behind their reluctance to open up a bioethical debate. In this sense, the politics of subterfuge operates to obscure the kind of political accommodation that serves their respective interests. By this we mean the interests of a medical elite to protect its self-regulatory domain, and the self-interest of the state to avoid being drawn too deeply into the political ramifications of a contestable medico-legal solution on abortion. Given the lack of democratic principles and the constraints on debate and participation within its structures, it is hardly surprising that the church's bioethical stance does not include a call for a more open and democratic debate amongst a plurality of views and values. Rather than engage in debate as a 'voice of social criticism' (Peillon 2001) – as it has in the United States – the Catholic Church in Ireland continues to see itself as an institutional power player.

It is clear that while the bioethics regulatory debate on ART in Ireland remains an emergent one, legislators, the medico-scientific community and the public at large will have to engage more fully with the ethical, social and legal implications of biomedical technology. While a comparative study of other EU countries with strong historical and institutional ties to Catholicism is beyond the scope of this chapter, our case study highlights the role of church-state relations in circumscribing bioethical debate and in laying a particular path for bioethical governance. Notwithstanding the historical differences, debates in countries with a strong Catholic influence at institutional levels such as Spain or Italy show the same difficulties in dealing with the legacy of the church regarding issues of ART and definitions of the embryo. What will be of interest, however, as the story of our case study unfolds, is the extent to which institutional inertia will prevail on bioethical regulation in line with the state's prevarication on abortion legislation. Even, procedurally, the opening up of a deliberative process on bioethical regulation is very much contained within the nexus of institutional power relations. As a political strategy, this is about maintaining an illusion of consensus to contain a widening dissensus. Hence, the deep contradictions between hegemonic and conservative social values encoded in the 8th Amendment, which are the very values at stake in the opening up of a bioethical debate on ART, and the lauding in cultural and political rhetoric of a post-Catholic plural identity, are avoided. The specific links between the church and the state have hampered a more pluralistic and diverse approach to bioethical issues and have not allowed for any meaningful public deliberative process that would represent a shift from biopolitics to bioethics.

Notes

1 Article 41 of the Irish Constitution states: 'The State shall, therefore, endeavour to ensure that mothers shall not be obliged by economic necessity to engage in labour to the neglect of their duties in the home. – The State pledges itself to guard with special care the institution of marriage on which the family is founded to protect it against attack' (41.2.1 and 2.2). This is a direct reflection of Pope Pius XI's encyclical *Quadrigesimo Anno*.

2 Against the background of the Beveridge Report (1942) in Britain, which became the framework for the National Health Service, this scheme was interpreted by both the Catholic hierarchy and the medical establishment as the thin edge of the wedge in the introduction of a national health service – or in the popular anti-communism lexicon of the time – 'socialised medicine' (Barrington 1987).

3 In correspondence with the government Archbishop McQuaid cautioned that '[t]he hierarchy cannot approve of any scheme which, by its general tendency, must foster undue control by the State in a sphere so delicate and intimately concerned with morals' (cited in Whyte, 1980: 446).

4 See how this argument is developed from perspectives within the Irish Catholic Church in Lane (2004) and McKeown (2003).

5 Liberal Catholics, anticipating changes to the church's rigid stance on sexual morality, were shocked and disappointed that *Humanae Vitae* maintained the status quo on contraception.

6 Conventional IVF involves the gametes of the 'infertile couple' being treated and limits the numbers of embryos produced, all of which are placed in the women's uterus.

7 Dr. Mary Henry's Bill, Regulation of Assisted Human Reproduction (1999) was defeated in its second reading in the Seanad (lower house of parliament) (Seanad Debates Official Report, 7 July 1999). The Bill provided for a statutory register of clinicians providing infertility services giving the state direct responsibility for the issuing and monitoring of licenses. It also provided for the establishment of an ethics committee to serve in an advisory capacity to the Minister for Health and Children. The only proscriptive elements of the Bill were to render surrogate contracts void and legally unenforceable, and to specify that donors had no parental rights to children born from donated gametes.

8   This sub-committee had been established in June 1996; while it issued its report in May 1999, this did not come into the public arena until after the defeat of Dr. Henry's Bill.

9   The report of the CAHR (April 2005) recommends that the Constitutional protection of the right to life of the 'unborn' be legally defined as beginning at implantation of an embryo in the womb of a mother.

10   See Smyth (2005) for an analysis of the recent repositioning of the medical profession, which emerged during the All-Party Oireachtas Committee public hearings on abortion (May 2000, Government of Ireland 2000).

11   Hospital ethics committees were first established under decree by the Archbishop of Dublin, Dr. Ryan in 1978 to ensure that Catholic ethics in reproductive medicine were adhered to by medical personnel. However, as long as hospitals remained within the ownership and authority of the church, a Catholic ethos could be maintained against the growing professional independence of medicine following the establishment of the Medical Council in 1979. This became a contentious issue between the state and the Catholic Church in the early 1980s during the negotiations of what has become known as the 'common contract', which effectively established the state as the employee of hospital consultants, including those working in voluntary hospitals. The main concern of the Catholic Voluntary Hospitals was that the new contract did not bind doctors to a Catholic ethos.

12   This document, also known as 'Instruction on Respect for Human Life in its Origin and on the Dignity of Procreation' was issued by the Congregation for the Doctrine of the Faith in March 1987 as a response to developments in the medical realm of assisted reproduction. The basis for its arguments against IVF as morally wrong are found in the encyclical *Humane Vitae*, which outlines the importance of the 'inseparable connection, willed by God [. . .] between the two meanings of the conjugal act: the unitive meaning and the procreative meaning' (Smith 1996: 98).

References

Barrington, R. (1987) *Health, Medicine and Politics in Ireland 1900–1970*. Dublin: Institute of Public Administration.

Beauchamp, T.L. and Childress, J.F. (1994) *Principles of Biomedical Ethics*. Oxford: Oxford University Press.

Commission on Assisted Human Reproduction (April 2005) *Report*. Dublin: CAHR.

Congregation for the Doctrine of the Faith (1987) *Donum Vitae*. Available from: <http://www.vatican.va/roman_curia/congregations/cfaith/documents/rc_con_cfaith_doc> [Accessed 24 September 2004].

Conrad, K. (2001) Fetal Ireland: national bodies and political agency, *Éire-Ireland: An Interdisciplinary Journal of Irish Studies*, 36, 3–4, 153–73.

Council of Europe (1997) *Convention for the Protection of Human Rights and Dignity of the Human Being with regard to the Application of Biology and Medicine*. Convention on Human Rights and Biomedicine, ETS No 164. Oviedo, Spain.

Fahey, T. (1994) Catholicism and industrial society in Ireland. In Goldthorpe, J.H. and Whelan, C.T. (eds) *The Development of Industrial Society in Ireland*. Oxford: Oxford University Press.

Fahey, T., Hayes, B.C. and Schnott, R. (2005) *Conflict and Consensus: a Study of Values and Attitudes in the Republic of Ireland and Northern Ireland*. Dublin: Institute of Public Administration.

Foucault, M. (1990 [1978]) *History of Sexuality Volume 1: An Introduction.* Translated by Hurley, R. New York: Vintage.

Fuller, L. (2002) *Irish Catholicism since 1950: the Undoing of a Culture*. Dublin: Gill and Macmillan.

Garvin, T. (2005 [2004]) *Preventing the Future: Why was Ireland so Poor for so Long?* Dublin: Gill and Macmillan.

Government of Ireland (1999) *Green Paper on Abortion*. Dublin: Stationery Office.

Government of Ireland (2000) *The All-Party Oireachtas Committee on the Constitution Fifth Progress Report: Abortion*. Dublin: Stationery Office.

Habermas, J. (1996) *Between Facts and Norms: Contributions to a Discourse Theory of Law and Democracy*. Cambridge: Polity Press.

Hesketh, T. (1990) *The Partitioning of Ireland? The Abortion Referendum of 1983*. Dublin: Brandsma Books.

Hug, C. (1999) *The Politics of Sexual Morality in Ireland*. London: Macmillan.

Inglis, T. (1998) *Moral Monopoly: the Rise and Fall of the Catholic Church in Modern Ireland*, 2nd Edition. Dublin: University College Press.

Inglis, T. (2003) *Truth, Power and Lies: Irish Society and the Case of the Kerry Babies*. Dublin: University College Dublin Press.

Irish Bishops' Conference (2004) *Notification on Recent Developments in Moral Theology and Their Implications for the Church and Society*, http://www.catholiccommunications.ie [Accessed 12 October 2004].

Irish Catholic Bishops' Committee on Bioethics (2001) Assisted Human Reproduction: Facts and Ethical Issues. [on line] <http://www.healthcare-ethics.ie/ahr.html> [Accessed 24 September 2004].

Irish Catholic Bishops' Committee on Bioethics (2003) Catholic Bishops' Letter to Taoiseach on Embryonic Stem Cell Research. [on line] <http://www.healthcare-ethics.ie/irlstemcells.html> [Accessed 24 September 2004].

Lane, D.A. (2004) Vatican II: the Irish experience, *The Furrow*, February, 67–81.

Le Bris, S. (1993) *National Ethics Bodies*. Strasbourg: Council of Europe.

Lee, J.J. (1989) *Ireland 1912–1985: Politics and Society*. Cambridge: Cambridge University Press.

Manning, P. and Smith, D. (2002) The establishment of a hospital clinical ethics committee, *The Irish Medical Journal* [on line], 95, 2. Available from:<http://www.imj.ie> [Accessed 2 March 2005].

McDonnell, O. (2001) New Reproductive Technologies and Public Discourse: From Biopolitics to Bioethics. Unpublished Ph.D. thesis. University College Cork.

McKeown, D. (2003) A changing church in a changing culture, *The Furrow*, May, 259–269.

Medical Council (1998) *Constitutions and Functions: a Guide to Ethical Conduct and Behaviour to Practice*, 5th Edition. Dublin: Medical Council.

Medical Council (2004) *Constitutions and Functions: a Guide to Ethical Conduct and Behaviour to Practice*, 6th Edition. Dublin: Medical Council.

O'Carroll, J.P. (1991) Bishops, knights – and pawns? Traditional thought and the Irish Abortion Referendum debate of 1983, *Irish Political Studies*, 6, 53–71.

Parliamentary Debates, Seanad Éireann (7 July 1999) Regulation of Assisted Human Reproduction Bill, 1999. Second Stage. [on line] http://www.gov.ie/debates-99/s7u99/sect5.htm [Accessed 29 November 2004].

Parliamentary Debates, Joint Committee on Health and Children (21 July; 15 September 2005) [on line] http://debates.oireachtas.ie [Accessed 25 September 2005].

Peillon, M. (2001) *Welfare in Ireland: Actors, Resources, and Strategies.* Westport, Connecticut: Praeger.

Smith, D. (1996) *Life and Morality: Contemporary Medico-Moral Issues.* Dublin: Gill and Macmillan.

Smyth, L. (2005) *Abortion and Nation: the Politics of Reproduction in Contemporary Ireland.* Hants: Ashgate.

Tong, R. (1996) Feminist approaches to bioethics. In Wolf, S. (ed.) *Feminism and Bioethics: Beyond Reproduction.* Oxford: Oxford University Press.

Twomey, D.V. (2003) *The End of Irish Catholicism.* Dublin: Veritas.

Whyte, J.H. (1980) *Church and State in Modern Ireland 1923–1979,* 2nd Edition. Dublin: Gill and Macmillan.

Wren, M-A. (2003) *Unhealthy State: Anatomy of a Sick Society.* Dublin: New Island.

11

Taking sociology seriously: a new approach to the bioethical problems of infectious disease

Mark Tausig, Michael J. Selgelid, Sree Subedi and Janardan Subedi

Introduction

After decades of neglect, bioethicists have begun to address the problem of infectious disease (Smith *et al.* 2004, Farmer and Campos 2004, Selgelid 2005, Francis *et al.* 2004, 2005). These preliminary forays into the ethical problems posed by infectious disease focus on several issues: (1) the severe consequences of infectious disease both in the past and, with the threat of avian flu and drug resistance looming, in the future; (2) the difficulty of implementing infectious disease control measures (such as quarantine) while preserving human rights; (3) the potential for infectious diseases to promote stigmatisation, panic and emotionally driven (policy) decision-making; and (4) the justice issues raised by the relation between poverty and infectious disease. When compared to the topics of abortion, euthanasia, genetics, cloning and stem cell research, however, bioethical attention to infectious disease remains in its infancy.

We believe that the bioethical questions raised by infectious disease present the opportunity to develop a new approach to the resolution of the ethical quandaries, not just of communicable disease, but of medicine and the life sciences. Our approach, which draws from the insights afforded by social science, fits well with the interdisciplinary tradition of bioethics. In the following pages we show how the work of bioethics can be broadened and improved by taking medical sociology seriously.

Bioethics and infectious disease

With the important exception of HIV/AIDS, infectious disease, until very recently, for the most part got 'left out' of bioethics. Francis and her colleagues (2005) describe the extent to which infectious disease has been absent in standard bioethics texts, and our internet searches offer further evidence of the paucity of bioethics work in this area. A *PubMed* search of titles and abstracts (conducted in May 2004)[1] for the terms 'ethics' and 'infectious disease' yielded a total of 195 citations; 'ethics' and 'AIDS' yielded 2,617; while 'ethics' and 'tuberculosis' yielded only 130, despite the fact that tuberculosis kills almost as many people as AIDS each year. 'Ethics' and 'genetics', in the meanwhile, yielded 8,400 citations; 'ethics' and 'euthanasia' yielded 8,288; 'ethics' and 'abortion' yielded 4,000. Although this kind of search is crude, the results are powerful and corroborate the notion that bioethics has paid relatively little attention to infectious disease.

As this citation search suggests, infectious diseases have not been *entirely* ignored by bioethicists. AIDS, for example, *has* received high profile attention in the bioethics literature. This coverage, however, has been limited in scope, extent and quality. Most early attention, which arose with the advent of AIDS, focused on doctor-patient relationship issues such as confidentiality, the ethics of mandatory testing and physicians' 'duty to treat' patients with AIDS (in spite of their fear of contagion). With regard to AIDS in developing countries, most of the attention has focused on international *research ethics* and the 'standards of care' debate in particular (*i.e.* the question of what should count as an ethically acceptable control arm in research involving human subjects) (see, for example, Schuklenk 2000). This latter debate has focused on controversial placebo-controlled studies (aimed at the prophylactic prevention of mother-to-child transmission of HIV in developing countries) that conflicted with the Declaration of Helsinki requirement that subjects in the control-arm should receive the 'best proven' or 'best current' treatment for their condition. Bioethics has otherwise paid surprisingly little attention to the overall justice of the healthcare situation in developing countries with regard to HIV and other infectious diseases, such as tuberculosis and malaria. An exception, however, is the growing body of bioethics literature addressing concerns that intellectual property rights in pharmaceuticals pose barriers of access to existing medicines and provide insufficient incentive for innovation in medicine (Schuklenk *et al.* 2002, Cohen *et al.* 2003, Sterckx 2004, Pogge 2005).

Increasing *public* attention to the problem of infectious disease – related to fears about bioterrorism, recent experience with SARS, the threat of a new flu pandemic, the growing danger of drug resistance, and the general increase in emerging infectious diseases during recent decades – suggests that bioethics can no longer afford to neglect this area. Indeed, there are several signs that bioethics is finally giving more attention to the topic of infectious disease, including the relatively new journal *Developing World Bioethics* (established in 2001), the recent appearance of a special edition of *Bioethics* on Ethical Issues in Infectious Disease (August 2005), and a growing interest in ethics and public health, illustrated by a number of books (Coughlin *et al.* 1998, Beauchamp and Steinbock 1999, Gostin 2002, Boylan 2004) and a special edition of *Bioethics* on Ethics and Public Health (November 2004). Since infectious diseases were primarily a problem for poor and developing nations during most of the second half of the 20th century, it was easy for bioethicists, most of whom work in the first world, to relegate them as 'problems of the other' and to focus on issues of more obvious domestic concern (Selgelid 2005). Now, with infectious diseases again clearly threatening rich and poor countries alike, and with the requisite rethinking of international healthcare distribution and public health measures, infectious disease has found a place on the bioethics agenda.

The social sciences have much to offer bioethics as it turns its attention to infectious disease and associated questions of justice. First, the ethical issues relating to infectious disease require a broader engagement with social sciences – such as history, anthropology, sociology, political science and economics – than is typical for a philosophically-oriented bioethics (Farmer and Campos 2004). Appreciation of the (in)justice of the infectious disease situation in developing countries requires empirical understanding of the causes and consequences of infectious diseases, an understanding that the social sciences are prepared to offer (Selgelid 2004, 2005). Second, we believe that the capacity for dealing with the bioethical problems of infectious disease will be enhanced by a shift away from the biomedical model toward a sociological model of disease causation that shows how the structures of society are related to health and healthcare outcomes.

Justice and the empirical facts

HIV/AIDS, tuberculosis and malaria together kill roughly six million people each year, primarily in developing countries. Of the approximately 40 million people currently infected with HIV, two-thirds live in Africa and 95 per cent reside in developing countries. While some may be tempted to think that AIDS' heavy toll in impoverished countries is somehow the fault of the individuals affected (a product of promiscuous sexual practices or reckless drug use, for example) or a matter of misfortune rather than injustice, the social scientific study of AIDS reveals that things are not so simple (see Webb 1997, Marias 2000, Whiteside and Sunter 2000, Barnett and Whiteside 2002, Farmer 1999, Farmer and Campos 2004, Farmer 2003, Hunter 2003). AIDS takes a heavy toll on the African poor because: (1) they lack good nutrition, which weakens their immune systems and increases chances of infection; (2) they lack options with regard to ways of making a living (and so women are pressured into prostitution and men must work in mines remote from their families and marital partners); (3) women are disempowered and have little control in sexual practices with male partners; (4) young women are often sexually abused by older males; (5) education, and thus public understanding of diseases like AIDS, is limited; and (6) life is generally so hard that fatalistic behaviour is common – and thus even those who are aware of the risk of AIDS are often undaunted, as a disease that might kill one 10 years from now is not any more frightening than risks that one faces on a daily basis.

While these factors increase the risk of infection with HIV, matters are made worse because of a vicious cycle of poverty and disease: the poor are unable to afford expensive AIDS medications; their weakened immune systems allow AIDS to progress with greater speed and severity; and their illness and death further compound the poverty of their families and contribute to the poverty of their communities. The poverty and disempowerment driving this cycle of disease in Africa is a product of a long history involving slavery, colonialism, racism, exploitation, and (in the case of South Africa, home to more HIV-infected individuals than any other country in the world) apartheid (Barnett and Whiteside 2002, Hunter 2003).

Like the causes of HIV/AIDS in Africa, the likely consequences of the disease – for developing and developed countries alike – are also extremely complex and relevant to justice. HIV threatens entire societies with collapse, and the current situation in sub-Saharan Africa may follow in parts of Asia and the former Soviet Union. Instability in affected regions, meanwhile, has serious health, economic and security implications for both wealthy and poor nations (National Intelligence Council 2000).

In less dramatic fashion but with equal importance, we must consider the *non-epidemic* prevalence of infectious disease in poor countries. Indeed, the illness burden of poor populations in developing countries is routinely defined in terms of all diseases, not just those that are epidemic (Murray and Lopez 1996). As a case in point we might consider the health conditions found in rural villages in Nepal (Subedi *et al.* 2000). The most prevalent health problems found in these villages include gastrointestinal, respiratory and genitourinary infections, and pelvic inflammatory disease. The life expectancy in Nepal is 58 years and infant mortality ranges from 100–115 per thousand – compared to 7–9 in the United States.

High rates of infection in the developing world are directly attributable to contextual factors such as contaminated water supplies, non-existent sanitary systems and the absence of modern healthcare resources. The typical villager in Nepal occupies a single-story two-room hut constructed of mud and brick with a dirt floor and an animal shed attached. Human-animal interaction is close. The rooms are crowded with multiple generations. There is no ventilation system and an open hearth is used for cooking and heat. The house is not insulated. There is no indoor lavatory and family members often use the latrine without wearing shoes. The water supply is routinely contaminated with faeces. The family diet lacks protein and micronutrients. There is no modern healthcare available except by travelling on foot for days. Infectious disease is a normal experience in such a setting but, as medical sociologists have long known, the high rates of disease are *not* attributable to individual health behaviours. Rather, they reflect the poverty of the socio-economic-biological environment (Subedi *et al.* 2000).

As bioethicists begin their systematic analysis of the ethical dimensions of infectious disease and health problems in developing countries, they will find the insights of the social sciences to be invaluable. In particular, the sociological explanation for illness will provide a richer and more appropriate framework for the study of these bioethical issues than the widely used (or presumed) biomedical model.

Because it does not capture the broader causes and consequences of health and medical care, the biomedical model of health and illness is of limited value in explaining the origin, treatment and prevention of infectious disease. In fact, the limited attention given infectious disease by bioethics may well be the result of the absence of an adequate understanding of the scope of the problem and, therefore, its ethical dimensions (Fox 1989). The link between poverty and infectious disease, for example, cannot be sufficiently explained by biomedicine. Understanding this link requires consideration of the origins of poverty and the poverty-related social mechanisms that increase exposure and vulnerability to infectious diseases. Those who adopt the broader, sociological perspective see issues of social justice that are otherwise not apparent. Indeed, as Fox argues, bioethics as a discipline has been disinclined to grapple with the relationship between poverty and illness because poverty is regarded as a *social* rather than an *ethical* issue.

Accounting for infectious disease

Critiques of the biomedical model are familiar (see, for example, Gordon 1988, Fee and Krieger 1993, Link and Phelan 1995). Gordon (1988) identifies two core presumptions of modern biomedicine that we regard as most germane to our argument. Biomedicine assumes: (1) that illness is located in the individual and (2) that nature is separate from the social order. The presumption that illness is located in the individual has, in fact, been linked to failures to adequately address public health policy (Fee and Krieger 1993, Porter *et al.* 1999, Smith *et al.* 2004). Porter, Ogden and Pronyk (1999) suggest that the emphasis on illness as an individual experience leads policy makers to develop 'micro' policies that address specific diseases at an individual, clinical level. They also argue that these policies are ineffective for dealing with the true character of infectious diseases such as AIDS or multi-drug-resistant tuberculosis (MDRTB).

Bioethics typically focuses on clinical relationships, reproducing the individualistic presumption of biomedicine that is focused on specific patients whose disease or disorder is explained by personal conditions (genetics, lifestyle, choices, etc.). Individualism as a moral value is a cardinal principle of bioethical thinking; this is partly illustrated by the high priority so often placed on 'autonomy' in bioethics discourse (Wolpe 1998, Francis *et al.* 2005). As a result, when ethical issues related to infectious disease and disease in developing countries are addressed, there is still an attempt to separate biomedical research from the 'unjust conditions where the research is con-ducted' (CIOMS 2002). In effect, this reinforces the notion that nature and society are two distinct spheres. Policy analysts, researchers and, lately, even some ethicists, have called for a disease model that takes into account the real conditions of people's lives and the social and material bases of disease transmission (Smith *et al.* 2004, Porter *et al.* 1999, Fee and Krieger 1993).

Most public health models are attentive to the social contexts of illness, and yet they are not sufficient for understanding disease causation and its implications for bioethics. While public health models recognise the environment as a source of disease (risk), the 'socio-medical' approach they offer is based on epidemiological studies that associate disease with specific segments of the population or behaviours. The focus remains on *individual* risk, *single* vectors, and policies aimed at controlling a *specific* source of illness (Porter *et al.* 1999, Potvin *et al.* 2005). Public health models do raise bioethical issues regarding the relationship between contagion and personal liberty, but they remain focused on individuals and the population-based strategies aimed at reducing *individual* risk. They are not adequate for explaining how macro-structural conditions affect general exposure to infectious disease (*i.e.* create risk). Public-health-inspired community interventions often lead to significant health improvements, but they do not dissolve class differences in morbidity and mortality (relative risk).

The sociological explanation for illness

Because the sociological model of illness does a better job of explaining the origins of infectious disease and the capacity to respond to illness, it makes the ethical issues related to infectious disease more apparent. Epidemiological studies often point to differences in mortality and morbidity that are linked to social factors such as socio-economic status, race/ethnicity and gender. Lacking a theoretical framework, however, these studies are of limited use (Potvin *et al.* 2005). We need a theory that links social conditions and health/infectious disease at the structural level rather than at an individual – or even aggregated individual – level (Farmer 1999, 2003, Farmer and Campos 2004, Robert and Smith 2004). Medical sociologists have developed an account of illness that offers a structural explanation of disease. When we recognise that social structure actually causes illness (creates risk), we are able to see the otherwise invisible connection between illness and society. The fact that tremendous differences in material resources between rich and poor countries are mirrored by equally large disparities in mortality and morbidity suggests that material conditions are central to explanations of illness. Awareness of this is crucial to the development of bioethical principles.

The sociological explanation for illness starts not with individual biologic capacity but with observations about the structured risk of biologic disruption. For example, the sociological explanation for why poor people have higher mortality and morbidity points to the ways a shared social status affects exposure to health risks and the ability to deal with those risks. Most physicians are aware that rates of illness and mortality vary by socioeconomic status, ethnicity and gender. The socio-medical (public health) interpretation of these differences is that they are related to differences in genetic characteristics and health behaviours such as diet, exercise, cigarette smoking and other lifestyle choices that vary by class, ethnicity and gender. Factors such as socioeconomic status are correlated with mortality and morbidity simply because people's lifestyles differ by socioeconomic levels. This is a useful *first* step, but it is a limited explanation of the relationship between social structure and illness because it does not recognise that social status differences in and of themselves cause disease.

The sociological perspective views socioeconomic status differences as considerably more than mere variations in lifestyle. Socioeconomic status reflects broad access to resources such as money, knowledge, prestige, power and beneficial social connections that enable individuals to avoid risks (including health risks) and to deal with adversity when it occurs (Phelan *et al.* 2004, Link and Phelan 1995). And, as risk factors change, persons in better socioeconomic positions are better able to adjust to changing conditions. When the association between smoking and lung cancer became known, for example, reductions in smoking were more immediate and significant in upper socioeconomic strata. Hence, those who were already in better possession of resources were able to take advantage of the new information to protect their health. Public health models are partial reflections of this observation. At any given historical moment, the social, economic and physical environmental conditions that more directly cause an illness may be modified to reduce the incidence of new cases. It is however notable that public health programmes, while they have reduced mortality and morbidity for many diseases, have not eliminated the 'social gradient' related to mortality and morbidity. Socio-economically-disadvantaged groups still have higher rates of morbidity and mortality despite public health programmes.

The sociological explanation for illness, then, emphasises the effects of socioeconomic differences in resource possession as a causal factor in health and illness. Its application in very poor countries as an explanation of health status relative to richer countries is thus evident. Health statistics at the national level show the gross differences in mortality and morbidity between rich and poor countries. Poor countries face different levels of risk and have different access to health-protective resources than rich nations in part because they are embedded in a political-economic world-system. This perspective places political-economic critiques of global resource distributions, and criticism based on the higher and qualitatively different disease burdens in poor countries, within a common framework of international and internal socio-economic structure. Wilkinson (1992, 1994) and Kennedy *et al.* (1996) have shown that income inequality across countries affects relative mortality and morbidity.

But we cannot stop our analysis at the level of inter-national differences. The explanation applies within countries as well. Income inequality directly affects access to personal resources including education, housing and nutrition – factors that affect exposure to health risks. In addition, the social distribution of resources includes the distribution of infrastructure resources such as safe drinking water, electricity, schools, healthcare and health providers, and economic opportunity. Each of these factors has been identified previously as a factor related to individual and population health. What the sociological explanation provides is an underlying connection based on the idea that these resources are allocated unevenly across and within societies based on stratification systems. Indeed, Link and Phelan (1995) call social conditions 'fundamental' causes of illness because, even if a disease-specific causal mechanism is altered (say by improving the quality of the food supply to eliminate nutrition-related disorders), the social gradient that was associated with risk of nutrition-related disorders will remain and will be associated with other illness via other mechanisms of exposure and vulnerability. Social causes of mortality and morbidity are fundamental because they influence multiple-disease outcomes and affect disease outcomes through a number of risk factors. Structural inequalities persist over time, and they involve access to resources that can be used to avoid risk or minimise the consequences of disease once it has occurred (Phelan *et al.* 2004).

The biomedical remedy for exposure to cholera in drinking water is to change the source of drinking water. Public health practitioners will agree with this remedy, but they will go further, pointing out that in order for an individual to *drink* untainted water, she will need a better income and the opportunity to obtain fresh water. But neither of these responses to cholera infection will eliminate the continued threat of infectious disease *unless* it is recognised that exposure and vulnerability to illness are related to social resource differences. It is clear (perhaps clearest in developing countries) that access to income and water is also related to the social distribution of resources and enduring differences in access to those resources based on social status. Incorporating this level of understanding of disease causation makes it easier to think about the *bioethical* matters entailed and the kinds of measures required to improve the status quo from an ethical perspective.

Application of the model for a bioethics of infectious disease

In very poor developing countries the normal fabric of daily life exposes individuals to many sources of infectious and other forms of illness. As in our description of life in Nepal, a poor farmer may live in an overcrowded, unventilated house with farm animals, no electricity or fresh water, eating tainted, nutrition-deficient food, using unsanitary toilet facilities. Modern healthcare will be both beyond his means and geographically distant. Moreover, the farmer will not understand how his life chances are affected by these conditions and, even if he did, there would be almost no changes that the farmer could make to improve any of these conditions. The sociological model of illness causation is helpful in understanding the aetiology and pathology of illness in this setting because it allows one to incorporate these daily conditions, borne of social structure and economic conditions, into an illness-causation model. An ethical- or justice-oriented health intervention would clearly need to deal with the impoverished material and social position of the farmer – an outcome not apparent using a biomedical model of illness.

Our sociological model allows us to specify areas in which bioethical principles need to be developed, especially regarding infectious disease in very poor countries. A bioethics derived from our model will focus on distributive justice and benefits measured at the population level (Bhutta 2002, Macklin 2001, Laurell and Arellano 2000, Kidanemariam 1995). In sociological models of illness, illness is a *normal* consequence of the organisation of social resources. This means that bioethical principles must account for the role that social organisation plays in determining health status, including the important but rarely acknowledged role of political-economic arrangements.

Two useful principles follow from our analysis. The first is that risks, benefits, and equity must be defined in terms of the international, national and local contexts and not just in terms of individual health. The sociological model makes it evident that health conditions originate in socio-economic conditions that need to be 'treated' to have an impact on the health status of individuals. Related to this first principle is a second: the need for a less restricted conception of the distribution of benefits that can account for the poverty of national and local healthcare systems as a function of social structure. At its core, the value of a sociological explanation of illness for bioethics lies in its implications for addressing the problem of justice. '[I]f we do not understand the broader social factors that are responsible for generating or exacerbating the health needs of developing world populations, we are unlikely to attend to the root causes of a community's health problems' (London 2005: 28).

Conclusion

We are convinced that a bioethics of infectious disease will benefit from adopting a sociological explanation of illness. Infectious diseases warrant more attention from bioethics because their consequences are so severe, because they raise difficult ethical/philosophical questions of their own, and because they are intertwined with issues of justice. As bioethicists begin sustained analysis of the problems posed by infectious disease, it is important that they recognise the limitations of a biomedical model of disease causation. A sociological model of disease causation recognises infectious disease as an issue of justice (and thus bioethics) and allows the formulation of bioethics principles appropriate to the contexts in which infectious diseases thrive.

Will bioethics embrace the topic of infectious disease as one of its core topics? While we celebrate the recent attention given to infectious disease by bioethicists, we are aware that obstacles to a thorough-going bioethics of infectious disease remain. Some scholars argue that bioethics suffers from a low level of rigour because bioethics discourse requires expertise in both ethics/philosophy and biomedical science. This difficulty is compounded in the context of infectious disease where rigorous discourse also requires an in-depth understanding of social science (Selgelid 2005). It remains to be seen whether or not bioethics educational institutions – so heavily dominated by philosophy and first-world universities – are up to the task of incorporating social sciences and developing world perspectives more deeply into their curricula.

Note

1   This search was done by our colleague, Kathleen Montgomery.

References

Barnett, T. and Whiteside, A. (2002) *AIDS in the Twenty-first Century: Disease and Globalisation*. New York: Palgrave Macmillan.

Beauchamp, D.E. and Steinbock, B. (1999) *New Ethics for the Public's Health*. New York: Oxford University Press.

Bhutta, Z.A. (2002) Ethics in international health research: a perspective from the developing world, *Bulletin of the World Health Organization*, 80, 114–20.

Boylan, M. (ed.) (2004) *Public Health Policy and Ethics*. Kluwer: Dordrecht.

Central Intelligence Agency (2003) Our darker bioweapons future. Available at http://www.fas.org/irp/cia/product/bw1103.pdf. [Accessed 15 January 2007].

CIOMS (Council for International Organizations of Medical Sciences) (2002) *International Ethical Guidelines for Biomedical Research Involving Human Subjects*. Geneva: CIOMS.

Cohen, C.J. and Illingworth P. (2003) The dilemma of intellectual property rights for pharmaceuticals: the tension between ensuring access of the poor to medicines and committing to international agreements, *Developing World Bioethics*, 3, 1, 27–48.

Coughlin, S.S., Soskolne, C.L. and Goodman, K.W. (eds) (1998) *Case Studies in Public Health Ethics*. Washington D.C.: American Public Health Association.

Farmer, P. (1999) *Infections and Inequalities: the Modern Plagues*. Berkeley, CA: University of California Press.

Farmer, P. (2003) *Pathologies of Power: Health, Human Rights, and the New War on the Poor*. Berkeley, CA: University of California Press.

Farmer, P. and Gastineau Campos, N. (2004) Rethinking medical ethics: a view from below, *Developing World Bioethics*, 4, 1, 17–41.

Fee, E. and Krieger, N. (1993) Understanding AIDS: historical interpretations and the limits of biomedical individualism, *American Journal of Public Health*, 83, 10, 1477–86.

Fox, R.C. (1989) *The Sociology of Medicine*. Englewood Cliffs, NJ: Prentice-Hall.

Francis, L.P., Battin, M.P., Botkin, J., Jacobson, J. and Smith, C. (2004) Research ethics and infectious disease: the moral significance of communicability. World Congress of the International Association of Bioethics, Sydney.

Francis, L.P., Battin, M.P., Botkin, J., Jacobson, J. and Smith, C. (2005) How infectious diseases got left out – and what this omission might have meant for bioethics, *Bioethics*, 19, 4, 307–22.

Gordon, D. (1988) Tenacious assumptions in western medicine. In Lock, M. and Gordon, D. (eds). *Biomedicine Examined*. The Netherlands: Kluwer Academic Publishers.

Gostin, L. (ed.) (2002) *Public Health Law and Ethics*. Berkeley, CA: University of California Press.

Hunter, S. (2003) *Black Death: AIDS in Africa*. New York: Palgrave Macmillan.

Kennedy, B., Kawachi, I. and Prothrow-Stith, D. (1996) Income distribution and mortality: cross-sectional ecological study of the Robin Hood index in the United States, *British Medical Journal*, 312, 1004–7.

Kidanemariam, A. (1995) Health and development in the third world: the political economy of infant mortality in Brazil. In Gallagher, E.B. and Subedi, J. (eds) *Global Perspectives on Health Care*. Englewood Cliffs, NJ: Prentice Hall.

Laurell, A.C. and Arellano, O.L. (2000) Market commodities and poor relief: the World Bank proposal for health. In Navarro, V. (ed.) *The Political Economy of Social Inequalities: Consequences for Health and Quality of Life*. Amityville, NY: Baywood Publishing.

Link, B.G. and Phelan, J.C. (1995) Social conditions as fundamental causes of disease, *Journal of Health and Social Behavior* (Special issue), 80–94.

London, A.J. (2005) Justice and the human development approach to international research, *Hastings Center Report*, 35, 24–37.

Macklin, R. (2001) After Helsinki: unresolved issues in international research, *Kennedy Institute of Ethics Journal*, 11, 17–36.

Marias, H. (2000) *To the Edge: AIDS Review 2000*. Pretoria: University of Pretoria, Centre for the Study of AIDS.

Murray, C.J.L. and Lopez, A.D. (eds) (1996) *The Global Burden of Disease: a Comprehensive Assessment of Mortality and Disability from Diseases, Injuries and Risk Factors in 1990 and Projected to 2020*. Cambridge, MA: Harvard School of Public Health, Harvard University Press on behalf of The World Health Organization and The World Bank.

National Intelligence Council (2000) The global infectious disease threat and its implications for the United States. Available at http://www.odci.gov/nic/PDF_GIF_otherprod/infectiousdisease/infectiousdiseases.pdf. [Accessed 10 May 2005.]

Phelan, J.C., Link, B.G., Diez-Roux, A., Kawachi, I. and Levin, B. (2004) 'Fundamental causes' of social inequalities in mortality: test of the theory, *Journal of Health and Social Behavior*, 45, 265–85.

Pogge, T.W. (2005) Human rights and global health: a research program, *Metaphilosophy*, 36, 1/2, 182–209.

Porter, J., Ogden, J. and Pronyk, P. (1999) Infectious disease policy: towards the production of health, *Health Policy and Planning*, 14, 4, 322–8.

Potvin, L., Gendron, S., Bilodeau, A. and Chabot, P. (2005) Integrating social theory into public health practice, *American Journal of Public Health*, 95, 591–5.

Robert, J.S. and Smith, A. (2004) Toxic ethics: environmental genomics and the health of populations, *Bioethics*, 18, 6, 493–514.

Schuklenk, U. (2000) Protecting the vulnerable: testing times for clinical research ethics, *Social Science and Medicine*, 51, 969–77.

Schuklenk, U. and Ashcroft, R.E. (2002) Affordable access to essential medication in developing countries: conflicts between ethical and economic imperatives, *Journal of Medicine and Philosophy*, 27, 2, 179–95.

Selgelid, M.J. (2004) Ethics, economics and AIDS in Africa, *Developing World Bioethics*, 4, 1, 96–105.

Selgelid, M.J. (2005) Ethics and infectious disease, *Bioethics*, 19, 3, 272–89.

Smith, C.B., Battin, M.P., Jacobson, J.A., Francis, L.P., Botkin, J.B., Asplund, E.P., Domek, G.J. and Hawkins, B. (2004) Are there characteristics of infectious disease that raise special ethical issues? *Developing World Bioethics*, 4, 1, 1–16.

Sterckx, S. (2004) Patents and access to drugs in developing countries: an ethical analysis, *Developing World Bioethics*, 4, 1, 58–75.

Subedi, J., Subedi, S., Sidky, H., Singh, R., Blangero, J. and Williams-Blangero, S. (2000) Health and health care in Jiri, *Contibutions to Nepalese studies; the Jirel Issue*, January, 97–104.

Webb, D. (1997) *HIV and AIDS in Africa*. London: Pluto Press.

Whiteside, A. and Sunter, C. (2000) *AIDS: The Challenge for South Africa*. Cape Town: Human and Rousseau.

Wilkinson, R.G. (1992) Income distribution and life expectancy, *British Medical Journal*, 304, 165–8.

Wilkinson, R.G. (1994) The epidemiological transition: from material scarcity to social disadvantage? *Daedalus*, 123, 61–77.

Wolpe, P. (1998) The triumph of autonomy in American bioethics: a sociological view. In De Vries, R. and Subedi, J. (eds) *Bioethics and Society: Constructing the Ethical Enterprise*. Upper Saddle River, NJ: Prentice Hall.

12

Biobanks, bioethics and concepts of donated blood in the UK
Helen Busby

Introduction

Recent years have witnessed the emergence of a number of large-scale national and regional genetic biobanks[1]. One irony of this development is that countries with a national health system and comprehensive population health records are of particular interest to commercial organisations, which view such systems as a unique resource that contains valuable, well-characterised data (Fears and Poste 1999). Importantly, in the cases of Iceland, Estonia, and now the UK, this private commercial interest dovetails with national economic strategies aimed at promoting biotechnology as an indispensable component of a modern knowledge economy (Rose 2001, Fletcher 2004, Biotechnology Innovation and Growth Team [BIGT] 2003). Both government planners and biotechnology entrepreneurs envisage public-private partnerships. The eventual success of these ventures depends upon participation of national populations. Citizen participation involves populations of interest donating blood samples and making information about themselves available for use in multiple unspecified research projects over a long-term period. Although in all cases public officials who advocate the development of biobanks expect a significant level of commercial involvement, each national plan has markedly different aims, operational arrangements and regulatory regimes. The development of such biobanks, then, poses new challenges for policy-makers, regulators and the bioethicists who are consulted on questions of public policy[2]. In the face of both a growing awareness of the multinational holdings of such data and the ease of circulating these data, a prominent approach has been to call for the information in biobanks to be treated as 'global public goods' (Human Genome Organisation [HUGO] Ethics Committee 2003)[3].

In this chapter I use an historical approach to understand the framing of policy debates about genetic databases and biobanks in the UK to date. The rationale for analysing a distinctive 'British' approach to these debates is to provide an empirical case to explore Jasanoff's observation that political culture shapes debates about biotechnologies in significant and important, if unappreciated, ways (Jasanoff 2005: 12). An important dimension for understanding 'ethics' involves showing how presumptively 'natural' and taken-for-granted assumptions about the 'right' way to organise biobanks, or for that matter any public good, are embedded within tacit cultural schema, social structures and collectively shared historical narratives.

Blood donation in the UK: social and political landscapes

In Britain, technologies of blood donation are widely accepted, having first been used systematically for the treatment of war casualties. Indeed, blood donation became woven into a myth of nationhood in which altruism and solidarity featured prominently. A blood service organised around the principles associated with the National Health Service (NHS) was established shortly after the foundation of the health service itself (National Blood Authority 1996). The idea of a blood service resonated with these principles and ideals, drawing on images of aristocrats and commoners alike responding to war-time emergencies by queuing to donate blood.

Titmuss' *The Gift Relationship* (1970) portrays a period in which blood donation was conceived of as an altruistic act within a framework of national solidarity. This paradigm continued to hold sway over the following several decades. Ironically, in the clinical and policy literature on blood donation, an interpretation of Titmuss has been taken up that heralds donated blood as an indicator of the altruism of *individual* blood donors. This interpretation transforms a book about the social organisation of health services with particular reference to blood donation into a celebration of individual altruism. This distorted and highly truncated reading of Titmuss continues to be pressed into service in the ongoing policy debates about the nature of biobanks as a national resource (Busby 2004).

Of all the national institutions in the UK, the NHS became a symbol of shared provision for the common good, and has an iconic place in British political life (Page 1996). Just as the political and welfare settlement of the post-war years shaped the history of the NHS, so did it shape the development of a blood service that was famously different from the US commercial market system: blood banks in Britain were to be sustained by the free, unpaid donations of citizens (Oakley 1996). To foreshadow the discussion below, the image of the early years of the blood service shaped the language for policy discussions about the use of donated blood and tissue in subsequent years. As a consequence, formative discussions about the emergence of global markets in the information derived from blood were shaped by associations of gifted blood, that, because of their long history in political discourse in the UK, were arguably even more influential than declarations issued by international organisations.

Meanwhile, despite an unchanging quality of discussions about blood in political arenas, technological developments in the use of blood during the 1970s and 1980s rendered the system almost unrecognisable from the system described by Titmuss. The uptake of technologies for more effective blood testing combined with more stringent selection of donors eroded the notion of universal blood donation (Martlew 1997). Moreover, the notion of a national blood supply was undermined by the practice of importing blood from other nations when required (O'Neill 2003). Finally, the National Blood Service (NBS) that eventually incorporated the precursor local and regional services developed an expanded portfolio of activities that included the banking of a range of human tissues, as well as undertaking research using donated blood. Nevertheless, the trust that donors place in the NBS remains informed by the politically potent cultural image of a national blood bank existing to provide immediate help to NHS patients who encounter accidents or serious illness (Busby 2004). Questions of identity are rarely raised in relation to blood donated in these contexts, nor are the processes of transforming raw blood into blood products seen as problematic. For these reasons amongst others, the uses of blood donated to the NBS have escaped close scrutiny or definition as problematic 'ethical issues'.

The emergence of an 'informational' economy

Historically, in Britain, the act of donating blood provided – or was at least thought to provide – a direct benefit to others in one's community. The management of such blood was a domain outside of and separate from commercial markets. However, the uses to which donated blood are put have diversified throughout the second half of the 20th century. Recent technological developments allow for genetic analyses to be undertaken on a large scale with small samples of blood (Hirztlin *et al.* 2003). Consequently, donated samples have become an immensely valuable resource for both commercial and public health research. The involvement of new commercial actors, notably pharmaceutical companies, has contributed to the emergence of an 'informational economy' within which blood is exploited (Tutton 2002: 537).

At the same time, products derived from donated blood continue to be essential in the treatment of patients following blood loss in serious accidents and acute illnesses. Despite attempts to manufacture synthetic blood, medical treatments still rely on donated blood and other corporeal donations. Blood has become a valuable commercial resource while it remains an irreplaceable public good. The dual nature of blood provides a certain elasticity to the deployment of blood and blood products in public discourse. Policy advocates for development of biobanks find it quite easy to switch registers in their framings – here it is a public good and then in a flash it is a resource to be exploited in the development of the new information economy – blood in political discourse is both priceless and valuable.

Commercial companies have for some time held banks of donated tissue, often from their own clinical trials or from public sources such as hospitals, and there is an established trade in the information derived from such tissue (Lewis 2004). In addition to the development and expansion of commercial tissue banks, population biobanks that draw on data across a regional or national population via public health systems exist in a number of countries. In general, such biobanks propose to obtain broad consent for an unspecified set of studies and for an undefined period of time (Austin *et al.* 2003). In the UK case, the stated rationale for investment in a national biobank is to provide a resource for commercial and public health research (Medical Research Council [MRC] 2002). Although plans to develop a new national biobank have generated only a limited public debate in the UK, the initiative has the potential for considerable controversy, destabilising the consensus about the basis for the state's involvement in blood and tissue banking.

My research focuses on the role of expert bioethics bodies in the intersecting debates about the banking and uses of donated blood and tissues for medical research. In this context, ideas of 'altruism' and gifted blood have been wrenched from the post-war sentiments in which they were sedimented, and now circulate through these debates, providing an apparently unifying reference point to what are, in fact, highly divergent positions.

The development of UK Biobank

For some time, there has been in the UK a number of known collections of tissue and genetic information, most of which are disease specific, and enrol participants through clinicians in contact with patients with the specified disorder. In addition, there is an established national 'blood spot' collection from newborn babies screened for phenylketonuria (PKU)[4]. More recently, several regional collections of genetic data have been established (Chase *et al.* 1998, see also www.alspac.bris.ac.uk). The idea for a national biobank was initially proposed in 1998 when the Medical Research Council (MRC) was given additional funds to establish a DNA collection (Barbour 2003). An expert panel published a report on a DNA collection in March 2000, recommending the creation of two prospective cohort studies, one of middle-aged people, and the other a birth cohort. The idea of studying a cohort of middle-aged people (aged 40–69) has been taken forward on the assumption that as the older cohort aged, the normal morbidity associated with ageing would provide useful data sooner (Barbour 2003). At government level, the project, now known as UK Biobank, is nested within a series of policy initiatives designed to secure a place for the UK in the emerging global knowledge economy. Its sponsors' efforts at consultation and market research notwithstanding, critics argue that a closed circle of decision-makers has prevented the project's scientific rationales and protocols from being subject to open scrutiny and genuine public debate[5].

The UK Biobank recently confirmed that it will recruit its subjects through the NHS. Participating subjects allow access to their health records on an

ongoing basis, answer detailed health and lifestyle questionnaires and provide blood samples. Potential subjects will be asked to give their 'broad
consent' to the use of their tissue and data for public and commercial
research. Potential subjects will consent or refuse to participate in the
Biobank in its entirety, but will not be informed, in advance, of the purpose
of the research for which their samples and data will be used (UK Biobank
2004, Newton 2004). This stipulation adds a dimension of uncertainty and
contingency to the burden of obtaining 'informed consent'[6]. Despite calls for
greater community involvement no plans currently exist to involve donors
or the wider collectivity in discussions about the priorities and boundaries
for the UK biobank (GeneWatch 2003, Kaye 2004, Tutton, Kaye and
Hoeyer 2004, Williams and Shroeder 2004)[7].

Science governance in the UK

No major political or parliamentary debate about the development of a
national biobank in the UK has taken place. Given the absence of a wide-
ranging political debate, experts who have been asked to advise on the development of the UK Biobank have a curious role to play. Selected on the basis
of their expertise in particular fields, they are implicitly being asked to identify
policies acceptable to a wider public. While this is not an unusual role for
bioethicists, it nonetheless conflates the policies that are deemed socially and
politically possible with those that are considered 'acceptable'. The rationale
for adopted policies then becomes hard to locate. What criteria are used to
determine what is socially and politically 'acceptable'? Whose interests are
represented in such determinations? How are conflicts resolved when policies
are acceptable to one group but not another? Because the policy role of the
bioethics adviser substitutes rule by experts for more inclusive democratic
processes, opaqueness replaces transparency in the formulation of policy.

Because many of these expert groups have been only recently established,
analysis of the role they play in British public life is only beginning to emerge.
In the US, where public bioethics bodies have played a more prominent role
in policy-making and agenda-setting, Kelly (2002) has suggested that such bodies
are 'flexible but stable spaces in which scientists and other interested bodies
struggle over the boundaries between science and politics . . .' and called 'for
greater attention to the complex relationship between ethics, science, and
policy in governance' (2003: 357). The 'discursive ambiguity' (Kelly 2003:
357) that Kelly identifies as a feature of ethics advisory bodies in the US has
a parallel in the multivalent notion of gifted blood in the UK.

'Public anxieties over technical change have become a recognised feature
of science and technology policy', in the UK and a number of other European
countries (Irwin 2006). The problem of trust is particularly acute when
issues of human genetics are involved (Jones and Salter 2003: 21). Public
officials have responded to these perceived crises through strategies to

promote public engagement and civic participation at various levels of government. Nonetheless, one area of policy rarely considered within the scope of public participation is the regulation of commercial involvement in research (Kerr 2003). This is so even though new intersections of public information and private enterprise pose new community-level challenges.

In the UK, as elsewhere, the cultural and economic importance of retaining a leading role in the development of biotechnology is a recurrent theme within government and policy debates. Early discussions about a national biobank project referred to innovation, international competitiveness and the UK's place in the global knowledge economy. Advocates for the development of the biobank claimed that partnerships between the NHS and commercial organisations were critical for realising the government's scientific and economic agenda (Gould 2003). The 2003 Genetics White Paper highlights the kind of collaboration sought by government (Department of Health 2003). A recent official report by the Department for Trade and Industry's BIGT, argues for the promotion of clinical research in the UK:

> The NHS is a unique institution globally, providing a gateway to the largest single pool of patients in the world, and caring for those patients from cradle to grave . . . The NHS should be a leader in clinical innovation, with the infrastructure and the expertise to support cutting edge clinical research that improves patient care. Such a capability would provide a significant competitive advantage for the UK bioscience sector, which no other country would be able to match. It would act as a clear incentive for companies to establish themselves in the UK (BIGT 2003: 7).

The aim of keeping 'at the forefront of modern health research and technology' (MRC 2002) encompasses the twin goals of providing health benefits and generating wealth through the biotechnology industry.

Although a view of the NHS as a resource for the national economy is evident in these policy statements, mechanisms for both recognising and then reconciling conflicts with more traditional concepts of welfare have not as yet been addressed. In particular, the implications of deploying the NHS patient population as a 'central resource for an emerging market in genetic information' (Martin 2001: 181) are rarely addressed in these discussions. Nor do the new regulatory and governance frameworks, described below, fully confront the challenges the absorption of patient information into 'novel regimes of ownership, informed consent and privacy' present to balancing commercial with community and individual interests (Brown and Webster 2004: 96, see also Brown and Rappert 2000). In summary, a new agenda for medical research involving extensive public-private collaborations has emerged within a more traditional framework that fails to acknowledge conflicts, tensions and disjunctures between commercial interests and public sector research.

Bodies of experts and the governance of medical research

Traditionally, regulation of medical research in the UK has depended very much on self-regulation by the medical profession (Martin 2001, Hazlegrove 2002). However, the initiative to develop a national UK biobank coincided with a period of change in both the political landscape and the regulation and governance of medical research in the UK. For the NHS itself, this overhaul culminated in a new regulatory framework that replaced a traditional reliance on professional codes of ethics with legal statutory requirements on institutions, including NHS trusts (Department of Health 2001, Kerrison, McNally and Pollock 2003).

Public debate and regulatory innovation surrounding the treatment of genetic data in medical research focused primarily on the 'stuff' of blood or tissue. The conjunction of the early discussions about the biobank with an intense debate about the use of human tissue in medical research, followed and, to some extent, was a consequence of the discovery of the use of organs retained in hospitals and research institutes after post-mortem without relatives' consent (Hansard 2003). The enactment of the amended *Human Tissue Act 2004* can be seen as a compromise between the government's desire to put patients' consent at the heart of the legislation and the research lobby's requirements. By announcing its intention to make the unauthorised use of DNA analysis an offence, the government made a symbolic statement about a new regime in which patients' interests were more explicitly underscored. Meanwhile, a more expansive archiving of NHS patient information, an activity crucial to the biobank project, has attracted less attention. Despite attempts to clarify the legal rules that protect individual medical records, there is a good deal of uncertainty about the new regulatory regime (McHale 2004). For example, how the differing and often competing interests and voices of the various stakeholders in medical research in the UK are to be resolved remains an open question of critical salience.

Unlike some other European countries, the UK has no national bioethics committee. As a result, a shifting, informal ad hoc network of local, national and international expert bodies informs and shapes discussion of developments in the biosciences. National Health Service research ethics committees are primarily concerned with regulating clinical research involving NHS patients and staff. Current guidelines for the review of research protocols do not require consideration of the collective implications of proposed research and it is not clear that an ethics committee has the authority to attempt such a review.

The most prominent of the non-governmental bioethics bodies in the UK, The Nuffield Council, was established in 1991 'to identify, examine and report on the ethical questions raised by recent advances in biological and medical research'. The Nuffield Council subsequently received support and funding from the Wellcome Trust and the MRC. Council members are mostly senior clinicians, lawyers and philosophers. The MRC plays a major role in this policy network if only because it has established behavioural standards that operationalise the ethical guidelines to which its funded researchers must adhere. The MRC is a powerful agent and policy advocate in its own right, proposing guidelines for the use of human tissues in research and lobbying the government on the Human Tissue Bill[8]. Drawing on its position as the major non-governmental funder of medical research in the UK, The Wellcome Trust also plays a significant role in sponsoring conferences that often serve as a first step in articulating frameworks for discussion of research ethics and governance. These organisations distribute intellectual, social, cultural and political capital to experts whose credibility rests on the investments made in them.

Despite this selective and focused investment, an absence of social consensus about biotechnologies in particular and science in general has allowed a proliferation of expert groups in this domain. Amongst these, the Human Genetics Commission (HGC) is the organisation most relevant to this discussion. At the government's request, the HGC has provided advice for and published a number of reports on the use of human genetic information. The HGC has extended its role to include conducting consultations and commissioning surveys on the public perceptions of these issues (HGC 2000, 2002). The task of promoting dialogue with members of the public has fallen to, or been seized by, the HGC, to a greater extent than is typically the case with expert advisory groups in the UK. The HGC is more explicitly involved in negotiating, establishing and reinforcing a consensus in this field (Jones and Salter 2003).

Both the Nuffield Council and the HGC place their advice in the context of the network of international bodies that effectively make up an 'international genre of ethical and social decision-making' (Kerr 2003: 148). Amongst these is the Human Genome Organisation (HUGO) ethics committee, which has published ethical guidelines on genetic research and more specifically on the use of genetic databases (HUGO 1996, 2003). Genetic databases are depicted as 'global public goods' in these guidelines and recommendations are made for benefit sharing. However – as in other areas of bioethics – transactions between individuals are easier to propose and to monitor than those across the wider social fabric. In addition to the difficulties of providing both workable and enforceable operational definitions for benefit sharing, consensus has yet to be reached on international agreements that regulate the commercialisation of human tissue or products derived from it.

Another level of bioethical discussion takes place amongst the bodies advising the European Commission, such as the European Group on Life Sciences and the European Group on Ethics in Science and New Technologies to the European Commission (EGE). As Kerr has noted, the pronouncements, soundings and concrete advice of national and supranational expert bodies commonly restate but do not resolve the key questions raised by public-private partnerships in biotechnology:

The spirit of capitalism involves investment, innovation and
scientific progress for the public good, balanced with the need
to reward individuals and corporations for their inventions
(Kerr 2003: 149).

As with these international discussions, discussions about genetic research
in the UK have taken place against a backdrop of shifting relationships
between commerce and the public sector.

Yet, in Britain, a powerful narrative about the NHS as a central component of the welfare state celebrates the role of that institution in mediating
national identity and, historically, reinforcing a national solidarity. A
counter-narrative that highlights the tensions at play between commercial
interests and the values underlying the NHS is not part of political discourse.
In the context of these shifting relationships the revival of the metaphor of
donated blood as a gift puts a gloss on some very different ideas about how
those relationships should be constituted and governed[9].

Blood and commerce: 'gift' as a mediating concept

Just as donated blood circulates through different contexts, so too does the
trope of 'the gift' as a description of the relationships constituted by the
voluntary donation of blood. The idea of gifted tissue appears in several
phases. First, the Nuffield Council and the MRC published ethical guidelines
on the use of human tissue in medical research. These guidelines became
necessary as a consequence of emerging controversies about the patenting of
genetic information (Nuffield Council 1995, MRC 2001). Initially, the issue
was mainly conceived as one of professional ethics. Next, appeals to patient
altruism served as a basis for discussions addressing the policy frameworks
about the uses of genetic information and genetic databases. These discussions explicitly ask the public to provide help for future generations of NHS
patients. Appeals to professional ethics, on the one hand, and patient altruism,
on the other, are powerful because of the echoes they find in the views of
donors and other members of the public.

The Nuffield Council's report *Human Tissue: Ethical and Legal Issues*
reviewed the ethics of the use of human tissue, including new problems
arising from applications for gene patenting. In summarising its conclusions,
the report refers to the importance of 'the gift relationship' between donors
and recipients, without referencing Titmuss' work directly (Nuffield Council
1995: 68). Similarly implicit reference to Titmuss' work is made in the
MRC's guidelines on the use of human tissue (MRC 2001). Tutton's analysis
of these guidelines places them squarely in the context of commercial interests'
involvement in biomedical research and the public uncertainty surrounding
the acceptability of such involvement (Tutton 2004). Both the MRC and the
Nuffield Council seek to protect human tissue from commodification,

whilst also underscoring the necessity of commercial involvement in research.

If we pursue the proposals for the use of human tissue further, we find that the metaphor of the gift is used to describe the transfer of property. This signification of gift, indicating that tissue, having been freely given, becomes the *property* of the researcher or institutional custodian, is one that was already used in consent forms for research participants. The gift language of professional guidelines formalises an ethical discourse, incorporating while delimiting property rights for the use of tissue. The subsequent distinction between tissues themselves and the information derived from them, begins to allow 'a boundary to be delineated between two economies, that of non-commercial tissue donation complete with a discourse of altruism, and the commercial realm of genetic information that can be transformed into property' (Tutton 2004: 33). If products do eventually come to market as a result of use by commercial companies of a public biobank, these delineations will be extremely important. The Biobank's 'Draft Intellectual Property (IP) Strategy' states that 'intellectual property arising out of research using the resource will vest in the investigator creating it, his or her institution, or in appropriate cases, their assignees' (UK Biobank 2005).

Subsequently, the image of altruistic blood donation, as a 'gift to strangers' was revived in discussions about tissue donation for genetic research in general and proposals for a national biobank in particular. In the House of Lords report on *Human Genetic Databases*, for example, the principle of establishing a national biobank is strongly endorsed, and members of the public are asked to provide help for future generations (House of Lords 2001). The ideal of 'genetic solidarity and altruism' as one of the bases for public policy in this field was subsequently made explicit by the HGC, and reiterated in the Government's *Genetics White Paper* (HGC 2002: 18, Department of Health 2003: 78). References to citizenship and altruism and – again – to the desirability of seeing donated blood as a gift are also featured in industry workshops undertaken by the UK Biobank (UK Biobank 2003). Importantly, these references are echoed in the findings of focus groups with potential participants conducted on behalf of the Biobank (People, Science and Policy 2002: 11).

When we unpack the discourse of patient and donor altruism in the context of the development of a UK biobank, we see that the gift metaphor is not a rhetoric imposed on an unwilling public. Rather, the power of the particular public representations of gifted blood lies in the extent to which they mobilise associations about the NHS and welfare state. However, the invocation of selfless altruism sits uneasily with more politically and historically informed ideas about the NHS, which stress mutual interests as the basis for it and related welfare institutions (Baldwin 1990). Further, it is difficult to find a logical place for them in an information economy where the value of genetic material and data is measured in commercial terms.

Conclusions

Social scientists and ethicists are only now beginning to confront the implications of new inter-relationships between genetic research, commerce and the state. A critical focus for examining these inter-relationships is the formation of national biobanks to promote commercial ventures in genetic research. Whereas some bioethicists in their role as 'legislative intellectuals' focus on policies that are formed to reflect universal principles, social scientists are more concerned with examining the fit between the rhetoric invoking universal principles and the practices – the bundle of tasks, work routines and social accounts – said to reflect these principles (Haimes 2002, Bauman 1992: 11, Bosk 1999). Both bioethicists and social scientists use, although often in different ways, a language that depends upon distinctions between 'public' and 'private', and references to altruistic behaviour and the metaphor of gift. These same terms, when used in policy discussions, often mirror the discourse of bioethicists and social scientists.

As UK Biobank moves towards a more detailed consideration of the policy questions it confronts, invocations of altruism have receded. Nevertheless, the legacy of this approach is contained in many iterations of public policy. In the midst of uncertainty and controversy surrounding contemporary developments in genetic research, the utility of the concept of altruism in a policy context is found in its fluidity. Depending on the context, altruism refers to the generosity of individual donors or to the appropriate response of citizens to promised therapeutic developments in genetic research and to the national commercial benefits that they will provide. The appeal to altruism, however, when combined with the metaphor of donated blood as 'gifted', has come to obscure the choices that are to be made about the organisation and boundaries of a public genetic research biobank. The nostalgic cast of this metaphor has obscured discussion about the research uses of diverse collections of genetic material held by public bodies in the UK, and has limited the scope of formative policy discussions about oversight of the new national biobank.

Acknowledgements

My thanks go to Robert Dingwall and Paul Martin. I would also like to acknowledge a recent doctoral training grant from the Wellcome Trust Biomedical Ethics programme, and the support of a postdoctoral fellowship from the ESRC. Conclusions drawn, however, are my own, and do not represent the views of these organisations.

Notes

1   Population genetic biobanks hold data and tissue samples for very large numbers of people, selected on demographic criteria from the members of a regional or national population (Austin *et al.* 2003, Kaye 2004).

2   Increasingly, an analysis of the ethics of blood donation and of the collection of genetic material must take account of global flows in the circulation and exchange of such material and related data (Parry 2004). However, this paper cannot describe the global flows of such data, not only because of limitations of space, but also because further empirical work is needed to track these flows.

3   My own view is that national biobank projects enrol participants through reference to an imagined national community (Busby and Martin 2006, with reference to Anderson [1991]). I have therefore advocated that their organisational hosts and sponsors pay more attention to the question of ethical and geographic boundaries than has been done to date, and explore the acceptable limits of commercial exploitation of genetic data amongst these communities (Busby 2004).

4   The PKU screening programme began in the 1960s, and was extended to a national programme in which blood spot cards were stored. These small blood samples are routinely held for five years, with a consultation underway about a further extension of storage and research use (Oliver *et al.* 2005).

5   See Wallace (2002), and the reply by Radda *et al.* (2002). The scientific and ethical peer reviews were subsequently made public after the GeneWatch group called for their release under the Freedom of Information Act. These reviews can now be seen on the MRC's website at <www.mrc.ac.uk/strategy-biobank> (Accessed November 2005).

6   Longstanding critiques of informed consent, *i.c.*, as a pillar of ethical relations between researchers and human subjects, are to some extent complicated by this notion of broad consent. Those opposing *i.c.* on the grounds that it is difficult, impossible or burdensome for individuals to assess information about research projects, might conceivably find comfort in the notion of broad consent. The issue of *i.c.* has been discussed extensively. See, for example, Wolpe (1998) on the trajectory and application of the principle of autonomy and its analogue in American bioethics; Corrigan (2003) for a recent critique of the positions taken in the UK, and Kaye (2004) for a specific critique of the application of 'broad consent' in the context of UK Biobank.

7   An Ethics and Governance Advisory Council is charged with advising on the compliance of its own Ethics and Governance Framework, and 'more generally on operating in accordance with the interests of participants and the general public'. (www.ukbiobank.ac.uk/ethics)

8   The Bill as originally conceived involved a degree of emphasis on patient consent which was seen to compromise the interests of the research community. See Hansard (2003).

9   I draw here on the idea of a 'mobilising metaphor', developed by Shore and Wright in their work on the language of policy and the construction of legitimacy (Shore and Wright 1997: 20).

References

Anderson, B. (1991) *Imagined Communities*. London: Verso.

Austin, M., Harding, S. and McElroy, C. (2003) Monitoring ethical, legal, and social issues in developing population genetic databases, *Genetics in Medicine*, 5, 6, 451–7.

Baldwin, P. (1990) *The Politics of Social Solidarity*. Cambridge: Cambridge University Press.

Barbour, V. (2003) UK Biobank: a project in search of a protocol? *The Lancet*, 361, 1734–8.

Bauman, Z. (1992) Legislators and interpreters: culture as the ideology of intellectuals. In Bauman, Z. *Intimations of Postmodernity*. London: Routledge.

Biotechnology Innovation and Growth Team (2003) *Bioscience 2015: Improving National Health, Increasing National Wealth*. http://www.dti.gov.uk/bio-igt/downloads.html. Department for Trade and Industry.

Bosk, C.L. (1999) Professional ethicist available: logical, secular, friendly, *Daedalus*, 128, 47–68.

Brown, N. and Rappert, B. (2000) Emerging bioinformatic networks: contesting the public meaning of private and the private meaning of public, *Prometheus*, 18, 437–52.

Brown, N. and Webster, A. (2004) *New Medical Technologies and Society: Reordering Life*. Cambridge: Polity Press.

Busby, H. (2004) *Reassessing the 'gift relationship': exploring the meaning and ethics of blood donation for genetic research*. PhD Thesis: University of Nottingham.

Busby, H. and Martin, P. (2006) National Biobanks and imagined communities: the case of UK Biobank, *Science as Culture*, 15, 3, 237–51.

Chase, D., Tawn, E., Parker, L., Jonas, P. and Burn, J. (1998) The North Cumbria Community Genetics Project, *Journal of Medical Genetics*, 35, 413–16.

Corrigan, O. (2003) Empty ethics: the problem with informed consent, *Sociology of Health and Illness*, 25, 3, 768–92.

Department of Health (2001) *Department of Health Research Governance Framework for Health and Social Care*. London: Department of Health.

Department of Health (2003) *Our Inheritance, our Future: Realising the Potential of Genetics in the NHS*. HMSO (Cm 5791-II).

Fears, R. and Poste, G. (1999) Building population genetics resources using the UK NHS, *Science*, 284, 267–8.

Fletcher, A. (2004) Field of genes: the politics of science and identity in the Estonian gene project, *New Genetics and Society*, 23, 1, 3–14.

GeneWatch UK (2003) Main ethical questions about genetic sampling sidelined in biotech industry's favour: GeneWatch UK response to UK Biobank 'Ethics and Governance Framework' (Press Release). <www.genewatchuk.org/press> (accessed 10/11/2005)

Gould, M. (2003) Group calls for agency to boost UK bioscience industry, *British Medical Journal*, 237, 1183.

Haimes, E. (2002) What can the social sciences contribute to the study of ethics? Theoretical, empirical and substantive contributions, *Bioethics*, 16, 2, 89–113.

Hansard (2003) Human Tissue Bill explanatory notes. http://www.parliament. the-stationery-office.co.uk/pa/cm200304/cmbills/009/en/04009x–.htm. London: The Stationery Office.

Hazelgrove, J. (2002) The old faith and the new science: the Nuremberg code and human experimentation ethics in Britain, 1946–73, *Social History of Medicine*, 15, 1, 109–35.

Hirtzlin, I., Dubreuil, C., Preaubert, N., Duchier, J. *et al.* (2003) An empirical survey on biobanking of human genetic material and data in six EU countries, *European Journal of Human Genetics*, Vol 11, 475–88.

House of Lords (2001) *Fourth Report of the Select Committee on Science and Technology: Human Genetic Databases: Challenges and Opportunities.* London: HMSO.

Human Genetics Commission (2000) *Whose Hands on your Genes? A Discussion Document on the Storage, Protection and Use of Personal Information (Consultation document).* London: Human Genetics Commission.

Human Genetics Commission (2002) *Inside Information: Balancing Interests in the Use of Personal Genetic Data.* London: Human Genetics Commission.

HUGO (Human Genome Organisation) Ethics Committee (1996) Statement on the principled conduct of genetic research. Reprinted in *Bioethics*, 1, 1, 32–3.

HUGO (Human Genome Organisation) Ethics Committee (2003) Statement on Human Genetic Databases. Reprinted in *Bioethics*, 1, 1, 38–9.

Irwin, A. (2006) The politics of talk: coming to terms with the 'new' scientific governance, *Social Studies of Science*, 36, 2, 299–320.

Jasanoff, S. (2005) *Designs on Nature: Science and Democracy in Europe and the United States.* Princeton: Princeton University Press.

Jones, M. and Salter, B. (2003) The governance of human genetics: policy discourse and constructions of public trust, *New Genetics and Society*, 22, 1, 21–41.

Kaye, J. (2004) Abandoning informed consent: the case of genetic research in population collections. In Tutton, R. and Corrigan, O. (eds) *Genetic Databases: Socio-ethical Issues in the Collection and Use of DNA.* London: Routledge.

Kelly, S. (2003) Public bioethics and publics: consensus, boundaries, and participation in biomedical science policy, *Science, Technology and Human Values*, 28, 3, 339–64.

Kerr, A. (2003) Governing genetics: reifying choice and progress, *New Genetics and Society*, 22, 2, 143–58.

Kerrison, S., McNally, N. and Pollock, A. (2003) United Kingdom research government strategy, *British Medical Journal*, 327, 553–6.

Knoppers, B.M. (2005) Biobanking: international norms, *The Journal of Law, Medicine and Ethics*, 33, 1, 7–14.

Lewis, G. (2004) Tissue collection and the pharmaceutical industry. In Tutton, R. and Corrigan, O. (eds) *Genetic Databases: Socio-ethical Issues in the Collection and Use of DNA.* London: Routledge.

Martin, P. (2001) Genetic governance: the risks, oversight and regulation of genetic databases in the UK, *New Genetics and Society*, 20, 2, 157–83.

Martlew, V. (1997) Transfusion medicine towards the millennium. In Oakley, A. and Ashton, J. (eds) *The Gift Relationship: from Human Blood to Social Policy, by Richard Titmuss.* London: LSE Press.

McHale, J. (2004) Regulating genetic databases: some legal and ethical issues, *Medical Law Review*, 12, 1, 70–96.

Medical Research Council (2001) *Human tissue and biological samples for use in research: operational and ethical guidelines.* London: MRC.

Medical Research Council (2002) The UK Biobank study gets funding go-ahead. http://www.mrc.ac.uk/index/public-interest/public-news-4/public-news_archive/public-news_archive_1_2002/public-biobank_uk.htm. (Accessed 10/5/2004.)

National Blood Authority (1996) *National Blood Authority Annual Report 1996.* London: National Blood Authority.

Newton, J. (2004) UK Biobank briefing note. http://www.ukbiobank.ac.uk/Documents/long%20briefing%20paper.pdf. (Accessed 3/11/2004)

Nuffield Council on Bioethics (1995) *Human Tissue: Ethical and Legal Issues.* London: Nuffield Council on Bioethics.

Oakley, A. (1996) Blood donation – altruism or profit? *British Medical Journal*, 312, 1114.

Oliver, S., Stewart, R., Hargreaves, K. and Dezateux, C. (2005) *The Storage and Use of Newborn Babies' Blood Spot Cards: a Public Consultation*. London: Social Science Research Unit, Institute of Education, University of London.

O'Neill, K. (2003) A vital fluid: risk, controversy and the politics of blood donation in the era of 'mad cow disease', *Public Understanding of Science*, 12, 359–80.

Page, R. (1996) *Altruism and the British Welfare State*. Aldershot: Avebury.

Parry, B. (2004) *Trading the Genome: Investigating the Commodification of Bio-information*. New York: Columbia Press.

People Science and Policy Ltd. (2002) *Biobank UK: A Question of Trust*. London: The Medical Research Council and The Wellcome Trust.

Radda, G., Dexter, M. and Meade, T. (2002) The need for independent scientific peer review of Biobank UK: Reply from UK Biobank, *The Lancet*, 359, 2282.

Rose, H. (2001) The commodification of bioinformation: The Icelandic Health Sector Database. *http://www.wellcome.ac.uk/assets/WTD003281.pdf*, 2001. http:// www.wellcome.ac.uk

Shore, C. and Wright, S. (1997) Policy: a new field of anthropology. In Shore, C. and Wright, S. (eds) *Anthropology of Policy: Critical Perspectives on Governance and Power*. London: Routledge.

Titmuss, R. (1970) *The Gift Relationship*. London: Allen and Unwin.

Tutton, R. (2002) Gift relationships in genetic research, *Science as Culture*, 11, 4, 523–42.

Tutton, R. (2004) Person, property and gift: exploring languages of tissue donation to biomedical research. In Tutton, R. and Corrigan, O. (eds) *Genetic Databases: Socio-ethical Issues in the Collection and Use of DNA*. London: Routledge.

Tutton, R. Kaye, J. and Hoeyer, K. (2004) Governing UK Biobank: the importance of ensuring public trust, *Trends in Biotechnology*, 22, 6, 284–5.

UK Biobank (2003) Report of UK Biobank consultation with industry workshop. http://www.ukbiobank.ac.uk/docs/Industry-Workshop.pdf (accessed 01/09/04).

UK Biobank (2004) UK Biobank Ethics and governance framework: Summary of comments on version 1.0. http://www.biobank.ac.uk/ethics

UK Biobank (2005) *UK Biobank: Policy on Intellectual Property (IP) and Access*. Draft, 11 January 2005. London: MRC.

Wallace, H. (2002) The need for independent scientific peer review of Biobank UK, *The Lancet*, 359, 9325.

Williams, G. and Shroeder, D. (2004) Human genetic banking, *New Genetics and Society*, 23, 1, 89–103.

Wolpe, P. (1998) The triumph of autonomy in American Bioethics: a sociological view. In De Vries, R. and Subedi, J. (eds) *Bioethics and Society*. New Jersey: Prentice Hall.

13

Embodiment and ethics: constructing medicine's two bodies
David Armstrong

The body of the profession

In a celebrated initiative of 1847 the newly formed American Medical Association (AMA) published a *Code of Medical Ethics*. Unlike the emerging medical profession elsewhere which relied on the good character of its members to guarantee ethical behaviour, the AMA chose to endorse a 'contract' model in which the rights and obligations of all parties were clearly specified (Baker 1999). In consequence, its *Code of Medical Ethics* set out formal descriptions of roles and responsibilities; these underwent regular revision over the following decades. This written record provides a unique resource for mapping the field of medical ethics from 1847 to the present.

The first *Code of Medical Ethics* of 1847 was organised in terms of the reciprocal obligations between doctor and patient and between profession and public. Yet despite this contractual format much of the actual content of the *Code* – reflecting its origins in Percival's (1803) profession-centred approach to medical ethics – was concerned with professional etiquette. Description of the duties of the physician to his (sic) patient was fairly brief and involved due attention and consideration for the sick so as to 'inspire the minds of their patients with gratitude, respect and confidence' (1803: 93). The reciprocal obligations of the patient towards the doctor mainly required recognising and engaging only qualified practitioners: 'The first duty of a patient is, to select as his medical adviser one who has received a regular professional education' (1803: 95). This duty was reinforced by advice that 'Patients should never allow themselves to be persuaded to take any medicine whatever, that may be recommended to them by the self-constituted doctors and doctresses, who are so frequently met with, and who pretend to possess infallible remedies for the cure of every disease' (1803: 96).

Emphasis on maintaining a distance from unqualified practitioners while promoting the interests of regular medicine was particularly strong in the section on the duties of physicians to each other and the profession at large. 'For the support of professional character' physicians were instructed to 'avoid all contumelious and sarcastic remarks relative to the faculty, as a body' (1803: 97). And they were advised against advertising their services or boasting of cures as 'these were the ordinary practices of empirics, and are highly reprehensible in a regular physician' (1803: 98). In similar vein the duties of the profession to the public with regard to responsibilities for public health also extended to protecting the community from unqualified practitioners: 'It is the duty of physicians, who are frequent witnesses of the enormities committed by quackery, and the injury to health and even destruction of life caused by the use of quack medicines, to enlighten the public on these subjects . . . The public ought likewise to entertain a just appreciation of medical qualifications' (1803: 106).

The struggle of 'regular' against 'irregular' medical practitioners in the 19th century is well documented (Berlant 1975, Larsen 1977, Starr 1982). From public appeals for recognition to legislative action to gain exclusive rights, the mid-19th century marked a point when the 'legitimate' medical practitioner was achieving professional status. The new collegiate style of practising medicine required the policing of clear boundaries around the nascent profession so that those who did and those who did not belong could be clearly identified. Indeed, the AMA's *Code of Medical Ethics* can be seen as just one more of the various mechanisms physicians used to ensure the exclusion of quacks (Abbott 1983). Whether by enjoining patients to avoid irregular practitioners, prohibiting doctors from interacting with or copying their rivals, or 'protecting' the public good by seeking legal recognition, the medical profession was engaged in a process of occupational closure.

The mobilisation of an ethical code in pursuit of professional aims is unsurprising given the early stages of professionalisation then in progress. That so much of the code should address the threats from quacks and charlatans is also explicable in terms of the attempts to define the profession as a clearly bounded entity within which there was homogeneity and accord ('It is of great importance that physicians should act in concert' (1983: 96–7)), and outside of which were the threats posed by unregulated healers. An ethical code based on exclusion of unqualified practitioners therefore served both to recognise and constitute a professional body that was distinct from the competing claimants to the healing arts who threatened its fragile integrity. Yet, at the same time, and apparently independently, the second of medicine's two bodies was being formed with the application of homologous strategies across the field of public health[1].

The delineation of corporal space

In the mid-19th century, coincident with the emergence of a bounded medical profession, a new approach to public health appeared that largely replaced the older system of quarantine (Rosen 1993). Quarantine had been a means of containing epidemics by isolating the putative source of the illness, which might be a ship, a town, or even a country. By preventing the passage of individuals or objects across specified quarantine boundaries it was believed that an epidemic could be contained until it died out. Quarantine can therefore be expressed in terms of a simple classification system based on a series of geographical spaces with lines of exclusion (the 'cordon sanitaire') preventing the ebb and flow of hazards of place. The danger could come from any object, animate or inanimate; policing was therefore not just directed at anonymous individuals but also at any threat that might allow one space to intrude into another.

In the mid-19th century, quarantine was replaced by Sanitary Science as the primary approach to public health (Smith 1866). Sanitary Science also drew and maintained a boundary, but whereas quarantine threw a cordon sanitaire around geographical places, Sanitary Science established a line of separation around a different object, the human body. This reconfigured cordon sanitaire was not a barrier of total exclusion but a permeable boundary: it had to allow a controlled passage for the air, water and food that needed to 'enter' the space of the body and the waste matter that had to be removed.

The central problem that Sanitary Science addressed was crystallised in the concept and substance of dirt. Dirt could contaminate air, water or food on its inward passage, or it might fester in the environment if body waste (exhaled air, urine, phlegm, sweat, faeces, etc.) was not immediately removed and decontaminated. Moreover, although Sanitary Science mainly policed a line around the body, it also engaged with a volume at those points of entry and exit at which the body's interface was poorly defined. Was food in the mouth in the body or still outside? Were the colon's contents, poised for evacuation, still part of the body or had they already been discarded? (Parkes 1873). These were topics of debate for a sanitary theory and practice that explored and stabilised the anatomical envelope of the human body.

The integrity of the new corporal space defined and constructed by Sanitary Science is also revealed in the major sanitary problem of 'disposal of the dead' (Wilson 1892). The body had been made distinct from nature through the activities of Sanitary Science but when it died that process had to be reversed. Inevitably the transition between life and dust was full of sanitary dangers – the hazards of the decaying corpse, the contamination of burial grounds, the terrors of premature burial, the (Gothic) threats of the undead – that called for inventive forms of sanitary hygiene that extended from clinical practice to administrative rules and sanitary law.

Sanitary Science was a geography of anatomical space, mapping the contours of the human body so as to identify those areas in which dirt could penetrate or hazards could be stored. It was both a population and an individualising strategy: it was concerned to establish and protect a healthy population yet did so through a focus on vulnerable anatomies. Water purification and sewage systems that protected the population were joined to intimate tasks such as the management of focal sepsis in the mouth (particularly by the professionalising 'mouth police' of dentistry) and proscription of masturbation in which bodily fluids were discharged without proper sanitary surveillance (Darby 2003). The goal was a vast network for the purification of substances destined for entering the body and the decontamination and dispersal of substances leaving it, all centred on the process of monitoring and managing anatomical boundaries. Sanitary Science both distilled out the form of an anatomical body from a population mass and redefined the population as a collection of separate anatomical bodies. As Virchow noted 'The body is a free state of equal individuals, a federation of cells, a democratic cell state' a view that was entirely congruent with his famed observation that 'Medicine is a social science, and politics is nothing else but medicine on a large scale'.[2]

Morphological parallels

Although apparently independent and distinctive strategies, there is a remarkable correspondence between the mid-19th century strategies of Sanitary Science and the contemporary policies dictated by the medical profession's new ethical codes. Both were centrally concerned with delineating and monitoring the boundaries of a new body, the anatomical body located in a population space in the case of Sanitary Science and the body of the practitioner/profession in the case of medical ethics. Indeed, dirt for Sanitary Science and the quack or charlatan for ethics were equivalent in the threat they posed for the space they defined and the constant risks of 'pollution'. The constancy of the 'milieu interieur' of the human body that Bernard ([1875] 1927) identified in the second half of the 19th century applied equally well to the contemporary stabilisation and realisation of the body of the medical profession.

On the one hand, the discrete space of the individualised anatomical body was defined by the constant monitoring of Sanitary Science (while its internal structures were mapped by the newly popular anatomical atlases such as that by Henry Gray published in 1858). On the other hand, the conduct of ethical behaviour served to identify and reinforce the separate body of the regular practitioner/professional. In effect, within a few years in the middle of the 19th century two new 'bodies' materialised, two new identities that were to form the bedrock of clinical encounters over the following centuries. It was the patient as anatomical body that entered medical practice – a site for the diagnosis of pathology and an object for observation and examination in the hospital bed. And it was the newly professionalised body of the physician that crystallised out of the mass of heterodox healers: a lifetime identity and vocation that constituted the new practitioner in the clinical setting.

Yet, despite these strong morphological parallels, there was relatively little connection between the world of medical ethics and Sanitary Science. True, the 1847 *Code* did refer to some of the public health-related duties of the physician. For example, it was reported that 'on subjects of medical police, public hygiene, and legal medicine . . . it is their province to enlighten the public in regard to quarantine regulations, – the location, arrangement, and dietaries of hospitals, asylums, schools, prisons, and similar institutions, – in relation to the medical police of towns, as drainage, ventilation, &c., – and in regard to measures for the prevention of epidemic and contagious diseases' (1847 Code: 105). These responsibilities, however, were simply part of the beneficial public services that the (regular) medical practitioner might provide. Further, the origins of Sanitary Science lay more in the drive of Victorian engineers than it did in the professional elite that promoted an ethical code. So, despite their similarities, the contemporaneous emergence of medicine's two bodies, both involving active strategies for marking and policing boundaries, would seem to be independent developments – except that later transformations of medical ethics were also fairly closely matched by changes in public health.

The body's internal dynamic

In 1903 the AMA revised its *Code of Medical Ethics* to produce a new *Principles of Medical Ethics*. The new document removed reference to the 'duties' of patients and the public, expressed fewer concerns about outsiders undermining the profession and instead focused almost exclusively on the relationship between *qualified* doctors. Unlike the 1847 *Code*, which was directed towards the threat posed to the collegiate integrity of the profession by doctors competing with irregular practitioners for clients and fees, the revised ethical code addressed the perceived growing problem of internal challenges to professional cohesion. In the closing years of the 19th century a number of services emerged that provided free or subsidised care for the poor. Dispensaries, government-funded hospitals, Friendly Societies, etc., began to offer basic medical care outside of the more usual consultation-for-a-fee-based clinical practice. These competing organisations were staffed by qualified doctors so they could not be opposed on the basis that they were outlets for quackery. Equally, these doctors, in accepting a largely salaried service, were not individually under-cutting their colleagues in private practice, though their organisations might well be. Hence when the new *Principles* removed the older section on the responsibilities of the patient, this was because the patient was no longer seen as culpable in bringing about conflict between practitioners. And when it continued to emphasise appropriate etiquette between practitioners this now referred to groups or categories of doctors (private, salaried, etc.) as well as individuals. These challenges to the internal unity of the profession were also seen in the threat posed in the early 20th century by increasing specialisation (Stevens 1971), a force that might also potentially undermine the collegiate cohesion of the profession.

The new concern with internal threats at the beginning of the 20th century was only possible because the integrity of the profession had largely been secured over the preceding 50 years. Indeed, there was a debate over the so-called 'consultation clause' as some doctors wanted the freedom to deal with some 'alternative' practitioners such as homeopaths (Baker *et al.* 1999). There was now no need for a professional etiquette focused on advising against critical or sarcastic remarks about the profession or describing the precise choreography involved when two doctors attended the same patient. Instead there was a new sense of professional identity as in the instruction to observe the laws laid down for the government of the profession and the need to 'honour the fraternity as a body'. The new task was to instil and maintain order and stability within now well-recognised professional boundaries. In part this could be engendered by entertaining due respect for 'those seniors who, by their labours, have contributed to its (the science and art of medicine) advancement' (1999: 2). But physicians were also instructed – as part of their ethical code – to identify with their local professional group (if one did not exist they should create it) and to ensure appropriate affiliation to state associations and, through them, to the AMA itself. Even when in dispute with another physician over the same patient the advice was not to seek a third physician as in 1847 but to refer the matter to 'the arbitration of a sufficient number of impartial physicians'. In other words, the situation facing medical practitioners in the early 20th century was very different from a half century earlier. By 1903 the profession was well organised, had seen off the threat from irregulars and was more concerned with the threats posed by medical practitioners to one another.

At the beginning of the 20th century public health also underwent a major reconstruction. In Britain this new form of public health was called Interpersonal Hygiene, in Europe, Social Medicine (a term eventually used in place of Interpersonal Hygiene in Britain), and in the United States, Preventive Medicine. Yet the term Interpersonal Hygiene perhaps best captures the nature of this new project: the concern was not with external threats but dangers of harms transmitted within the aggregation of anatomical bodies. The significance of this plurality of bodies was recognised in both the concept of a 'population' as developed within the new statistics and the 'social body' as promoted by the new discipline of sociology.

The 'internal' dangers that underpinned Interpersonal Hygiene were partly expressed in terms of the physical transmission of disease within the population/society. Tuberculosis, for example, the major killer of the 19th century, which had been a disease of dirt and unsanitary conditions, was reconfigured as a disease of human contact, of the dangers of coughing and spitting: the problem was less dirt crossing the body boundary and more dirt (in its new manifestations) crossing the narrow space between bodies. Human phlegm acquired a new-found danger as shown in the removal of spittoons from public houses or the covering of the mouth with the hand or handkerchief whilst coughing (Mackenzie 1906). In schools, a system of quarantine was apparently revived with the introduction of a new policy of excluding contagious diseases (Gulick and Ayers 1908), but the underpinning logic was not one of separating places but policing physical contacts between bodies in school and bodies in the community.

Perhaps the archetypal disease of the new framework of public health was venereal disease. Here was a public health threat that was passed through the population by the intimate contact of one body with another and whose public health management was the extension of surveillance throughout the population by means of educational programmes about sexual liaisons and attempts to track the threads of the disease through contact tracing. The latter, as it were, began to draw a map of the spatial dimensions of this new geography as the lines of interconnectedness of individuals were superimposed on the cartography of the traditional geographical atlas.

The space between the population's bodies, however, was not only a physical space but also a space of 'relatedness' with psychological and social dimensions. The contemporary newly institutionalised disciplines of psychology and sociology began the analysis of this inter-corporal space and its inchoate dangers. From Freud's contention that it was the bond between parent and child – a relational space – that determined future mental health to Durkheim's claim that it was the existence of the social sui generis that could explain even individual acts such as suicide, this new public health space was constituted as an analytic unity.

The fact that the new public health dangers came from within the body of the population can be seen in broader reconstructions and extensions of medical knowledge. The main causes of infant mortality, for example, were transformed from immutable biological and meteorological factors that were external to the body to problems of motherhood, nutrition, illegitimacy and social class (Lewis 1980, Armstrong 1986). It was less unsanitary conditions (as it would have been a decade earlier) that underpinned the explanation of the poor state of British recruits for the Boer war but nutrition, a failing of family or society. The child became a particular focus of Interpersonal Hygiene given the contemporary belief in the 'relationship' threats it underwent during its growth and development (Mackenzie 1906). Not least this interconnectedness of one body to another in space was physically expressed in early 20th century interest in physical exercise and synchronised movement.

The practical implications of Interpersonal Hygiene were very different from those of Sanitary Science. The latter was concerned with ensuring that dirt from the environment did not penetrate the body; the interpersonal hygienist was concerned with whether contamination passed between individual bodies. This latter was not the same dirt as in Sanitary Science where it had functioned as the medium through which nature polluted anatomical space; in Interpersonal Hygiene dirt carried elements of anatomical space itself, allowing one body to contaminate another. This new threat required new cadres of health workers deployed amidst the population and new healthcare structures embedded in a developing medical space outside the hospital, developments that were to dominate much of 20th-century healthcare provision.

The emergence of Interpersonal Hygiene marked a new way of thinking about public health. Dangers did not come (through dirt) from un-decontaminated nature but from the dangers of mixing with other bodies. And the management of the threats emerging from the space between bodies functioned to define a new body, that of the human aggregation or population or society. Exactly in parallel, codes of ethics also changed. Both the new code of ethics and Interpersonal Hygiene recognised 'internal' rather than 'external' threats to their respective body's integrity. In the case of public health it was the threats that lurked in passing noxious material from one person to another; it was the dangerous individual who now threatened the integrity of the new social body. In the case of ethics it was the dangers that one group of doctors posed for another; dangers came from internal differentiation which threatened to fragment newly-won professional unity.

Once more, although the mechanism for maintaining the integrity of bodies in both medical ethics and public health were remarkably similar there seems little direct influence between the two fields. The professional elite, fretting about unity and revising its ethical code accordingly, and public health, still a marginal medical activity, pursuing the dangers that lurked in the social domain, were separate worlds. Indeed, searching for the existence of 'influences' between medical ethics and public health is hardly likely to yield results, given the lack of a language through which communication could occur. How would the interpersonal hygienist have 'read' the political problem of a salaried practitioner in terms of a strategy for meeting the challenges of contagious disease? And how could the turn of the century ethicist have related the hazards of coughing and spitting to the fissiparous tendencies of a fragmenting profession?

Modern dangers

In the second half of the 20th century, ethics underwent yet another fundamental change. This was reflected in a new revision in 1958 of the *Principles of Medical Ethics* that emerged as a brief document of 10 sections. These sections continued the advice on professional etiquette, including advice not to associate with those who practiced forms of healing not 'founded on a scientific basis' and some encouragement to probity (not allowing pecuniary rewards to interfere with clinical judgement, not paying for referrals, etc.), but the most novel feature of the new *Principles* was a section on the potential dangers of physicians for their patients: 'The medical profession should safeguard the public and itself against physicians deficient in moral character and professional competence'. Within a few years this new focus on the dangers of the medical profession to patient well being was further consolidated under an approach characterised as 'bioethics'.

There are extensive histories of bioethics describing its emergence from the Nuremburg trials and various post-war 'scandals' in medical research (Callahan 1973, Martensen 2001, Jonsen 1998, Rothman 1991). The actual name had a 'bilocated birth' in 1970/1971 (Reich 1993, 1994, 1995) and represented a sea-change in the focus of medical ethics. The problem was no longer the medical profession and its internal relationships but the potential threats that the medical profession posed for the patient. The new task of ethics was to protect the patient from medicine itself.

The idea of a potentially dangerous medicine extended from individual acts of 'unprofessional' conduct – carelessness, incompetence, error, etc. – through to the injurious consequences of the actions of the medical profession as a whole. Harm could come to the patient from any aspect of clinical practice as echoed in Illich's celebrated opening sentence to his contemporary book on *Medical Nemesis* (1974), 'The medical establishment has become a major threat to health'. The use of foetal tissue in experimentation and the deliberate infection of patients as part of medical research might have helped launch the new ethical focus but it was continued in terms of obtaining the maximum protection for patient welfare consonant with the necessary risks that medical intervention implied.

The new perspective was reinforced in the AMA's 1980 revision to the *Principles of Medical Ethics*. This reduced ethics to seven pithy statements, the majority of which were concerned with ensuring that physicians did not harm patients. Physicians had to offer care 'with compassion and respect for human dignity'; they had to expose the dangers in those 'deficient in character or competence, or who engage in fraud or deception'; they had to seek changes in the law when requirements were 'contrary to the best interests of the patient'; and physicians had to respect the 'rights of patients, of colleagues, and of other health professionals'. The 1999 report from the Institute of Medicine, *To err is human*, which brought the problem of medical error centre-stage, can be seen as a summary statement of the potential dangers inherent in medicine. Certainly medicine maintained its core therapeutic role but there were hidden dangers in its claim to promote wellbeing. From the risks of accidental harms to deliberate abuse, patients now had to beware of engaging with the medical enterprise and equally the medical profession had to protest its good intentions through its new ethical codes.

At the same time as ethical codes were identifying dangers from medicine and medical practitioners, public health was beginning to identify a new set of threats. The post-war New Public Health located health hazards in the wider ecological environment. It was the products of social activity and interaction – depletion of the ozone layer as a result of burning fossil fuels, contamination of food by chemical additives, exhaust fumes in the atmosphere, pesticides in the food chain, pollution in the ground water, radiation from phone masts, mobile telephones and nuclear power stations, and so on – that created a dense web of 'industrialised' threat. As Dubos noted, it was the dangerous mixing of Man and environment particularly through technology that produced contemporary diseases (Dubos 1959, 1966). Ecological thinking and 'green' solutions constituted the new directions for public health as lifestyle (a 1970s invention) and the risks of self to self, in terms of 'risky' behaviours (Ogden 1995), came into increasing prominence.

None of these new environmental hazards could be prevented by strict monitoring at boundaries as in earlier public health regimes. There was no cordon sanitaire to police, no boundary lines to maintain, only a vast range of unseen dangers that could come from anywhere and from everywhere. The new imperative was, therefore, constant vigilance. Whereas in the 19th century nature had been the ultimate source of the dirt that threatened the integrity of the anatomical body, in the second half of the 20th century, a reconfigured nature had become the beneficent presence that afforded some hope of protection. Indeed, a new 'dirt hypothesis' suggested that many modern illnesses might be due to a failure to allow dirt to challenge developing immunological systems (Weiss 2002). In other words, a totally sanitised world – that dream of 19th-century public health – had become a harmful environment: better the dirt of the farm than the cleanliness of modern urban life. But lifestyle, in terms of diet and behaviour, and the external costs of industrial production from energy use to environmental pollution, constantly threatened the potential rapprochement with a reconstructed nature.

Just as the New Public Health was discovering dangers everywhere, so clinical medicine found that everyone was 'at risk'. From diagnosing diseases in those who were ill, clinical medicine moved increasingly towards the identification of risk profiles for both ill and healthy (Armstrong 1995). Disease became less a threat to corporal identity and more a challenge to (multi-dimensional) quality of life. The public health strategy of surveillance was, therefore, both supported and reinforced by parallel changes in the clinical field.

Exactly as Sanitary Science had emerged alongside ethical codes for newly professionalising medical practitioners in the mid-19th century, and Interpersonal Hygiene had been mirrored in the 1903 revised *Principles of Medical Ethics* in the early 20th century, the appearance of the New Public Health occurred in conjunction with the new regime of bioethics. Both the New Public Health and bioethics opened up dangers from the confines of the traditional doctor-patient consultation. Both stressed the risks from interacting bodies – social bodies working together to generate pollution, practitioner bodies working together to threaten patient health and safety. Neither of these threats could be managed by simple rules of exclusion as promoted by earlier sanitary frameworks and ethical codes: both demanded on-going vigilance, a cautionary regime to protect against hidden and unsuspected dangers that had insinuated its logic into both 21st century public health and ethical theory and practice.

For over a century medical ethics and public health had been separate enterprises but now, in a world of generalised hazards, their paths converged. On the one hand, the research that was needed to study the new public health threats could not be conducted without prior ethical sanction (as might not the researchers constitute an even greater threat to their 'subjects' more than the risks they studied?). Equally, the dangers that medicine itself posed – side-effects of investigations and treatments, harms of radiation, substance-addicted doctors, dangers of antibiotic-resistant organisms, etc. –

became part and parcel of the environmental challenge targeted by the new regime of public health.

Narratives of continuity

Changes in both ethics and public health have been described in terms of shifts in classification boundaries and permeability that established new sources of danger. This description resonates with Douglas's analysis of classification and pollution in her 1966 book, *Purity and Danger*. Following Durkheim's work in *Primitive Classification* (co-authored with Mauss ([1903] 1967) and *Elementary Forms of the Religious Life*, ([1912] 1995), she observed that all classification systems were social in origin. Whether an animal was to be classified as a fish or a bird did not depend on what it 'really' was; rather, the categories of fish and bird were human constructs through which people made sense of the world around them. But in any classification there were anomalies, cases that did not fit the pre-established cells of the classification table, and these, she observed, were usually construed as impure or polluting. Moreover, for good reason, a category that did not fit a classification system was a threat to the system's integrity, so was potentially dangerous. This quality of danger – that was a property conferred solely by the classification rules – was then transferred to the object in question. For example, in Leviticus (many of her examples were drawn from the Bible), Jews divided the natural world into animals with feet on the land, fishes with scales in the sea and birds with wings in the air. So how were the biblical Jews to understand crabs that had feet but lived in the sea or other shellfish that lacked scales? Her answer was that they would be construed as unclean and dangerous.

Douglas's ideas about purity and danger and her identification of hygiene as a fundamental aspect of ordered social life reflected closely on different systems of public health. Public health is a spatial science: it is about classification, about spaces and their associations, about questions of cleanliness and pollution. Dirt as Douglas (1966) observed, quoting Chesterton, was 'matter out of place'. Dirt was fine in the garden, the basis of good crops, but it did not belong in the space of the body. Thus, Sanitary Science can be seen as a simple case of purity and danger: the anatomical body and its external environment had to be kept separate; the danger of pollution was expressed through the idea of dirt that constantly threatened the 'purity' of corporal space; the task of public health was therefore to ensure hygiene at those body boundaries across which there could be transmission.

An exactly analogous social process occurred in the relationship between the new idea of medical ethics and the professional body in the mid-19th century. Again, there were threats to the integrity of the body through the 'dirt' of irregulars, charlatans and quacks. The principal task of ethics was to 'police' the boundary around the profession, ensuring the integrity of professional identity. Then, in the early 20th century pollution became an 'internal' problem for both public health and ethics. The integrity of the respective body – patient/population and practitioner/profession – was threatened by interior movements of dirt and its like. And finally, in the mid-20th century, there was a great reversal as bodies – professional and social – became themselves potential sources of pollution. For the new bioethics it was the threat of the medical profession to its patients; for the New Public Health it was the dangers inflicted by the social body or population on the environment. And in each case the integrity of the former body began to falter. For the profession it was recognised in commentaries on deprofessionalisation and medical proletarianisation (Haug 1973, McKinley and Stoeckle 1988) and the problematisation of the unquestioned patient's body was reflected in the books on corporal identity that began to emerge in the early 1980s (Armstrong 1983, Turner 1984).

Conventional histories of medical ethics and public health, however, have worked in isolation from each other and with an underlying focus on discovering continuity. Jonsen (2000), for example, in typical fashion, opened his history of medical ethics with the statement 'The ethics of medicine in Western culture has its roots in Hellenic, Hellenistic, and Roman medicine, beginning in the fifth century BCE [before the common age] and extending to the third century CE [the common age]'. This idea of continuity pervades the history of ethics but, as described above, within the last two centuries alone, medical ethics has shown remarkable shifts in focus and it requires a major effort to link each of the recent strands – from questions of appropriate etiquette to protecting the patient from the doctor – with a long distant past. Yet the history produced by ethics' most recent incarnation rewrites past histories. For example, while the 19th-century ethical codes were celebrated in their time they can be dismissed as mere rules of etiquette from the point of view of 20th-century ethics (Leake 1927, Waddington 1975).

For its part, public health elicits histories that celebrate progress (Rosen 1993) or at least never questions the constancy of the underlying 'body' it addresses nor the way in which threats are products of an underlying classification system (Porter 1999). And public health regularly rewrites its history. Historical explanations produced in the era of the New Public Health, for instance, acknowledge the importance of components of Sanitary Science (such as ensuring a clean water supply) and decry the error of other aspects (such as miasmatic theory), without recognising the coherence of the underlying explanatory framework (Chave 1984, Halliday 2001, Aycliffe and English 2003). Thus, the connections between disposal of the dead, warm drinks and good ventilation (Parkes 1873) lie in a displaced theory and practice that managed permeable body boundaries, just as the link between etiquette and ethics is embedded in a reconfigured medical profession and practitioner identity.

These separate 'disciplinary' histories that stress continuity are largely self-serving as they legitimate a configuration of knowledge that constructs danger – and the role of ethicists and public health officials to combat it – as a phenomenon whose existence requires no explanation. Thus, it is only by inventing a history going back to Hippocrates that bioethics can demonstrate its universal and timeless truths (in particular the imperative not to usurp the patient's rights) even though it has had such a brief existence. And it is only by selecting out the 'correct' aspects of Sanitary Science that the New Public Health can sustain the centrality of an ecological model of health without the need to engage with a rival explanatory framework that cast nature as the source of problems.

The alternative, as described in this chapter, is to recognise both the historically constructed nature of domains of knowledge and the major discontinuities that lie between them. From Percival's first use of the word 'patient' as a general descriptor for the person being attended by a doctor (Baker 1999) to the subsequent parallel spatialisations of ethics and public health, medicine's two bodies can be seen to have been forged and transformed in tandem. Doctor and patient, profession and population, are not only locked together in analyses of consultations and healthcare systems but in the morphogenetic spaces of their own histories. By treating the field of medicine's two bodies as one and by searching for major shifts in perception, public health can be reread as a mechanism for constructing the human body and ethics as a device for realising a professional body.

Over the past decade or so sociology has started to engage with the substantive content of bioethics in exploring opportunities for collaborative or mutually improving cross-disciplinary work (De Vries and Conrad 1998, Haimes 2002, Hedgecoe 2004, Lopez 2004) or in engaging with the professionalising tendencies of ethicists (De Vries 1995, De Vries and Subedi 1998). This chapter, however, tries to prepare the ground for a sociological analysis of medical ethics that can be joined to the sociological exploration of the human body over a period beyond the very recent reign of bioethics. In this wider history, public health and medical ethics can be represented in terms of spatial relationships and boundary-maintaining mechanisms; they can be expressed as the parallel unfolding over the last two centuries of a joint project that constructed medicine's two bodies, that of the doctor (as professional) and that of the individualised patient.

Notes

1   The following sections on the history of public health draw heavily on Armstrong (1993 and 2002).
2   See Ackerknecht 1953.

References

Abbott, A. (1983) Professional ethics, *American Journal of Sociology*, 88, 855–85.
Ackerknecht, E. (1953) *Rudolph Virchow: Doctor, Statesman, Anthropologist*. Madison, Wisconsin: University of Wisconsin Press.

American Medical Association (1847) *Code of Medical Ethics.*

American Medical Association (1903, 1958, 1980) *Principles of Medical Ethics.*

Armstrong, D. (1983) *Political Anatomy of the Body: Medical Knowledge in Britain in the 20th Century.* Cambridge: Cambridge University Press.

Armstrong, D. (1986) The invention of infant mortality, *Sociology of Health and Illness*, 8, 211–32.

Armstrong, D. (1993) Public health spaces and the fabrication of identity, *Sociology*, 27, 393–410.

Armstrong, D. (1995) The rise of surveillance medicine, *Sociology of Health and Illness*, 17, 393–404.

Armstrong, D. (2002) *A New History of Identity: A Sociology of Medical Knowledge.* Basingstoke: Palgrave.

Aycliffe, G.A.J. and English, M.P. (2003) *Hospital Infections: From Miasmas to MRSA.* Cambridge: Cambridge University Press.

Baker, R. (1999) The American medical ethics revolution. In Baker, R., Caplan, A.L., Emanual, L.L. and Latham, S.R. (eds) *The American Medical Ethics Revolution.* Baltimore: Johns Hopkins University Press.

Baker, R., Caplan, A.L., Emanual, L.L. and Latham, S.R. (eds) (1999) *The American Medical Ethics Revolution.* Baltimore: Johns Hopkins University Press.

Berlant, J.J. (1975) *Profession and Monopoly.* Berkeley: University of California Press.

Bernard, C. ([1875] 1927) *Introduction to the Study of Experimental Medicine.*

Callahan, D. (1973) Bioethics as a discipline, *Hastings Center Studies*, 1, 66–73.

Chave, S.P.W. (1984) The origins and development of public health. In Holland, W.W., Detels, R. and Knox, G. *Oxford Textbook of Public Health Volume 1.* Oxford: Oxford University Press.

Darby, R. (2003) The masturbation taboo and the rise of routine male circumcision: a review of the historiography, *Journal of Social History*, 36, 737–57.

De Vries, R. (1995) Towards a sociology of bioethics, *Qualitative Sociology*, 18, 119–28.

De Vries, R. and Subedi, J. (eds) (1998) *Bioethics and Society: Constructing the Ethical Enterprise.* Upper Saddle River, NJ: Prentice Hall.

De Vries, R. and Conrad, P. (1998) Why bioethics needs sociology. In De Vries, R. and Subedi, J. (eds) (1998) *Bioethics and Society: Constructing the Ethical Enterprise.* Upper Saddle River, NJ: Prentice Hall.

Douglas, M. (1966) *Purity and Danger.* London: Routledge Kegan Paul.

Dubos, R.J. (1959) *Mirage of Health: Utopias, Progress and Biological Change.* New Jersey: Rutgers University Press.

Dubos, R.J. (1966) *Man Adapting.* New Haven: Yale University Press.

Durkheim, E. ([1912] 1995) *The Elementary Forms of Religious Life.* New York: Free Press.

Durkheim, E. and Mauss, M. ([1903] 1967) *Primitive Classification.* Chicago, University of Chicago Press.

Gulick, L.H. and Ayers, L.P. (1908) *Medical Inspection of Schools.* New York: Russell Sage.

Hamies, E. (2002) What can social sciences contribute to the study of ethics? Theoretical, empirical and substantive considerations, *Bioethics*, 16, 89–113.

Halliday, S. (2001) Death and miasma in Victorian London, *British Medical Journal*, 323, 1469–71.

Haug, M. (1973) Deprofessionalization: an alternative hypothesis for the future, *Sociological Review Monograph*, 2, 195–211.

Hedgecoe, A.M. (2004) Critical bioethics: beyond the social science critique of applied ethics, *Bioethics*, 18, 120–43.

Institute of Medicine (1999) *To Err is Human: Building a Safer Health System*.

Illich, I. (1974) *Medical Nemesis*. London: Caldar Boyars.

Jonsen, A. (1998) *The Birth of Bioethics*. New York: Oxford University Press.

Jonsen, A. (2000) *A Short History of Medical Ethics*. New York: Oxford University Press.

Larson, M.S. (1977) *The Rise of Professionalism: A Sociological Analysis*. Berkeley: University of California Press.

Leake, C. (ed.) (1927) *Percival's Medical Ethics*. Baltimore: Williams and Wilkins.

Lewis, J. (1980) *The Politics of Motherhood: Child and Maternal Welfare in England, 1900–1939*. London: Croom Helm.

Lopez, J. (2004) How sociology can save bioethics . . . maybe, *Sociology of Health and Illness*, 26, 875–96.

Mackenzie, W.L. (1906) *The Health of the School Child*. London: Methuen.

Martensen, R. (2001) The history of bioethics: an essay review, *Journal of the History of Medicine and Allied Sciences*, 56, 168–75.

McKinlay, J. and Stoeckle, J. (1988) Corporatisation and the social transformation of doctoring, *International Journal of Health Services*, 18, 191–205.

Ogden, J. (1995) Psychosocial theory and the creation of the risky self, *Social Science and Medicine*, 40, 411–14.

Parkes, E.A. (1873) *A Manual of Practical Hygiene*, 4th edition. London: Churchill.

Percival, T. (1803) *Code of Medical Ethics*.

Porter, D. (1999) *Health, Civilisation and the State: A History of Public Health from Ancient to Modern Times*. London: Routledge.

Reich, W.T. (1993) How bioethics got its name, *Hastings Center Reports*, 23, S6–7.

Reich, W.T. (1994) The word 'bioethics': its birth and the legacies of those who shaped it, *Kennedy Institute of Ethics Journal*, 4, 319–35.

Reich, W.T. (1995) The word 'bioethics': the struggle over its earliest meanings, *Kennedy Institute Ethics Journal*, 5, 19–34.

Rosen, G. (1993) (expanded Edition) *A History of Public Health*. Baltimore: Johns Hopkins University Press.

Rothman, D.J. (1991) *Strangers at the Bedside: A History of how Law and Bioethics Transformed Medical Decision Making*. New York: Basic Books.

Smith, S. (1866) *The Common Nature of Epidemics and their Relation to Climate and Civilisation*. London: Trubner.

Stevens, R. (1971) *American Medicine and the Public Interest*. New Haven: Yale University Press.

Starr, P. (1982) *The Transformation of American Medicine*. New York: NY Basic Books.

Turner, B.S. (1984) *The Body and Society*. London: Sage.

Waddington, I. (1975) The development of medical ethics: a sociological analysis, *Medical History*, 19, 36–51.

Weiss, S.T. (2002) Eat dirt – the hygiene hypothesis and allergic diseases, *New England Journal of Medicine*, 347, 930–1.

Wilson, G. (1892) *A Handbook of Hygiene and Sanitary Science*. Philadelphia: Blakiston.

Index